——————

LIGHTHOUSE
IN MY
L·I·F·E

LIGHTHOUSE
IN MY
L·I·F·E

PHILMORE B. WASS

DOWN EAST BOOKS

Cover and text design by Edith Allard
Printed at Capital City Press, Inc., Montpelier, Vt.

10   9   8   7   6

Down East Books / Box 679 / Camden, Maine 04843

C·O·N·T·E·N·T·S

Photographs section begins on page 181.

DON WASS

F·O·R·E·W·O·R·D

IT IS a hard person who has no soft place in his or her heart for lighthouses. Their physical presence speaks of absolute service to mankind, and their lights, beaming across a dark wilderness of sea, are widely recognized as beacons of care, integrity, and perseverance. And no wonder: the number of lives saved and the amount of property protected can never be known. How often has a glance at their white glimmer corrected a course or reassured a weary mariner?

The earliest lighthouses in America were built along the New England coast. New England's lighthouse towers came to be architectural and cultural archetypes as their design and layout were replicated on other coasts around the country. Of all the images that Americans associate with New England and Maine, lighthouses surely top the list.

The arrangement of buildings at each lighthouse station was unique to its lonely and forbidding location, but each complex was an integrated whole of form and function: the clapboard-sided Cape where the keepers lived was carefully arranged in relation to the brick or granite light tower and the associated bell tower or whistlehouse, sheds, and barns. This tight arrangement of buildings in a rugged location bespeaks the light station's practicality and self-sufficiency.

As with so many of the "improvements" brought about by modern technology, lighthouse automation proves to be a mixed blessing. We have eliminated the problems associated with maintaining a staff on remote and dangerous locations, but in doing so we have abandoned irreplaceable pieces of our cultural heritage. Like the corner candy store and the in-town railroad depot, manned lighthouse stations are now superfluous. It is technologically feasible, and certainly cheaper, to flip the switch of an automatic beacon and a pure-tone fog signal from some central location rather than rely on lighthouse keepers and their families to attend the lights and horns. The more remote the lighthouse, the more expensive and difficult it becomes for the U.S. Coast Guard to maintain the now "useless" buildings that once sheltered the keepers and their families, livestock, and boats.

Here on the Maine coast, our last lighthouse is scheduled to be automated ("unmanned") in 1989. At dozens of light stations—particularly those on islands—whole buildings, walkways and ramps, bell towers, sheds, oil houses, barns, and even schoolhouses already have been demolished—erased from the landscape. Tragically, only now do we begin to perceive that buried in the rubble of these demolished structures are important notions of who we were and are as Americans, as New Englanders, and as Mainers. The light towers themselves remain (except where lights have been mounted more cheaply on steel superstructures or floating buoys), but the human context of these powerful places is gone forever, and with it the ineffable connections to a humanistic maritime past.

But no matter what happens to the physical buildings, the images of lighthouses we see in our mind's eye are intimately tied to people such as Philmore Wass's family, who for twenty-one years attended the Libby Island light at the far eastern end of Maine. This book is an elegant and moving testament to the human qualities demanded by life on a remote light station:

abiding care, strong family bonds, an acute sense of responsibility, attention to detail, and physical endurance. These qualities were required at a moment's notice for the benefit of seamen the keepers would never meet and only rarely glimpse.

Philmore Wass's story is all the more moving because it details a childhood during which he was isolated from the kinds of activities we normally associate with growing up. And yet we sense throughout this story that from the isolation and occasional loneliness he has gained a kind of natural spirituality and polished the childlike imagination first shaped along Libby Island's wild shores.

Libby Island still has its lighthouse tower, but the human context—the buildings generations of keepers had maintained—is gone. Although the structures of the Wass's years can be seen no longer, the rich fabric of their lives is wonderfully captured in the pages of *Lighthouse in My Life*.

Libby Island is unusual. Its history is preserved in this book, but dozens of other light stations are slowly slipping into oblivion, their history unrecorded except as lifeless government records of gallons of paint used, tons of coal burned, keepers assigned and transferred, and, finally, of buildings demolished. Dozens more will disappear as the pace of lighthouse automation quickens. Surely we could find a way to utilize these still habitable buildings, providing opportunities for interested people to experience today the unique lifeways Philmore Wass describes.

— Philip W. Conkling
Director of The Island Institute
Rockland, Maine

P·R·E·F·A·C·E

IN WRITING this book, I wanted first of all to share my experiences and those of my family living on an isolated Maine island. All my life, people have expressed interest in my lighthouse background, and I have spent many hours answering their questions. Second, I wanted to preserve for future generations of our family this precious and unique part of their heritage. Third, I wanted to pay tribute to all the other families who have kept Maine's lighthouse signals burning brightly and sounding steadily since 1791, when the first one was established at Portland Head. Their experiences, I am sure, were not much different from ours. They all had to contend with the vagaries of the sea, and the sea does not change.

I want to express my thanks to my wife, Dorothy, for her constant encouragement and for listening critically to each sentence I wrote; to Jim Brown, associate editor of *Down East* Magazine, who talked to me willingly when I walked in off the street and told him about my plans for a lighthouse book and who has continued to encourage me; to Karin Womer and Kathleen Brandes, my editors, who also gave encouragement and in addition untangled my syntax and continually pressed me for more details; and to my brother Irwin, who emerges as a central character in my story. He shared most of the experiences I have recounted, and often his memory was far richer in details than mine.

I also want to thank my sister Hazel Woodward and her husband, George, who fell in love on Libby Island and went on to be lightkeepers at four other Maine lighthouses. Their memories and their lives greatly enriched my life and this book.

My sister Winona (now deceased) shared with me one of the outstanding experiences I have recounted in this book. She and I were among the first people to reach the *John C. Myers,* a three-masted barkentine wrecked on Big Libby Island in 1925. Without her adventuresome spirit, I might not have had that exciting opportunity, since I was only eight at the time.

Finally, I want to thank my younger brother, Arnold, a "late arrival" in our family, who brought the eyes of a child to many of our activities. He did not spend as much of his life as we did on Libby, but he nonetheless absorbed all the island ways.

I wish to dedicate this book to my father and mother, Hervey and Mabel Wass, who exemplified the very highest traditions of a Maine lighthouse-keeping couple. As parents they were always loving and forgiving, and they gave us a great deal of freedom. As lightkeepers, they made many sacrifices not required of those who work on the mainland. And their most costly sacrifice was having to live apart for a number of years so that their children could be educated. But they finally were rewarded with sixteen happy retirement years together. Father lived to be eighty-three and Mother died only a few months short of her hundredth birthday. My one regret is that I did not write this book sooner so that they could enjoy it.

All of the descendants of Hervey and Mabel Wass and the other lighkeepers who served on Libby Island can take great pride in the service these courageous and dedicated people rendered to all of the seafarers who sailed Maine's coastal waters during the first half of this century. They never sailed past Libby at night when the light was not burning brightly or in the fog when the fog signal was not booming out its warning.

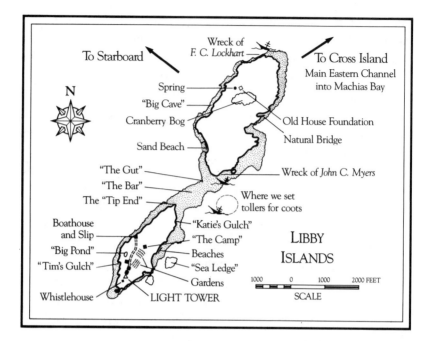

To Starboard

Wreck of
F. C. Lockhart

N

To Cross Island
Main Eastern Channel
into Machias Bay

Spring

"Big Cave"

Cranberry Bog

Old House Foundation

Natural Bridge

Sand Beach

"The Gut"

Wreck of *John C. Myers*

"The Bar"

The "Tip End"

Where we set
tollers for coots

Boathouse
and Slip

"Katie's Gulch"

"The Camp"

LIBBY
ISLANDS

"Big Pond"

Beaches

"Tim's Gulch"

"Sea Ledge"

Gardens

1000   0   1000   2000 FEET

Whistlehouse

LIGHT TOWER

SCALE

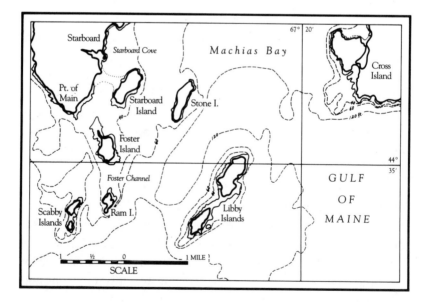

Starboard

67° 20'

Starboard Cove

Machias Bay

Cross
Island

Pt. of
Main

Starboard
Island

Stone I.

Foster
Island

44°
35'

Foster Channel

GULF

Scabby
Islands

Ram I.

Libby
Islands

OF

MAINE

½   0   1 MILE

SCALE

MAPS BY PATRICE M. ROSSI

1

A

LIGHTHOUSE

FAMILY

"DANNY, go out and start up your lobsterboat and see if you can pull Philmore's trailer into the water far enough so his boat will float off."

Danny agreed and quickly backed his boat into where our trailer and boat were stuck on the shingle beach in the tiny mainland community of Starboard, Maine. Richard Pettegrow, owner of the local boatyard, had tried to back us into the water with his truck, but a recent storm had built up an extra ridge along the shore. Just before we had enough water under our keel to float off, the trailer started rising.

Richard fastened a heavy line from Danny's boat to our trailer frame and Danny slowly headed offshore. When the line was taut, he pulled out the throttle. The line began to snap and crack as the tension increased, but the trailer did not budge. Danny finally pulled the throttle wide open and a cauldron of water burst from under his broad-beamed lobsterboat. Just as we felt the trailer begin to stir, there was a loud CRACK! As we watched, a whole plank was flying through the air from Danny's boat. He thought he had made the line fast to a solid cleat.

"Next time fasten to something solid, Danny," Richard

shouted over the roar of the engine. Danny circled and picked up the line. This time he must have found a more secure point. Again he opened up his throttle and we could feel our boat and trailer begin to rock. In another few seconds, the pebbles gave way and our *Puffin* floated free.

I got the motor started, shouted apologies and thanks to Danny and Richard, and headed for Libby Island Light Station, a trip I had been planning for many months.

All during the preceding winter of 1979-80 in Hawaii, where I spend about six months of every year, I had felt an overwhelming desire to return "home" to Libby Island. My father, Hervey H. Wass, was appointed head lightkeeper on Libby in 1919 and served there until 1940. I went there when I was only two years old, and Libby was home to me during my early growing-up years. Home was not Machias, where I had spent many of my elementary, high school, and early college years, nor Connecticut, where I had lived most of my adult life. Home was Libby Island, and I had a great yearning to return there in my own boat. I knew, as I subsequently proved, that it would have been easier just to ask a local lobster fisherman to land us on the island and return for us later in the day, but this did not satisfy me. I wanted to be in charge of the trip, as my father had been for so many years.

Being a cautious sailor, I prepared well, securing the proper charts. It was a thrill to note all the islands and ledges with which I was so familiar—they were stamped indelibly in my mind. I looked up the latitude and longitude: 44° 34.1' North; 67° 22.1' West. And I plotted courses, allowing for the strong current caused by the eleven-foot tides in case we were caught in the fog—which I fully expected, since this is one of the foggiest places in the world.

But this day was clear, unusual for July. There was not quite enough wind to sail, so I kept the motor running. As I looked back, Starboard appeared exactly the same as it had on our trips more than a half century earlier. The houses had not changed, nor had the great sweeping beach with a few lobsterboats anchored before it. I told Dorothy, my wife, who was accompanying me on this voyage, how happy we always were when we reached that secure harbor after some of our cold winter crossings from Libby.

Soon we rounded the end of Starboard (also called Ingalls) Island, and Libby Island came into view. I swept my eyes from east to west, taking in every detail. It still looked like a whale, lying on top of the water with a green cover stretched over its back. But I felt my stomach tighten when I saw that the western head was bare of houses. Only the tower and whistlehouse were left. Gone were our beautiful home, its attached hundred-foot-long rainshed, and the commodious duplex house that accommodated the families of the other two keepers. This came as a sad shock, even though on my previous visit, our house was the only building still standing. Now it had been demolished—as a training exercise for some amphibious army unit, we were told. Had I been there then, I think I would have felt like gathering up all our firearms, with which we were well supplied, and given them a more realistic exercise. This was my home!

As always, a southwest wind was making up outside of Ingalls. We raised the sails and soon were whispering through the water. How familiar it all was—the smell of the sea, the feel of the air on my face.

As we drew closer, more details became evident. I realized with sadness that the boathouse, which had offered us early shelter on return trips, had been razed. But the island was unchanged. I was familiar with every convolution of its grass-covered surface. Libby had no trees, although the many short stumps with grass grown over them were reminders of long-ago forests.

When we came under the lee of the island, we took down the sails, started the motor, and ran in close to inspect the slip. The tide was already down too far to land, and I realized that the lower third of the slip timbers had broken off, leaving jagged ends. The slip itself was also in bad shape, with protruding rusty nail heads and broken cleats. All the timbers, up to the high-water mark, were a mass of sea moss and seaweed.

We had run in farther than I had planned, and when I tried to steer away, I realized we were not turning as sharply as I had expected. The rocks began to loom closer and closer. In a second, I knew what was wrong: The large inflatable boat we were towing was hindering our turn. With a quick adjustment of the outboard motor and the rudder, we quickly came clear. For one fleeting moment, I remembered all the emotions I had so often felt in fighting to launch or land our government boat. Making a landing and getting away was going to be just as difficult as always. I decided to postpone our attempt to get onto the island until the next day. I knew it would be no picnic.

I swung Puffin's bow away from the slip and headed east along the shore, examining every feature of the island as we passed. I pointed out to Dorothy the "cowhole," where we landed all our cows, bulls, and horses. It did not look like a safe landing, but there was a small opening in the ledge where we brought in boats. We finally reached the Tip-End—the end of Libby's grassy cover —and started moving along the bar that stretched between us and Libby's sister island, Big Libby. Our island was officially forty-two acres, about a half mile long and a quarter mile wide. Big Libby was eighty acres. At low tide, the bar was entirely out of water and we could walk across to Big Libby, but at high tide it was completely covered. This deceptive bar had doomed many a ship trying to get through what appeared to be the main entrance to Machias Bay, just to the east.

The bar was about two-thirds out of the water. I had been busy telling Dorothy many things about the island when I glanced over and saw what appeared to be fog rising from the ledges. Fog could come in on a summer afternoon in a matter of minutes. Not wanting to get caught in a fog mull (we called it a "mow"), I quickly swung Puffin about and headed for Stone Island, following one of the compass courses I had carefully laid out. The tide was already running out of the bay and the current set us west toward Foster Island.

When we were about halfway back to Starboard, I could see out toward the open ocean and there seemed to be no sign of fog. Nor did it "smell" like fog. Anyone who has lived on this part of the

Maine coast can sense the approach of fog. I decided that what I had seen was condensation from the warm summer air striking the cold rocks of the bar. The wind was light but steady, a perfect sailing breeze, so I turned around and headed back toward Libby. These hours were too precious to waste.

Raising the sails, we returned quickly to the island. Skirting the southwest end, I pointed out interesting features as we sailed by. "Tim's Gulch," where one of our horses had fallen to his death, looked as mysterious as ever. Soon we were abreast of the whistlehouse and the tower. I explained that we had to take a wide swing around the end of the island because the water was shoal and dangerous breakers often made up there.

As we rounded the end of the island, we could now look all along Libby's coastline to Big Libby. I could hardly believe I was here. The outside (oceanward side) of Libby always had been forbidden territory for us. We seldom ventured here unless we were on a specific fishing trip, usually with Father. This was where huge waves formed that sometimes washed right into our yard—we were at least fifty feet above the high-water mark, so the waves had to be gigantic to come so close to reaching our house and the other keepers' duplex.

Soon we could see the beaches where we had enjoyed so many wonderful picnics. One beach had large, round, white stones— probably the broken ballast from wrecked ships. After a short sail, we could look back to the tower and the whistlehouse, which appeared lonely in the mist. The light was flashing, possibly activated by the low degree of light coming through the clouds. But there still seemed to be no sign of fog settling in.

By this time, the bar was nearly all exposed. I showed Dorothy the exact place where I had spotted a three-masted barkentine, the *John C. Myers*, smashed high on the rocks with her six hundred cord of pulpwood strewn over the ocean as far as one could see. Many ships were wrecked here in the 1800s, and we witnessed two wrecks in the 1920s, when shipping by sailing vessels had almost ceased.

The sailing was perfect—a fresh breeze and great ocean swells seemed to propel us along. Finally we reached the large beach on the eastern end of Big Libby. Here there had been a natural bridge that, as kids, we dared each other to cross. Through my binoculars I could see that it had not survived the half century since I had proved myself a man by walking over it. Rounding Big Libby's eastern point, I could see where the *F.C. Lockhart*'s captain had sailed his ship directly into the rocks. She had sat up as if in a cradle. My brother Irwin and my father had gone aboard and had lunch with the captain. Tugs never could pull the ship off the rocks. She broke up there in the winter storms. (More about our two shipwrecks appears in chapter 4.)

As we headed back toward Stone Island, we ran into an area of whirlpools—not substantial enough to be dangerous but enough to let us know the power of the tides. We steered far to the northeast to compensate for the current so we could make it around the eastern end of Stone Island. We sailed close under its forested shores, where the fragrance of the island spruces hung heavy in the air. Soon we were clear, and in a short time we were back in Starboard, laying at a mooring Richard had made available for us, secure for the night.

In the evening we rowed ashore in our inflatable. I had become concerned about trying to land on the broken-up slip at Libby in this clumsy boat for fear it might get punctured. After I shared my concerns with Richard, he agreed to lend me a small skiff—a type of sturdy, flat-bottomed boat used as a tender by lobster fishermen.

We chatted a while. Mrs. Pettegrow said that when she saw us heading for Libby in the morning she had thought that it must be quite a thrill for me, after all the years I had been away, to be going home. She was so right. It was also good to be in the Pettegrows' home. Richard's grandparents, "Aunt" Alice and "Uncle" Jim Sprague, had owned this farm, and they had provided sanctuary for us in the same house many times after we had made a stormy crossing from Libby.

As Dorothy and I sat in *Puffin*'s snug cabin that evening, playing cards and talking over our trip around Libby, I told her that I had just had one of the most thrilling days of my life. And we still had the landing on Libby to look forward to. About this time, the boat started rocking vigorously. I knew what was happening: the tide had risen over Ingalls Island bar, letting the ocean swells through. I began thinking to myself that if my "first mate" were ever going to be seasick, it would be now. She gave no heed to the boat's motion, however, and continued to beat me at cards.

Before "crawling under the kelps," my father's expression for going to bed, I went on deck to inspect our mooring line and to check the weather. The sky was clear. The Big Dipper and the North Star were sending down their sparkling light. The breeze was soft, bringing from the shore a multitude of fragrances. Tomorrow would be a good day—it had to be.

I went below and turned in. As I closed my eyes I visualized the jagged ends of the slip on Libby. In calm weather it would be a difficult landing; if any sea were running, it would be impossible. I had contemplated mooring *Puffin*. The Coast Guard had placed a large can buoy off the slip, and I had obtained permission to tie up there. But when I discussed plans for this trip with my two brothers, they warned me about the currents that had always twisted our government boat around and around our mooring pole in the same location. Perhaps I should anchor, but I did not trust the bottom. If the anchor broke loose while we were on Libby, *Puffin* would be gone and we also would have lost our only means of communication—our VHF radio. Finally the lapping of the waves lulled me to sleep.

We were on deck early the next morning. I could hardly wait to climb through the companionway to check the weather. The day was perfect, with a light wind off the land, and in the distance I could hear a "Tom Peabody" bird (white-throated sparrow) giving his many-syllabled call. I knew I was once again in Starboard.

After checking the tide table, we had breakfast and planned our departure time to coincide with the first feeble currents of the flood tide. We wanted to land at Libby precisely at the time the water would cover the end of the slip—which would give us maximum time before it dropped off again. There was not quite enough wind to sail against the flood tide, so we motorsailed. The sky, the smell of the air, the sounds of gulls, and the black figures of shags (cormorants) sitting on old weir stakes projecting from the water reminded me of home. And today, after many years, I would again be there.

We sailed close by bold-headed Stone Island, and I recalled the day Father had detected the disturbed cries of ravens as they flew back and forth close to the cliffs. Being curious, he swung the boat over, and there in the water were two baby ravens—one obviously dead but the other very much alive. Bringing the boat in close, he scooped the live one out of the water. We took him back to Libby, where he entertained and annoyed us for several years.

The distance to Libby, which once had seemed so long, now was shortened greatly. It was less than three miles. In forty-five minutes, we were at the Coast Guard buoy. Dorothy was able to reach out from the bow and pass *Puffin*'s painter through a ring in the top of the buoy. With motor shut off and sails down, *Puffin* was secure (we thought). I let out about thirty feet of scope on the painter and assumed that she would lay bow against the current, no matter what its direction.

We pulled the skiff alongside and I helped Dorothy aboard. Then I climbed in, fitted the oars in the oarlocks, and started rowing toward the slip. How often I had done this as a child. Someone always had to row about in the sixteen-foot peapod while Father landed the government-supplied powerboat, which would strike the slip with considerable force. The government boat had no neutral or reverse gear, and if the peapod had been in tow, she surely would have crashed through the big boat's transom.

Right at this moment I wished I had a peapod. These double-ended boats are stable, easy to row backward or forward, and very seaworthy. I had never liked a skiff and I did not like the one we were in now.

Fortunately, the sea was almost flat calm and we had arrived at precisely the right time. I headed into a small pool beside the slip, which the tide had flooded, and held onto it while Dorothy got out. I warned her to crawl up over the slippery weeds. After she made it safely, I got out and pulled the skiff farther into the pool and tied it. As I crept and walked up the slip, I looked about. The boathouse had been leveled, but the huge bulkhead that gave slight protection to the area was still intact.

As I stepped onto the grassy cover, I shouted, "I'm home! I'm home!" I could hardly believe I had made it.

We began our exploration, and since this was Dorothy's first trip, I tried to tell her about events that had occurred on almost every square yard of the island. First we headed along the southwest shore to where we could look over the "Big Pond" (about four hundred feet square), which provided us with skating in the winter. The water was gone. Just beyond that was the gulch where one of our cows had chosen to drop her calf. We were able to rescue it from the rocky shelf where it landed.

It was sad to see that the barn that had housed our cows and horses was no longer here. As we walked by where our home had stood and the edge of another gulch, I told Dorothy about Maude, the "wild" horse Father had unwittingly bought. (Some of Maude's escapades are recounted in chapter 9.)

Standing near the tower, we could look down over fifty-foot cliffs to the ocean where we had sailed the day before. I pointed out the delicate bird's-eye primroses that always bloomed at the base of the tower where a migrating bird must have dropped a seed. Here, too, we would pick up many small songbirds that had crashed into the light during storms.

Looking over the site of our home, I tried to describe to Dorothy the rich and wonderful family life we had enjoyed here. She, being a former teacher, was intrigued when I told her about the schoolroom in our house and the itinerant teacher who used to come several times a year to teach us. And then there were the trips Santa Claus and his reindeer made to our island home every Christmas.

Leaving the area where the keepers' homes had been, we walked along the path toward the boathouse, a route I had traversed so many times in the fog of summer and the cold of winter. We soon veered off from this path toward the Tip-End, and I pointed out the site where one summer—the best summer I ever spent on Libby—another boy and I built a camp that became a refuge and a playhouse for the whole family.

At this point, I realized that I had run out of film, and the rest of it was on board *Puffin*. I decided to walk back to the slip, launch the skiff, and row out to get it. Soon I was beside *Puffin*, but to my shock, I realized that my brothers' predictions had been right. She was hopelessly entangled, riding stern to the current, and rocking perilously close to the big metal buoy. I got aboard, retrieved my film, and then had to make a decision. I had either to spend perhaps an hour trying to untangle *Puffin*'s painter and have no further time on Libby, or to take a chance that there would be little if any damage and go ashore to finish my exploration. I refused to give up the opportunity to walk over more of Libby. The time already spent there had been too precious to me. So I returned and we resumed our walk.

We continued to the Tip-End and then cut back along the southern shore. Soon we were walking along the beaches where I had spent so many hours. Just as Dorothy and I reached the end of the two beaches, I saw a familiar sight: a flock of sea ducks (eiders) swimming just offshore. It was satisfying to know that Libby's wildlife was still intact.

As we turned and headed back across the top of the island, we found walking hard at times, because the grass was thick and matted—very different from when we lived on Libby and our horse and cows kept all the grass cropped short. We marveled at the beauty of the wildflowers—fields of yellow buttercups and hawkweed, with bluebells and wild iris showing through. Dorothy, an amateur botanist, felt certain the iris was a unique variety that might be indigenous to the area, or possibly even to

Libby. The view was spectacular from the top, with the yellow flowers blowing in the wind and the white breakers providing contrast along Libby's shores.

I wanted desperately to spend more hours just roaming about, but "tide waits for no man." Soon the water would be too low at the end of the slip, and we would have great difficulty launching our skiff. Some things never change. Our lives had always been circumscribed by the tides.

In my excitement at rediscovering Libby, I had forgotten about *Puffin*. As we approached the brow of the hill where I could view the mooring, I was very anxious to see how she had fared. What I saw was not good. It looked as though her transom was pounding against the side of the buoy.

We hurried down to the landing. The tide had already fallen several feet, leaving our skiff high on the rocks. Since the boat was light, I soon got it down to the water's edge. We would have to launch from the rocks, though. I looked for a particular flat place that we had used over many years. It was there, buried in seaweed as usual. I told Dorothy to climb down to the ledge and to get as secure a footing as possible.

"These waves will come in sets of six or seven," I said. "Then there will be a lull. When I tell you, get into the skiff as quickly as possible and I will shove off." We counted from one lull and, sure enough, another one occurred after six more waves. Dorothy quickly stepped into the skiff, going to the stern seat. I pushed the boat off, jumped in over the bow, grabbed the oars, and quickly rowed away from the rocks. I had made one more successful landing and launching on Libby. It pleased me that some of my old skills were still in place.

But our troubles were not over. As we got closer to the mooring, I became even more concerned about *Puffin*. I did not want her beautiful shiny hull marred with red and white paint from the buoy. We quickly climbed aboard and secured the skiff. Now I had to solve the problem of clearing the mooring line. I soon saw that it was twisted hopelessly around our keel, the motor, and the hull itself. Releasing it would take hours, and in the meantime I would run the risk of further scratches. There was only one answer—to sacrifice several feet of mooring line. I whipped out my rigging knife, climbed up on the bow, and in seconds we were free. I then had no problem untangling the line and hauling it aboard. Fortunately, we have an outboard motor, so I did not have to worry about the line being entangled in an underwater propeller. But *Puffin* now carried bits of the Coast Guard's colors. We were soon underway, headed for Starboard. The wind was fair, so we raised the main and jib, shut off the motor, and were again under sail.

I thought about all the years when lightkeepers had had to travel back and forth to the mainland in sailboats. It must have made life so much more complicated—although even during our time on Libby, we rowed over this same course many times in our peapods.

This had been the most satisfying "voyage" I had ever taken. And tomorrow, if the weather stayed clear, we could sail over toward Cross Island and perhaps west to Jonesport.

Our evening was restful, but that night, when I made my last check of the mooring line and the weather, something different was in the air—a cool dampness. The sky was clear, however, and there had been a red summer sunset. "Red at night, sailor's delight." But how could we expect three clear days in July? That would be unusual. When I emerged from the cabin in the morning, my worst fears were realized. The fog was so thick I could scarcely see the shore. Our Libby Island adventure had come to an end—albeit a successful one.

Richard pulled us out without difficulty, *Puffin* was secured on her trailer, and we were soon rolling along westward. Over the years of our marriage, I had told Dorothy a great deal about our lighthouse life, and I was pleased that she finally had been to Libby Island. But she had many more questions: "Tell me more about your schooling on the island." "How did your mother ever feed you all with no stores nearby?" "What did you find to do for recreation?" Finally, she had one last question: "When are you going to write your Libby Island book?"

This was something I had thought of doing over many years. Dozens of stories had been shaped in my mind because when our two sons were growing up, each night I told them Libby Island stories. It took me four more years to get started, but on Christmas Day 1984, I finally began writing my Libby Island book. Since it was Christmas, I first wrote about how we celebrated Christmas on Libby Island. This became chapter 10.

My first trip to Libby Island Light Station was quite different from the 1980 one I have just described. Father had put in a request to be transferred from Whitehead Light Station, off Spruce Head at the entrance to Penobscot Bay, to a station "down east," where he and Mother could be nearer to their relatives. In the spring of 1919, Father received a letter from the lighthouse superintendent's office stating that he had been appointed head keeper on Libby Island, a major offshore light that guards the entrance to Machias Bay.

The big lighthouse tender *Hibiscus* would be coming soon to move us, so the frenzy of packing began. (Since I was only two years old, I have had to rely on other members of the family for information about this move.) Finally, the day came—what excitement! We were excited not only about moving to a new island, but also about traveling on a "big" steamship. When everything was aboard—even my sister Hazel's piano—the *Hibiscus* weighed anchor. Everyone enjoyed the trip, particularly my brother Irwin, who loved exploring the ship and talking with all the sailors.

The trip was only about a hundred miles, but apparently we traveled overnight. As the end of our voyage grew nearer, I'm sure that we were all on the foredeck peering into the distance to try to be the first to sight our new island home.

Someone shouted, "Is that it, Father? I think I can see a white tower." Father confirmed the sighting. Our eyes were riveted on the island. Our excitement increased when Father pointed out our house—a large white and gray building standing on the high southwest head of the island.

I'm sure someone also shouted, "Father, where are the trees?" Whitehead had been heavily wooded. As we rounded the head of the island, the answer to that question was obvious. There were none.

Soon we were anchored near the boathouse and quickly loaded into the *Hibiscus's* tender—all six of us. Being lowered into the water was a little scary, but the motor started with a roar and we were on our way to the boat slip to make the first of many such landings. The keeper in charge had the steam-powered hoisting engine in operation, and it whisked us to the top of the slip. This was the fastest ride we ever had on this slip. Later, when we landed our own government boat, we would hoist it up with a muscle-powered winch. We were not supplied with enough coal to allow frequent use of the steam engine, and it took too long to get it started.

At last our feet were planted firmly on Libby Island soil. So anxious were we to see our new home that we rapidly covered the distance to it. The entrance was through a 100-foot-long shed built to catch rainwater, which was stored in underground cisterns. Inside the house, we admired the large, pleasant rooms, eight in all. Through every window we could see the ocean.

There was not much time to think about what life would be like on Libby, but one thing we were sure of—it would be different from Whitehead, where we were only a few minutes' row across a sheltered harbor to a village that had stores. Libby Island felt like it was in the middle of the ocean. Getting to a town from here would not be easy, as we quickly learned.

All day long, the men worked to move our furniture up to the house. They had the help of old Tim, a horse Father was to buy from the previous head keeper.

By nightfall we had beds to sleep in, and someone must have provided us with food for a few days. I doubt that any of us slept much that first night, because the fog signal would have started its baleful bellowing. Later, it would be like the ticking of a clock; we only woke up when it stopped—an infrequent occurrence in the summer. Fog was something we would have to learn to live with on Libby. That first July, the fog signal blew for more than 350 hours. We had never experienced fog this continuously on Whitehead.

My sister Hazel, who was sixteen, well remembers our landing on Libby. As she reports it, "That first night I sat on my trunk, out on the veranda, and looked across those miles of ocean to other islands and the mainland in the distance. I felt very lonely. I had left our sheltered life on Whitehead, my piano teacher whom I loved, and all my friends in Rockland, where I had been attending high school. Life here was going to be quite different. But not being one to mope around, I determined to make the best of it."

Sis, as I always called her, lived on the mainland during the school year in order to finish high school in Machias. But it was on Libby Island, of all unlikely places, that she found romance, love, and a husband. She has very happy memories of the summers and vacations she spent on Libby.

Winona ("Nonie"), my other sister, was ten when we arrived on Libby. She had left an environment where she was very happy. There was a school on Whitehead, as well as other girls her own age. She would never be content on Libby, perhaps because she would not attend a full year of regular school until she went to high school. She had no friends, either boys or girls, and enjoyed none of the activities that delight girls of this age. For a while, our cousin Orrie lived with us, but even her companionship was not enough to satisfy Nonie's yearning for normal relationships.

My older brother, Irwin, then aged seven, would attend school off the island only for the sixth and seventh grades. But the island environment was his element. By the age of twelve, he was a crack shot, supplying much game for the family table. He enjoyed everything about Libby, especially the boating, lobster fishing, and "gunning." During his growing-up years he gained the skills that would serve him well as he pursued a career in the U.S. Coast Guard.

I did not know any other home than Libby for many years, and I would always be bonded to the island where I first became aware of my surroundings. Even though I would spend part of my elementary-school years in Machias, Libby was where my earliest memories were formed.

My younger brother, Arnold, was born in August 1923. Mother was forty and Father was fifty when Arnie arrived on the scene, and the rest of the children were pretty well grown up. He would never live on Libby after he was two except for summers and vacations, because Mother lived ashore so we could attend school, but he fully absorbed all the island ways.

In 1919, my father was forty-six, well along in his career, having previously served eleven years in the Lighthouse Service and Coast Guard. As head keeper on a three-man offshore station, he had reached the peak of a lighthouse career. He remained on Libby until 1940, when he retired at the age of sixty-seven, after thirty-two years in the Lighthouse Service and the Coast Guard.

Mother was a young woman—thirty-six. Mabel Crowley Wass (Father often called her "Maybelle") would spend the next four years on Libby, making only infrequent trips off the island— almost none in the winter months. But if she missed her more varied life on Whitehead or her family of eleven brothers and sisters who lived in Jonesport and Addison, she never let anyone know. Libby was her home, and she seemed content to live there.

2

LIBBY'S LIGHTKEEPERS,
THEIR FAMILIES,
AND THEIR WORK

LIBBY Island Light Station was first established with only one man as keeper. Later, when a fog signal bell was added, a second man was required. Still later, when steam apparatus was installed to blow a fog whistle, a third man was needed.

The second keeper who arrived was a relative of the head keeper, so no new housing had to be built. But when a nonrelative replaced him, separate quarters became necessary. It took the Lighthouse Board (the national administrative agency, 1852-1910) many years of petitioning before the spacious head keeper's house was constructed and a two-story duplex was provided for the other two keepers and their families. The head keeper's house had eight large rooms, and the other keepers' homes had six—small but adequate.

During the twenty-one years our family occupied the head keeper's house, two families lived in the south side of the duplex reserved for the first assistant keeper, and six second assistant keepers and their families occupied the north side. This made a total of nine families who lived on Libby during Father's years as head keeper. If I have remembered correctly, more than forty people (counting children) shared some part of our Libby Island experience.

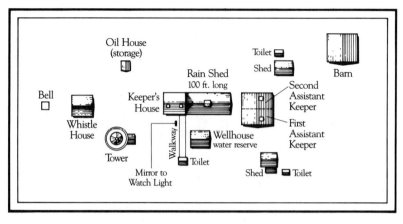

Dwellings and outbuildings at Libby Island.   MAP BY PATRICE M. ROSSI

Willis Clark, second assistant keeper, and his wife, Angelia, made no lasting impression on me, except that the gulch in front of their house always carried her name: "Aunt Gelia's Gulch." But the next keeper who came, in 1921, was to make a lasting impression on all of us. His name was George Woodward and he was a widower from Jonesport with two children, Coleman and Charlotte. He was twenty-six, intelligent, handsome, and mischievous. He came well trained, having served an apprenticeship on Petit Manan, a difficult station with the second-highest tower (123 feet) in the First Lighthouse District. His assignment just prior to Libby was Boon Island, which had the tallest tower —over 130 feet. Tending the light required a climb of approximately two hundred steps. Boon was a notoriously bad assignment for a lightkeeper. Landing was so difficult that it was necessary to lay in a complete store of food in the fall because shopping opportunities were few during the winter months. One retired keeper called Boon the most barren light station on the Maine coast. Just to have a few flowers, they transported soil from the mainland in boxes. Because the island is so low, sometimes seas surge over it completely. During bad storms in the past, waves have broken into the dwellings and washed everything movable into the sea. The island's name came from the local fishermen's practice of leaving a barrel on the island well stocked with food for shipwrecked sailors and fishermen.

After spending two years on Boon Island, George must have thought his assignment to Libby was a transfer to paradise. And it was on Libby that he truly found a "boon"—a kind, generous, pleasant, merry companion.

My sister Hazel had just graduated from high school and returned to Libby for her summer vacation before entering Washington State Normal School in Machias to train for teaching. George and Hazel fell in love that summer, and romance filled the air on Libby. We kids all thoroughly enjoyed this prospective new member of our family, and we often tried to find their trysting places. With forty-two acres, however, this was not easy. It was easier to pry up the cover on the heating hole in the parlor ceiling and spy from the upstairs bedroom.

I loved my big sister — "Sis," as I called her — and always looked forward to her coming home on vacations and being with us during the summer. Sometimes this required difficult trips; she often walked from Machias to Starboard over thirteen miles of dirt road. This must not have been easy for a young woman of under five feet who weighed close to 180 pounds. But she was anxious to be with us and her George.

During this early period of our life on Libby, Father had not yet bought our first car, so getting to and from Machias was difficult, although sometimes we made the trip up the river in the government boat. Father must have purchased a car while Sis was still in normal school, because I remember one very significant event connected with a visit to the school. We had gone to the girls' dormitory to get Hazel. When she came out, she wanted to take her "cute little brother" into the dorm to meet some of her girl friends. I remember enjoying this tremendously, but most of all I remember that she gave me a new box of crayons. I must have been only about six, but this kindness still gives me a warm feeling. This was also my first introduction to "higher education." I would later spend my first three years of college at that school.

Of course, relations among siblings—even between the eldest and the youngest—do not always run smoothly. One day Hazel was assigned the job of washing down the stairs from our entryway into the cellar. For some reason I wanted to get past her. In spite of her request that I wait, I tried squeezing around her and upset the water bucket. She says she thinks she gave me a slap, but I do not remember it. I do remember, however, being banished to an empty room. She says she passed the door a few minutes later and heard me singing to myself, "Tain't my brother nor my sister, but it's me, O Lord, a-standing in the need of prayer." Who could resist such a charming fellow? Since it was obvious that I had repented, I was released immediately. But in the process I had supplied material for a family story. The hymn, I am sure, was one that Sis had been playing for a hymn-sing, which we usually had every Sunday afternoon.

On Whitehead, Father's previous assignment, Hazel had had an opportunity to take piano lessons from the keeper's wife, a talented musician. Father loved music and bought Hazel an excellent upright piano that she had been able to bring to Libby. Passengers on any ship or yacht that approached close enough to Libby on a calm day must have been quite surprised to hear piano music drifting down from our cliffside house.

Although I am sure Hazel was very much in love with her "intended," she says she told George that she had plans to become a teacher, and if he wanted to marry her, he would have to wait. The course of true love never runs smoothly, and I remember one occasion when we thought this budding romance might suffer early blight. Hazel had a magnificent head of thick, brown hair that hung way below her waist. Apparently, this was very much a part of her charm for George. But disaster was about to strike. Hairstyles were changing, and women began to "bob" their hair. When Sis announced that the next time she went to Machias she was going to have her hair bobbed, George was adamant. He said, "If you get your hair cut, don't bother to come back—I won't want to see you again." He should have learned by this time that his bride-to-be had a mind of her own. This was probably the most effective way to ensure her visit to the barber. When she came home, her hair was only long enough to reach the bottoms of her earlobes. All the rest she carried in a bag. I do not know how the impasse was resolved, but somehow the romance continued to blossom.

George soon took his revenge. The happy pair was taking a stroll around the island when George, without warning, leaped down over the edge of the island, climbed to a high perch on a rock, looked back at Hazel, and began a loud maniacal laugh. At first she thought he was joking, but he did not look as if he were joking. He laughed and laughed, his loud cackling mirth echoing and reechoing among the cliffs and crags. Hazel stood it as long as she could. Then, completely convinced that her lover had gone mad, she started running for the house as fast as her short legs could carry her. Seeing what he had done, George started running after her, shouting, "I'm all right, Hazel! I'm all right!" But she never stopped running until she was safe at home. I wonder what any onlookers might have thought had they observed this strange scene.

These years (1921-23) were among our best on Libby. With Sis home in the summer, our whole family of six was together, and the new assistant keeper contributed greatly to our happiness. George remembers many baseball games with kids and adults playing together, our teams supplemented by government work-men who were often on the island for major building or repair projects.

During one summer vacation, Hazel realized that our island population numbered twenty—perhaps the most people who lived on Libby at one time. She decided to grab the opportunity to try out some of the skills she had learned in her teacher training. She got all the kids together and put on an entertainment. I recall that one number was a dance called an Irish lilt.

After graduating from the normal school in 1923, Hazel got a job in West Bath, Maine. That same year, George was transferred to Franklin Island, a one-man station in Muscongus Bay. They were married in Portland in April 1924. Before the end of the school year, when Hazel would join George permanently on Franklin, she decided to pay him a weekend visit. Arriving at the nearest harbor, she was able to find a lobster fisherman to take her out to the island. When she arrived off the end of Franklin's slip, she was quite concerned to see that waves were breaking across it. She watched George launch his rowboat successfully, and, although she noted that a wave had broken across the bow, she was not afraid. When George pulled alongside the lobsterboat to take his new bride aboard, he warned her to be careful, but his next words were most disconcerting.

"Hazel," he said, "When you get in, I want you to sit right down in the bottom of the boat, not on the seat." Wearing a new spring suit, she looked with dismay at the four inches of cold Atlantic covering the floorboards. She protested, but George was firm.

"We have to keep your weight low or the boat might tip over landing on the slip." She had no choice but to slide onto the floorboards. This was the way she began her first crossing to her new home.

Realizing that she might have avoided this unpleasantness had she not been carrying so much "ballast," Hazel was very receptive, after she moved to the island, to an article in the *Portland Press Herald* about dieting. Included was a detailed plan for losing weight. She immediately made up her mind to try it. She says, "I didn't have any scales, only a tape measure, but four months later, when I got ashore and weighed myself, I found, to my amazement, that I had lost sixty pounds." And, unlike most people, she never regained it.

After leaving Franklin in 1927, Hazel and George moved to Wood Island off Biddeford Pool in southern Maine, where the rest of our family visited them many times. From there they were transferred in 1934 to Rockland Breakwater, where he served eight years. Finally, they were moved to one of the most delightful lighthouses on the Maine coast, Owls Head, just south of Rockland.

Hazel and George contributed a great deal to our family. The fact that she, as the first child, sought higher education, made it easier for the rest of us to follow. Living "away"—as we called any place west of Washington County — opened up a new world to us. Otherwise, I am sure we never would have become familiar with Portland and the other cities we traveled through to visit them. Nonie chose to train to be a nurse at Trull Hospital in Biddeford, gaining support from her big sister, who lived nearby. And she finally settled in that area.

Later, when George and Hazel moved to Rockland, we became familiar with that area. Arnie chose to live permanently in that city and Irwin lived there for several years. A few years after Father retired in 1940, my parents moved to nearby Thomaston, across the street from where Hazel and George had recently bought a home after his retirement. Our favorite assistant keeper had helped to expand our island boundaries.

George and Hazel's lighthouse career was quite remarkable. Altogether George served on seven of Maine's lighthouse stations, with Hazel as his "assistant keeper" on three of them. (Rockland Breakwater, at the time, was not a family station.) She had followed in her mother's footsteps. After being married more than sixty years, George and Hazel continue their romance begun on Libby Island so many years ago. When someone recently asked George if he wanted to go to heaven, his answer was, "I don't know. I just want to go where Hazel goes."

I may not be wholly accurate in discussing the order of the five second assistant keepers and their families who came to Libby after George left, but I think I have recalled them correctly.

Everett Mitchell, his wife, Lena, and (I believe) two children came from the Harrington area. I do not remember a great deal about them except that Everett was a casual, relaxed individual who always wore his cap with the visor a bit askew. He was one of the few assistant keepers who used to pay social calls on us. Or perhaps he came in to talk with Father about something and stayed to visit. He loved to play cards and would accept an invitation readily to enter into one of our games. I can visualize him now, cap askew, concentrating on his next play. He never stayed very long, however, because soon after he became involved in a game, one of his kids would come in and tell him he was wanted at home. His wife must have been lonely. For anyone accustomed to a busy family and community life, Libby could be a dreary place.

It is difficult to imagine how the next two second assistant keepers—Bernard Small and James McCloud—ever became interested in the Lighthouse Service or got appointed. Neither of them had any experience with the sea or any training in the handling of boats. My guess is that they got in by exercising veterans' rights.

I was very interested when I heard about the impending arrival of Bernard and Abigail Small, from Ellsworth, because they had three boys—Edward, Gilford, and Charles. I hoped that Edward, although two or three years younger than I, might be a good playmate. And perhaps Gilford also might be old enough to enter into some of our games.

The day they arrived, I watched with eagerness as the three boys were helped out of the boat. I decided that I had never seen a scrawnier bunch of kids in my life. What a disappointment! I knew in a minute that they would be unable to keep up with our rough-and-tumble island games. They probably grew up to be burly high school football stars, but at that stage of their development, they looked very fragile to me.

Bernard himself had a near-impact on our family that might have been disastrous. When he arrived, Father was becoming restive about being separated from us because we were all away at school in Machias, and Bernard started telling him about a wonderful little farm that was for sale near his home in Ellsworth. Father was quite interested, and I think even went to inspect it. There was a productive apple orchard, plus wooded areas and ample arable land for farming. Knowing that Father was considering this proposition seriously, we kids began to think about moving to the "city." To us, Ellsworth was a metropolis.

During summers we had encountered enough "rusticators" to know that they did not speak our language. It seemed that the only letter they recognized in the alphabet was R. That, of course, was the one letter we did not recognize, so we began practicing sounding our Rs to better communicate with our new urban neighbors.

This was around 1928, and disaster struck in 1929. If Father had given in to the urge to end the isolation of being on Libby without his family for several months each year, we would have been faced with a far different future. But he put the security of the family first, and his selflessness meant that all through the Depression our family was rich compared with most of the people we knew. Anyone in eastern Maine who had a steady job during those years was wealthy, indeed.

James McCloud, a self-proclaimed Indian, came from Rhode Island. He was a bachelor, and the second to arrive with little knowledge or experience to prepare him for lighthouse work. The one talent he claimed was running, and he boasted about the many races he had won. Finally, Irwin could stand it no longer and challenged him to a race.

I well remember this contest. We laid out a course—not a long one, because Jim supposedly excelled as a sprinter. Word of the race spread quickly, so a "crowd" gathered. We used the traditional, "On your mark, get set, GO!" starting signals. Irwin took off at high speed and reached the finish line several lengths ahead of the "champion." After that, we heard little more about Jim's racing laurels.

Our next second assistant keeper was John Beal, one of our favorites. He and his family came from Jonesport, and he was an expert boat handler. Father could trust him with any of the functions of the station. John was good natured, a willing and capable worker, and a skilled pole vaulter. (More about that in chapter 7.) John and his wife, Katie, who seemed quite happy living on Libby, had four children: Dorothy, Roger, Jonathan (I believe), and Gloria. Roger was the pal near my own age I had dreamed about for many years. He was a bit younger than I, but sturdy, and we immediately formed a fast friendship. We were seldom out of each other's sight. Some of our elders predicted, "Oh, you'll be fighting before the summer is over." This made us all the more determined to get along. I can recall only one squabble, and that had something to do with Dorothy, but it was quickly resolved. (Chapter 7 describes our experiences in building a camp together.)

As far as I know, none of these second assistant keepers stayed in the service very long, finding lighthouse life not particularly to their liking. But Jasper Cheney, the next man to fill the post, stayed until after Father retired. He was competent, a reliable worker, and always wore a smile. His wife wanted no part of Libby Island life, and, after a summer of two, she remained at their home in Lubec. They had a son named Forrest who later joined the Coast Guard and a younger son named Roland. I believe there was also a daughter.

A few years ago, my wife and I visited Lubec, where I knew Roland was a barber. I found his shop, but he was out, so I left a message that we might drop by on our return from Campobello Island the next day. That night we stayed at a campground on Campobello and went to one of the two restaurants for dinner. When we walked out of the restaurant, I saw a man approaching. Although I had not seen him for years, I knew in one glance that it was Roland. He had been so anxious to see me that he had checked the campground, found we were not there, and decided, rightly, that we must have gone out to eat. Since there were only the two restaurants, he had checked them both.

There are strong bonds among those who have shared lighthouse living. We had a great conversation. He had some vivid memories about Libby and had enjoyed his summers there. (One experience he related was his encounter with an angry bull, a story recounted in chapter 9.)

During the 1920s, while several second assistant keepers and their families came to Libby and moved on, Justin Foss served continuously as first assistant keeper. He was already serving in that position when Father became head keeper and did not leave until 1932.

Justin and his wife, Ada, had four children: Millie, Arlona ("Loni"), Justin, Jr. ("Junie"), and Leo. Millie was two years younger than Irwin, Loni was one year older than I, Junie was a couple of years younger, and Leo was one year younger than his brother.

Justin, who came from Beals Island, was an excellent boatman and a skilled worker. He served a full career in the Lighthouse Service, transferring from Libby to The Cuckolds, a two-man station off Boothbay Harbor, where he became head keeper. Later he served at Blue Hill Bay and finally at Goat Island near Kennebunkport. He died before he could retire. But his lighthouse career—and his life—came close to ending during his early years on Libby, as recounted in chapter 5.

Ada raised all her children in the harsh and dangerous environment of Libby Island. When she and Justin accepted their assignment in 1916, Millie was three and Arlona about six months old. Although Ada returned to Beals Island for the births of Junie and Leo, they were raised on the island from infancy. Among their escapades, they survived some severe falls. Loni fell backward off a high breakwater at the boathouse, and Leo, as I recall, fell through the heating hole in a bedroom floor and "bounced" off the hot kitchen stove before hitting the floor. Fortunately, neither one sustained serious injury.

These were the kids who were our playmates during most of the time we were on Libby. Loni, in particular, was my very best friend in our early years, and I do not remember that we ever quarreled. But it was different with Junie and Leo. Because they were younger, they often got in our way. Still, they were part of our little gang, and all six of us spent hours playing our island games. Even though Junie was younger than I, he was tough and never hesitated to tackle any challenge we took on.

In addition to the Foss kids, there often were children in the other assistant keepers' families. During one year, our kid population was nine. We usually played together quite peacefully, but one day we had a quarrel that I shall never forget because it caused me a summer of acute anxiety. The long rainshed attached to our house—which I considered Wass territory—had been the scene of some dissension. The other kids always seemed to win these battles with words. Our epithets were so sanitized (due to our strict upbringing) that they carried little power, while most of the other kids seemed to have a full lexicon of cuss words. As we hurled epithets at each other, the "enemy" slowly retreated to the far end of the shed. Then I decided to hurry them along a bit. My air rifle was nearby and I knew the barrel was empty, because I had fired at targets several times outside and no pellets had emerged. I picked it up and fired in their direction, but at the roof. Immediately one of the kids set up a yowl and screamed back that I had wounded him. The next message was frightening: "The next time we go to Machias, we are going to tell the sheriff and he'll come and get you and put you in jail." I was quite certain there had been no pellets in the gun, and I knew I had fired at the ceiling. Since I was a hundred feet away, I also knew that even if a stuck pellet had emerged, the chance of its hitting anyone was remote. And even if it had, the force of the pellet would have been spent. But my reasoning did not help. I greatly regretted that one rash act. I think perhaps the worst aspect of the whole episode was that they did not tell my parents—I was the only one who knew about this "crime."

All that summer, every time the government boat went ashore, I lived in a state of paralyzing fear that reached its peak when I saw the boat returning from Starboard. I always went to the highest bluff and scanned the boat as it approached, trying to discern whether any strange men were aboard. If one of the other families had had a male visitor, I would have assumed immediately that he was the sheriff and would have gone into a state of shock. After viewing the boat from a distance, I would carefully make my way to the boathouse, still keeping out of sight, to observe the passengers at close hand. What a relief it always was when I saw only familiar faces. I was safe until someone took another trip ashore.

Justin Foss was replaced by Gleason Colbeth from Bucks Harbor. He and his wife, Lillian, had four children: Gleason, Jr., Julian, Weldon, and Hollis. A former lobster fisherman, Gleason was an expert in handling boats and a competent worker. He had a pleasant, kind disposition, and he and Father worked together amicably until Father retired from Libby. (They even had winter picnics together, as described in chapter 7.) They and Jasper Cheney made an excellent team.

Gleason and Lillian Colbeth also contributed to our island life with their two comely young relatives, Jenny and Marguerite Beal, who occasionally came for visits. During their stays, our fogbound island was transformed. Irwin's and my days were filled with joy and our evenings with romance. We could not have asked for a happier location. We were perfectly contented—until they left. Then the "fog" returned. In your teens, when you are in love (or think you are), who needs other people?

The head keeper on every light station was the boss. He planned the work, assigned the duties, and, of course, every day worked side by side with his assistants. Father was eminently qualified to be head keeper at a lighthouse station. As a young man he had served an apprenticeship as a blacksmith, and he used his metalworking skills frequently in making basic repairs. His ten years at sea as chief engineer aboard five-masted sailing ships had taught him many skills, particularly how to work with steam-powered hoisting equipment. This was useful in lifting the heavily loaded tenders from the *Hibiscus* and running the steam engines that, in the early years, blew our fog whistle. His years at sea also had given him perspective on the value of lighthouse signals. He knew what it meant to run for a light on a black night in gale-force winds. He also knew the terror of men clinging to wrecked ships. As a member of the Coast Guard (then the Life Saving Service), he had often participated in rescues made with boats that sometimes traversed twenty miles of open sea powered only by men pulling in unison on their long oars.

Not one of the men who served under Father on Libby approached the experience and training that he brought to the job of head keeper. In fact, I doubt if there were many keepers along the entire Maine coast who could match his qualifications.

Unlike most positions of authority, head keepers had no disciplinary power. They did not control pay increases, leaves of absence, or other rewards, nor could they terminate an assistant keeper's employment or even transfer him. The Lighthouse Service did not back up Father's authority very well, either. Several times Father had to report that one of the assistant keepers had in some way failed to do his duty. The assistant keeper, in turn, would file a "grievance" against Father. I do not know what would finally result—nothing, I think. I cannot help wondering why the superintendents were not more sensitive to the incompatibility problems that could so easily flare up on the islands. Working together in isolation—often without sleep because of long watches—and just the sheer boredom of a keeper's life must have caused tempers to wear thin on many light stations, but regardless of conflicts, the watches had to be stood and the work had to be done.

I can well remember how a keeper with whom Father might have had some differences during the day had to come into our house at night to call Father for his watch. I can still hear the voice calling up the stairs, "Mr. Wass, it's time for your watch." Father would acknowledge him and a few minutes later would go down to the kitchen. I could always tell when he got there, because I could hear him slide the covers in place on the iron kitchen stove. (They would have been left slightly ajar to "cool" the fire.) Then I could hear him pumping water into the teakettle to make hot water for a cup of tea.

Although Father occasionally had difficulties with his keepers, I believe he was always generous and fair with all of his men. One of the few privileges controlled by the keeper was the right to go ashore. I never knew Father to refuse a request, nor to take advantage of his position to go more often than the other men went.

Fortunately, any conflicts were sporadic, and months and perhaps years went by as the men shared their work and their watch duties without rancor. I have no knowledge of the interrelationships of the crews on other two- and three-man stations, but I suspect that conflicts were not uncommon.

The families on Libby never established close relationships. There was no interfamily visiting for meals or just socializing. We never had any island picnics or holiday celebrations. The nearest we came were our after-supper baseball games, which sometimes involved members of all the families. When I think of what a rich social life three families might have had, I realize what a great lack this was. During my growing-up years and through my adult life, I have never found it easy to form and maintain close relationships. I have often wondered if the root of the problem did not come from these early experiences when none of the "others" were looked upon as close frends. But perhaps this tendency of families to keep their distance might have been common on offshore stations. There might have been the fear that close relationships would lead to conflict or awkward situations.

Perhaps inevitably, there was some competition among families. I can remember Mother commenting that she needed to get up earlier than usual on Monday so that she could be the first to hang out her laundry. Another time, she and Hazel stuffed layers of newspaper in their berry pails, then topped them off with cranberries to show what "fast" pickers they were. We were convinced that our peapod and our cars were always superior to the others'—certainly *our* Overland Whippet was superior to any Ford or boxy Essex, and it could go up steeper hills without having to downshift.

This does not mean that there was no cooperation among the families, as I have already described. Cooperation was at its best with the Wasses and the Fosses. Haying was one of our joint ventures. Father and Justin were the only keepers who had cows.

They also worked together in killing and butchering pigs and cattle, standing watch for each other so that lobster traps could be hauled, and collecting the pulpwood that came ashore after the wreck of the barkentine *John C. Myers,* a story recounted in chapter 4.

Perhaps the only example of social cooperation was the arrival of Santa Claus. The parents in the three families must have gotten together each year and decided who would be Santa. I think Father and Mother always supplied the costume.

In 1932, Justin Foss was transferred after serving about sixteen years on Libby Island. We lost contact with the family after that, but one of the best outcomes of writing this book was receiving a letter from Patricia Machson, daughter of Arlona Foss. She had read my article, "The Inspector Pays a Visit," in the July 1986 issue of *Down East* Magazine and recognized that I was writing about Libby Island, where her mother had lived as a child. She urged me to call or write, which I did. She put me in touch with her mother, and Loni and I bridged more than half a century in a long telephone conversation.

Regardless of how well the keepers got along with each other, the work of the light station always had to be done. The first and most important job was designated by their title—they were light keepers. On stations with fog signals, they were also fog-signal keepers.

The light tower on Libby was ninety-one feet above high-water mark and, as I recall, forty feet tall. It was constructed out of granite blocks in the early 1820s. Some of the old slabs, not used, were still lying around the area. The light itself was like a Coleman lantern, except that it burned kerosene rather than gasoline. To increase its power, the light was placed inside a huge lens composed of prisms at the top and bottom and a thick magnifying glass in the center. This lens system, invented in France in 1822 by Augustin Fresnel, and named for him, came in seven orders or sizes, number one being the largest. Ours was a number four. These lenses focused the light of the lantern into a powerful vertical band of light that could be seen for many miles. Libby's light was visible for about twelve miles.

Kerosene for the light had to be carried from a storage building about a hundred feet away. The hard part was carrying it up the spiral staircase to the top of the tower. Another time-consuming job was pumping air into the pressure tank. The kerosene was sprayed, under pressure, through a jet. The vaporized fuel, when burned, heated the mantle, which glowed with an intense white light. We enjoyed helping Father with this chore, often pumping up the tank. When the light was burning satisfactorily, it gave out a loud roar and an extremely bright light. Somewhat blinded, we would carefully make our way down the stairs, hanging onto a rope attached to rings in the wall.

The light was started shortly after sundown and put out soon before sunrise, as soon as it was light. While the light was burning, it had to be watched because of the danger of "smoke-ups." Occasionally, even though the kerosene was strained carefully, small pieces of dirt would clog the jet and the kerosene would start burning as liquid, giving off large amounts of smoke and flame. This could be dangerous to both the lens and the interior of the tower, and it made standing watches necessary. The night was divided into three parts—the first watch went from light-up time to ten o'clock. (The length of this watch depended on the time of year.) The second or middle watch was ten to two, and the third watch from two until sunrise. This meant that each keeper was on duty approximately four hours each day. If one man was ashore on leave (which occurred frequently during the summer), this watch became six hours long. In addition to operating the light, they also cleaned it frequently to be sure the jet was clear, the mantle was whole, and the brass that held the sections of the lens in place was shining brightly. Unshined brass was not tolerated on a light station. "Smoke-ups" made the cleanup even more difficult. The soot collected on the lens and sometimes on the walls and roof of the tower. Outside the kitchen window, Father mounted a mirror directed toward the light, and it was frightening to see flames filling the entire glassed-in area at the top of the tower. Father would take off running as fast as he could, often without proper clothing, and I am sure he did not stop until he reached the top of the tower. The immediate first step was to turn off the kerosene. The next was to clean up the lens quickly and place one of the old lamps or a lantern inside so that the signal, although dim, would still be shining. A second light was always in readiness, but this took a few minutes to install.

Until 1923, during our time at Libby Island, the fog signal was powered by steam. There were two large boilers with all the related equipment to blast out a loud steam whistle four times a minute.

The steam fog signal required that about eighty tons of soft coal be delivered to the station each year. This had to be loaded by shovel at the boathouse, hauled to the whistlehouse, and then unloaded. An additional twenty-one tons of hard coal was supplied for use in the keepers' homes. Several cords of hardwood kindling were also landed to ignite the coal.

Libby Island was known as one of the foggiest places on the whole U.S. coast. In 1918, Libby Island held the record for all U.S. light stations: 1,906 hours of blowing the fog signal. When certain islands, used as markers, were obscured by the fog, the keeper who was technically on watch had to start the fog signal. This meant starting a fire with kindling, adding coal when it was hot enough, and opening all drafts to get up steam as quickly as possible. This took so long that when fog was threatening, which was most of the time in July and August, a low fire was kept burning under the boilers at all times.

In 1923, the system was modernized and diesel engines were installed. These blasted compressed air through a horn to provide the fog signal. I was only six at the time, but I remember the summer when these huge engines were brought by the *Hibiscus.* With all their related equipment, they completely filled the thirty-two-foot-square whistlehouse. (Everything was in duplicate in case of breakdowns.) My father, with the help of government workers, got the engines moved from the boathouse. He used our horse to move the engines on iron rollers along a track timbers, which was constantly rebuilt as the engines progressed. The horse and all the men succeeded in moving the engines to the whistlehouse in about a week. I have a clear picture in my mind of the engines, which looked like small locomotives as they made their way slowly along the primitive cart road that ran to the whistlehouse. It was an exciting event.

Even more exciting was the day when the trumpets let out their first blast—four times each minute. Unlike the steam apparatus, which was quiet between blasts, the diesels gave out a steady "Pom! Pom! Pom!" from their exhausts. We had a few sleepless nights getting used to this new sound.

But the diesel-powered whistle had many advantages over steam. There was no longer a delay in starting the signal when the fog closed in. The diesel oil came in fifty-gallon drums, much easier to handle than coal. Later, huge tanks were installed, and tankers filled them directly. But perhaps the greatest advantage for the keepers was cleanliness. The coal dust would infiltrate everywhere, making cleaning very difficult for both the men and the women. Although we still used hard coal for heating and cooking, this was clean by comparison.

During the summer months, when we lived in fog some part of nearly every day—and sometimes continuously for a week—the men's watches became onerous. They were required to stay at the whistlehouse whenever the fog signal was in operation. They were only relieved by one of the other men for their meals; otherwise, they stayed close to the machines. This was not only monotonous duty, because there was little to do, but the noise was deafening. Sometimes they protected their ears by stuffing them with the cotton waste used to wipe up oil. During the day, they would sit outdoors part of the time. We often went up and played horseshoes with Father or just visited with him. Sometimes he would prepare surprises for us. He would give us a six-inch ball made of newspapers and ask us to guess what was inside. We would frantically unroll it, finding a nickel or a dime, a piece of candy, or nuts and raisins.

During foggy periods, the watches were continuous—each man

was four hours on and eight hours off, around the clock. During the time off, the men had to sleep and do other work required around the station. The watches were rotated once a week. The man serving the first watch would move to the second, the second to the third, and the third to the first. This was done by two of the men serving what were called dogwatches—an extra watch of two hours so the change could take place.

The watches, of course, were stood seven days a week, which means that each man spent twenty-eight hours of the traditional forty-hour work week performing this duty. When the weather was foggy, the watch time increased to fifty-six hours.

In spite of the interruption of their normal sleeping patterns, and often insufficient sleep, the regular maintenance work of the station had to be continued. This was usually done during clear weather.

During most of the years we were on Libby Island, there were thirteen major buildings, including the tower and three outhouses, which had to be maintained.

In addition, there were several lengths of wooden fence skirting some of the more precipitous gulches.

The tower was a major project. The bottom section, made of granite, was whitewashed once a year and the top part, which housed the light, got a coat of black paint—except for the windows, which were trimmed in white. During this operation, the men had to do the work of steeplejacks. A staging was suspended from lines and pulleys attached at the top so that it could be lowered and raised. The barn and the whistlehouse also were whitewashed. Although not painted every year, the other buildings were kept in excellent condition. The Bureau of Lighthouses never seemed to lack money for paint. Minor repair projects were also done by the keepers. For major repairs, such as rebuilding the slip when it was damaged by storms, a special crew was sent. But during the Depression, when money was scarce, Father and the other men undertook major projects. One such project was removing the steam engine in the boathouse and replacing it with a modern gasoline-powered hoist. Besides the regular cleaning, washing of floors and woodwork, hauling coal and other supplies after the lighthouse tenders came, there were necessary trips to Starboard and later to Machias to get mail and to purchase groceries and other household items.

For Father, as head keeper, there was another whole set of duties: keeping records. He was required to keep a log of the hours the fog signal was in operation and any significant events that happened on the station. Each month this information was compiled into a monthly report. All supplies also had to be carefully inventoried, as described in chapter 3.

The winter workload was not nearly as heavy, since all outside work had to be done during the warmer months. In the winter, we did interior painting and scraped and varnished floors.

In spite of the many hours spent on lighthouse duties, the men still found time to farm, fish for lobster, hunt wild birds, and spend some recreational time with their families.

3

THE

"GUVMENT" IN

OUR LIVES

THE "guvment," as we referred to the United States Lighthouse Service, was an all-pervasive force in our lives on Libby Island. We lived in a government house, used government supplies to keep it painted and cleaned, heated it with government coal, and lighted it with government kerosene. Time was kept by a large government striking clock on the wall and the dates were kept by a government calendar. When we went ashore for mail and supplies, we used the government boat and kept to a time schedule decreed by the government—six hours from departure to return. Any delay had to be reported. Off-island vacation time was thirty days a year. Each leave had to be applied for and approved by the government. (More about our vacations appears in chapter 8.)

This outside force, which seemed to have great influence on our daily lives, had a major impact on me as a child. We always knew the name of the lighthouse inspector, because my parents often referred to him. The earliest one I remember was Inspector Luther. To me he was an all-powerful figure who had a great deal to do with Father's state of mind, which in turn affected Mother's state of mind and the happiness of the whole family.

At the same time, there was another great force that I was taught to respect and fear: God. Like the government, He played a major role in determining our activities, especially on Sunday. Because of Him we could not play games or play with toys, could not go swimming (no matter how hot it was), row a boat (for pleasure), ride a bicycle or velocipede, push a wheelbarrow, or shoot an air rifle. We were allowed to read, color, draw, or go for a walk. On our walks, we might take a picnic lunch. If Father set up a target for rock-throwing, He did allow that. He also strictly monitored our speech. Of course we could not swear, but we could not even use substitutes, such as, "Gosh dern." When we needed to express frustration, we were limited to such expressions as, "By gorry," "For gracious sakes," "You are so despisable [despicable]." This sanitizing of our language carried over to the parts of the body and its functions. Buttocks became *stern*, in true nautical fashion; penis, *pee wee*; its function, *pee*; and sh— became *kinney*. Mother monitored adherence to these rules very closely, and both she and Father modeled them, which made it easy for us to follow their example.

There was a time during my early years when these two all-powerful forces—God and Luther—became confused in my mind. I thought they were the same, the only difference being that Luther occasionally appeared in uniform. The only other familiar uniformed figure (besides my father, who seldom wore his) was the English "bobby" that appeared on one of the Old Maid game cards. These cards split the uniformed figure in the middle so that the cards and the figure were always right side up. I can remember clearly saying my prayers at night with both God and Luther combined in one all-powerful figure represented by the figure of the bobby on the Old Maid cards.

Twice a year the lighthouse inspector came to our station. Of all the events we experienced on Libby Island, inspection time surpassed all the others in sheer excitement, but it was excitement mixed with anxiety. The inspection was very thorough, particularly in the early years. It included not only all of the signaling apparatus—the light, the fog signal, and all related equipment—but also the houses, upstairs and downstairs.

These inspection tours were not scheduled; no one was sure when they might occur. Even the sight of the lighthouse tender was not a sure sign. She might be on other errands, such as delivering supplies. But the keepers did have one way of getting a warning of the imminent arrival of the inspector.

There were two lighthouses near us: Little River in Cutler (to the east) and Moose Peak (to the west), off Jonesport. When the tender arrived at either of these stations with the inspector's flag flying, the keepers immediately would phone Father. (An underwater telephone cable connected us with the mainland, the Cross Island Coast Guard station, and other light stations.)

When this call came, Father made an announcement that set off a flurry of excitement and activity. Although Father maintained a good station, everything had to be shipshape for inspection, and each of us had a special job to do. My job, I remember well, was to clean all the brass around the house, including all doorknobs and the dustpan. It was a joy to see them sparkle.

Not long ago, a man was polishing brass in a hotel elevator in which I was riding, and that smell brought back vivid memories. Apparently the polish formula has not changed.

Irwin had the job of sweeping up the rainshed attached to our house. The womenfolk cleaned the house from top to bottom, washing and dusting until the whole house shone like the brass. Father and the two assistant keepers cleaned the signaling apparatus. The glass prisms and brass framework of the lens took the most time.

When someone shouted, "The *Hibiscus* is coming," we would all dash outside to see a black hull on the horizon. The black plume of smoke rising from her stack indicated that she was coming full speed ahead for Libby.

Until my first visit to Hawaii, *hibiscus* meant only this familiar black ship that so often brought excitement to our lighthouse island. I have often wondered who chose that name, since the hibiscus is a tropical flower.

This was one of the occasions when Father wore his lighthouse keeper's uniform. He would later in the day don new overalls and a blue denim jacket (over the uniform), because this was not wholly a ceremonial affair.

One of Father's first jobs, when he heard the *Hibiscus* was coming, was to rush to the boathouse to start a fire under the boiler to get up steam for the donkey engine used to hoist the inspector's yawlboat up the slip. The acrid smoke would fill the air as the soft coal ignited.

By the time the *Hibiscus* came to anchor near the boathouse, all of us had assembled, usually high on a bank where we could see everything. All eyes were on the *Hibiscus* as we waited for her yawlboat to be lowered. The yawlboat was a big, bluff-bowed craft capable of carrying large quantities of supplies. Since the water drained off the end of our slip at low water, the captain had to read his tide tables carefully in order to arrive when the tide was high and rising.

We treated our own government boat and the slip with great care, always landing as gently as possible, but the inspector's yawlboat received no such respect. The first mate would bring her in at top speed, running her high up on the slip's stringers. One of the keepers was always there to hook the steel cable onto her bow. Then he would raise his white-gloved hand and Father would manipulate the levers on the donkey engine to put the winch in gear and start edging the boat up the slip. A great hissing, roaring, and rattling from the steam engine accompanied the yawlboat as it surged toward the boathouse.

At the appropriate point, Father would ease off the steam lever, apply the brake, and lock the gears. Having done this, he would doff his overalls and descend steps to a lower platform to greet the inspector, who, by this time, would be descending a ladder from the yawlboat. This was always a moment of high drama—Father, resplendent in his uniform, brass buttons shining, stepping forward to meet this godlike giant, Inspector Luther. Every eye of the audience was riveted upon them as they shook hands, turned, and marched through the boathouse and up the grassy path toward the houses. The urge to follow was too great to resist, so, keeping a safe distance, we all fell in behind— mothers with babes in arms, all the children, and, often, the horse, cow, and dogs. It was quite a parade.

As soon as we reached the houses, we older children turned and ran back to the boathouse, where more excitement was about to begin. Usually, when the *Hibiscus* brought the inspector, she also brought supplies—particularly coal. By the time we got back to the boathouse, she would be unloading her cargo into the yawl- boat. Soon the yawlboat would again approach the slip at full speed. The donkey engine, hissing and belching steam and smoke, would whisk her to the top of the slip, where the crew would jump out, ready for unloading. I do not know where these crewmen came from, but most of them had much darker skin than we had, and we called them "guineas." I presume they were from some coastal Massachusetts cities where many Portuguese immigrants had settled. To us they seemed like demigods.

The coal came in heavy burlap bags that we called crocus sacks. Each of these must have weighed more than a hundred pounds when filled. One of the first things each crewman did was to take an empty sack (they may have brought some with them) and push one of the bottom corners into the other. This made a hood, which each one wore on his head and back for protection, making them all look like giant elves. And they worked like fiends. Carrying a bag of coal on his back, each man would run (or go at a running walk) up the steps, through the boathouse, and outside to where the coal was stored. When he reached the summit of the pile, which accumulated quickly, he would turn and stand with his back to the pile. Another crewman, with a very sharp knife, would slice the restraining cord at the mouth of the bag, which was carried upside down. The coal would go streaming out while the man stepped clear. Without stopping, he would head back for another bag. Finally, there was an endless chain of men who be- came blacker by the minute. But they did not stop until the yawlboat was empty and had to return to the *Hibiscus* for an- other load. For weeks afterward, we would use old grain sacks to make hoods for our heads and play "unloading the coal," using some steep-sided knoll for a coal pile.

As the tide fell, more and more of the slip would be exposed. Whenever our government boat was lowered down, everyone took the greatest care to protect her propeller from the rocks as she swayed from side to side. The "guineas" showed no such concern for their yawlboat. When the coal was unloaded, they all piled in, cast off the restraining lines, and went plummeting down the slip, hitting the water with a great splash. As far as we were concerned, these were brave, if somewhat reckless, adventurers. No other performance since then, circus or otherwise, has ever thrilled me as much.

After the coal was unloaded, there often were other supplies to come in: equipment for repairs, kerosene in five-gallon cans (we used a lot of it for the light signal and lighting our homes), and all the other items the government provided for us.

One of those crewmen, named Jimmy, stands out in my mind. He was short and smaller than most of the others, but he would carry gigantic loads. During one of the visits of the *Hibiscus,* I saw him carry a two-hundred-pound water pump as easily as he carried the bags of coal.

When the inspector's visit was over, he would board the yawlboat and be lowered into the water somewhat more ceremoniously, with Father at the controls of the donkey engine. Shortly after the yawlboat was hoisted aboard, the *Hibiscus* weighed anchor and headed away from Libby. At that moment there was not a single child who did not dream of someday joining her crew.

On one of her later visits when I was about eight, I managed to realize a bit of that dream. At least I had a short passage on the *Hibiscus.* I heard a new inspector, named Sampson, ask my father if he would follow the *Hibiscus* into Starboard and drive him to Machias so he could get the train for Portland. Father kept our car garaged in Starboard, so of course he agreed. Immediately an idea hatched in my mind. Why not board the yawlboat with the inspector, stay aboard the *Hibiscus* on the three-mile trip to Starboard, and then get off with the inspector when my father came alongside?

When I proposed this idea, I fully expected that it would be rejected, but Father agreed readily. Since then, I have often wondered how many fathers of that generation would have risked having a son do something that could have reflected poorly on his reputation with his boss.

I cleaned up quickly, changed my clothes, and was ready when the inspector mounted the ladder into the yawl. I could hardly believe that I was following him into the boat, but I was disappointed that we did not take a speedy ride down the slip, although we did go much faster than our usual cautious pace. We were soon beside the *Hibiscus* and hoisted up to deck level. Everything was like a dream. Since earliest childhood I had seen from a distance what seemed to be a gigantic ship. Now I was actually on her deck. No one instructed me, so I began a leisurely inspection on my own. A short time later, a steward appeared and said, "Mr. Sampson wants you to join him for dinner." I cannot remember what was served, but I do remember a meticulously clean white room and my feeling that this man I had regarded with awe must have a very kind heart. Shortly afterward, the *Hibiscus* lowered her anchor and the inspector and I climbed down a ladder into our boat, which Father had skillfully brought alongside. One of many unforgettable experiences had come to an end.

In addition to the lighthouse keepers and inspectors, other men worked for the Lighthouse Service as carpenters and machinists. They were another source of excitement in our sometimes monotonous lives. As I mentioned in chapter 2, these men came when there were major repairs to be done to buildings, new structures to be built, new machines to be installed, existing machines to be overhauled, and repairs required on the slip. During the time we were on Libby, the entire steam system for blowing the fog signal was converted to diesel.

There was no other place for these men to stay except with the keepers, so they became boarders with the three families, who took turns taking them in. The introduction of these strangers into our small society brought some changes. One was the odor of tobacco smoke. No one in our family smoked, so it was strange to have the odor of cigarette and pipe tobacco permeating our house. It was not oppressive, however, because the men seemed to respect our tobacco-free household and did all their smoking outdoors or in the rainshed, but this did not prevent fumes from entering.

We children always looked forward to having these visitors stay in our home, because there was an immediate improvement in the menu. About our only regular dessert was cookies and various types of canned fruit, although Mother sometimes baked pies and cakes. But when the boarders were with us, we had dessert twice a day. One dish I particularly remember was a cornstarch pudding with orange slices in it and meringue on top.

Sometimes these men also added to our family's store of humor. One man occupied the room that Irwin and I usually shared. We then slept on the floor, on a mattress in the sewing room. Our room had a low window opening onto a sloping roof. I do not know where the rumor originated, unless telltale signs were discovered, but we all came to believe that instead of using the chamber mug (which we called the "whistle pitcher"), this man used the window. My brother and I thought this was hilarious, but my father did not. The water from that roof ran directly into the cistern that contained our water supply, so Father nailed the window shut.

I have a very happy memory of another worker, Mr. Webster. I can still visualize him, with his black moustache and jet-black hair. I would climb up into my high chair for meals and he would pick me up, chair and all, and carry me to the table. He often talked with me and was the only one of the workers who ever paid attention to us young children. How little we realize what simple gestures can mean to a child. Many years later, I saw Mr. Webster and was able to thank him for his kindness.

Whenever I hear anyone saying that the government cannot run anything without a great deal of waste, I have to tell them a few stories about the Lighthouse Service.

The government supplied all basic items related to the operation and maintenance of the station. This included not only such items as coal and kerosene for signal operations and heating but also such minor supplies as soap, cleaning cloths, dustpans, brooms, and paintbrushes. Careful invoices were kept on the semidurable items so that my father could account for all existing stock. When such items as paintbrushes had to be replaced, the worn-out ones had to be turned in when the inspector came; otherwise, no new ones would be issued. Boxes of these used items were offloaded to the *Hibiscus*. We never knew what happened to them, but we presumed that at some point they were dumped overboard. One tale alleges that a keeper who wanted to be sure he always had used equipment to return would watch with his spyglass to see where the items were dumped. After the tender was out of sight, he would retrieve the ones that did not sink. Many times Father had to buy paintbrushes with his own funds because the old ones had been misplaced.

The keepers' homes were heated with steam furnaces, but there never was enough coal supplied to provide heating throughout the houses. Consequently, we confined our living to the kitchen, heated by a coal- and wood-burning stove. In the winter, every other part of the house felt like the Arctic. There were a few radiators, but the upstairs was warmed only by the scanty supply of heat that rose through grates between the floors. A radiator at the head of the stairs gave off little warmth.

On the other hand, it seemed that there was always plenty of paint—white and battleship gray. The buildings were always well painted and we did have tints for the interior walls and trim. All of us took our turns at painting, and I well remember how proud I was when Father assigned me to paint the interior of our outhouse. The seating area went very well. I painted carefully around the three holes—one for Father, one for Mother, and one for the children. But when I painted the floor, I made a major error: I started at the threshold and painted my way in. It was not until I had nearly finished that I discovered I had left no way out without stepping in the wet paint. I took one giant step, then reached back and repainted my track as best I could.

An item *not* supplied by the government was toilet paper. In the history of the human race, I suppose, many things have been used for this purpose—corncobs, hay, leaves, bark, and who knows what else—but we used outdated mail-order catalogs. As soon as a new catalog appeared, the old one went immediately to the outhouse. Anyone familiar with such catalogs knows that some of the pages were quite thin and pliable. These were not too uncomfortable to use, but by the end of the season, the supply of good pages would be exhausted. Only the shiny pages would be left, and they were both uncomfortable and ineffective. The only way to improve them was to crinkle them and rub them together vigorously, which softened the surface. In addition to being eager to get the new catalogs to see what new fashions and items were for sale, we always were anxious to allocate the old ones to the outhouse.

Not only did the catalogs serve a cleaning function, they also provided entertainment. Many a dream of Christmas gifts, or purchases made with carefully saved money, was born during a visit to that outhouse.

There was one fixture in the outhouse that always aroused my curiousity when I was small. It was a three-sided metal bracket with one side screwed to the wall. On the two protruding ends, small disks were affixed. Many times I studied this device, trying to figure it out. One day I made an amazing discovery. I reached up, pulled on one of the disks, and let go. To my surprise, it made a quite musical humming sound. Then and there I decided it was a simple musical instrument installed by the government to help while away the outhouse hours.

It was not until several years later, on the mainland, that I discovered the real purpose of this simple instrument—to hold a roll of toilet paper. It must have been installed during some previous progressive administration of the Lighthouse Service. In the interest of economy, toilet paper later was removed from the list of lighthouse supplies.

I do not know how other keepers handled this basic problem, but I assume they also used the catalogs. I vividly recall that one of the keepers became quite hostile toward a mail-order firm over a mismanaged order. In his final letter severing all relations with the company, he stated emphatically that he would no longer even use their catalogs for "a—— paper."

The home supplied to us by the government was commodious and comfortable, but the outhouse was an example of poor design that caused us considerable discomfort. Set at the end of a plank walk about seventy-five feet from the house, ours was fully exposed to the elements. On a cold evening with rain or snow falling and the wind hurtling around the house, there was no more disturbing sensation than nature's call. No matter how hard one might try, it usually could not be denied. Using the chamber pots was not considered acceptable except in the middle of the night. There was no alternative but to don rubber boots and foul-weather gear, light the lantern, then leave the cozy kitchen and enter the maelstrom. Sometimes we young ones would make a dash for it, but older family members moved carefully, holding onto the lantern with one hand and the railing with the other. The process was rushed as much as possible because with the temperature often below zero in winter and the wind blowing under our seats, our bodies became chilled rapidly. Sometimes very high waves would send their last frigid fingers directly under the building.

This was an experience we all dreaded, but none of us, young or old, could avoid it. With a bit of better planning, however, the government could have eliminated this discomfort. Most Maine farmhouses had sheds that connected the house to the barn. Somewhere in one of these sheds, close to the house, an inside "outhouse" usually was provided. Although there was no heat, it was not necessary to go outdoors to get there. Ignoring this architectural invention, which was based upon years of wintry outhouse experience, the designers of our government outhouse decreed that when nature called, lighthouse keepers and their families had to face the full fury of the elements. There were plenty of places where a toilet could have been located within our extensive sheds, or a covered passageway could have been built, but this never was done.

The Lighthouse Service supplied us with two boats: the broad-beamed, square-sterned, motorized craft that we used for getting supplies and a narrow-beamed, double-ended rowboat called a peapod to be used as a tender to get from our mooring in Starboard to the shore.

The pod, a boat common to the coast of Maine, was never used; it always remained hoisted up near the ceiling of the boathouse. My father declared it unsafe. Because of its very narrow beam, he was convinced it was too cranky. One wrong move and it would tip over. Since we often had four or more people, plus supplies, to ferry from mooring to shore and return, he would not run the risk of capsize. Another fault was that the pod had a keel, which made it difficult to pull across rocks and sand. When the tide was low at Starboard, the pod might have to be pulled up several hundred feet to clear the high-water mark before it could be left there. Not using this boat actually created no problem, since each keeper had his own peapod, much more stable in design.

The government boat was a more serious problem. These boats apparently were designed to be lowered into the water from a hoisting apparatus, because they were unfit to enter the water from an unprotected slip. Often, when we launched, the wind would be blowing directly toward us, creating sharp waves that would crash against the flat stern of the boat, not only impeding progress but also sending spray over everyone on board. In summer this was uncomfortable, but during the cold weather, which seemed to extend through most of the year, it could have created dangerous conditions of exposure. The boat should have been designed with a pointed stern to make it easier to enter the water. The only protection was a spray hood stretched over a part of the boat. But this was old, often mended, and always seemed to leak

ISLAND LAUNCHING

Winter's cold irons
pried at the fabric of garments
seeking the warm flesh beneath.
The ice-encrusted rocks rejected footprints
and the eagle-winged wind
beat upon faces,
filling the air with violence.

The sea at the cliff's feet
was beaten to foaming and
its liquid roar drowned the wind.

The black staccatoed sounds of motors
crackled in eardrums
and the great gray hull
pointed heavenward,
then dropped slowly seaward.

The waves parted to receive it.

On this day a boat was launched
and life was lost from the island.

P.B.W

just where people were seated. I can still feel the discomfort of streams of icy-cold North Atlantic pouring down my neck.

The design was only one of the problems that we had with this boat. The engine was totally inadequate. An ancient, one-cylinder, upright, make-or-break engine, it had no transmission. If you pulled up on its huge flywheel in one direction, it would run backward; the other way, forward. To shift from one direction to the other, you had to stop and restart the engine. Years after the local lobster fishermen had engines equipped with transmissions, we still were struggling with our antiquated "one-lunger."

Since it was not possible to launch the boat with the engine running because the propeller could strike the rocks, Father would start the engine, making sure it would run, then shut it off until we were free of the slip. But this meant that sometimes we were facing heavy winds and waves without power, and there was no guarantee that the engine would start as easily the second time. Often we had to grab oars and paddle madly to clear the rocks and give Father enough time to nurse the engine back to life.

Landing created a similar problem. Coming into the slip in rough weather required a wait for lulls in the waves, but with this engine, it was impossible to idle in neutral. The only alternative was to circle, wait for a lull, then dash at full speed (there was no speed control) onto the slip, all the while hoping the boat could be hooked on and winched up the slip before a wave could smash us onto the rocks. This never happened, although once a wave lifted the boat onto the other side of the slip. We were fortunate; one boat lay on a nearby bank, totally wrecked, mute testimony that this was a dangerous place.

The keepers on duty always kept a sharp eye out for the return of the government boat. (When one of the keepers was ashore, sometimes I was sent to a high bluff, as lookout. I can still vividly remember the low, gray hull plowing through the seas, sending showers of spray over her entire length.) We always knew that someone would be on the slip to hook the winch rope to our bow ring and pull us clear of the danger of a breaking wave.

Father would quickly jump over the bow of the boat to hold her on while the keeper who had helped us land ran the length of the slip, a hundred feet or more, up to the winch to help the third keeper start the slow process of retrieving us from the water.

There was another step in this landing process that I mentioned in chapter 1—a job that usually fell to Irwin or me. To prevent the pod from crashing into the transom when the big boat hit the slip, she had to be brought in separately. I can almost hear Father saying, "Philmore, you get in the pod and bring her in after we pull the big boat clear." I must have started doing this by the time I was nine. Sometimes it was rough and windy, but I never remember having a single moment of fear. I suppose I reasoned that my father would not have asked me to do something dangerous—which, of course, it was. As an adult, I think I would view the task with a good measure of trepidation.

We had life preservers, but I never remember seeing them used except as cushions—they were big, cumbersome vests made of cork sewn into canvas.

For most of the years we were on Libby, we hauled the government boat up the slip with a hand winch. It took too long to get up steam to use the donkey engine, and coal was in short supply. On each end of the winch were large metal handles that turned cogwheels and, in turn, the drum that wound up the line. These handles were arranged so that at least two people could crank on a side and even more could get a hand on. We all pitched in, often including the women. The slip was long and steep, and the boat literally moved by inches, but eventually she would reach the top. Then, in the winter, came the precarious process of getting her into the boathouse. This was accomplished with some people cranking on the winch while others supported the boat on each side. Rollers were strategically placed so that when she tipped down and leveled off, she rolled easily on $1^1/_2$-inch pipes.

After the big boat was in, next came the peapod. All of us would grab onto the painter and, with my father coordinating our efforts by chanting, would bring her up, one tug after another. Father would use chants he had learned during his seagoing

years from black crews unloading railroad ties and other cargo. I
remember one of these was: "Oh! Oh! Ram him! Oh! Oh! Drive
him! Oh! Oh! Lord." The rhythm would result in three powerful
tugs. Sometimes he made up these chants as he went along.

In the mid-1930s, a gasoline-powered hoist was installed, and
it quickly whisked the boat up the slip. But in a way we missed
the old hand winch that brought us all together in a common
effort.

I do not know the age of the government boat we used during
most of our years on Libby Island, but it was in very bad condition.
I can remember Father sticking his jackknife blade into its
planking and encountering little resistance. Year after year, he
reported this boat's condition to the Lighthouse Service, but
nothing was done. Finally, word came that the *Hibiscus* would
take the boat in for repairs. For several months we had to depend
upon our peapods, rowing to the mainland—a trip that took more
than an hour in favorable conditions. When the boat finally was
returned, Father gave it a careful inspection. He discovered that
it merely had been renailed through the partially rotten planking. The men on Libby all decided that this boat was unsafe, that
they would be safer using their pods and oars. So the government
boat was hauled into the boathouse, where it was stored with
the government pod.

Eventually the station received a new boat. That was a great
day. The new boat had a dependable four-cylinder engine with a
transmission. Its only fault, again, was the design. The Lighthouse Service designers, none of whom probably had ever been on
an offshore station, had retained the same square stern. But at
least we had power for backing off, and we no longer had to circle
to dash in between the waves.

An aspect of our isolation that weighed heavily on all island
families was the fear of being cut off from the mainland. This not
only increased our sense of loneliness but it also was dangerous.
We were always totally isolated during severe storms—we could
not launch a boat and no one could land, not even the Coast Guard.
A regular aftermath of these storms was the loss of our slip and

our telephone. This made getting off the island extremely difficult and calling for help impossible. After a severe gale, we would often discover that the lower ends of the slip timbers were broken off and the great bolts that had held them fast to the ledges were twisted and bent. The same storms usually broke the underwater telephone cable that linked us with the mainland. Without the telephone, we could not report on lobster fishermen and other boats that might be in trouble or overdue, nor could we call for medical help.

It was sometimes many months before the slip and cable were repaired. Mother often expressed great fear during these times and always warned us to be careful because there was no way for us to get to a doctor or even to consult one by telephone.

Mother had one such consultation when I developed a serious infection. One rainy day I entertained myself by rolling a rusty iron hoop in the rainshed. Every time I turned it, the edge cut into my thumb. I did not mention this to Mother because she had a single cure for all wounds: iodine, which inflicted a severe sting. Two days later, to my amazement, I found an ugly red streak running from my thumb along my arm to my armpit. I was scared. The time for concealment was over; I had what was then called "blood poisoning." Mother immediately called the doctor, and his prescription was hot poultices made from bread and milk. Whether it was the bread or my body's healing power, within a week my thumb was healed, but I still bear the scar.

Although we often complained about the inadequacy of some of the government equipment, the delays in getting repairs, and the needless restrictions (such as the six-hour limit for going ashore, which created real hardship), generally we all accepted our role in keeping the light and the fog signal. And we all participated in nearly every phase of the operation. We felt that any hardships we encountered came with the territory. In general, the "guvment" was a generous employer, providing us with a livelihood far better than that of most of the families living on the nearby mainland.

4

The Libby Islands—Hazard to Sailing Ships

IF THE Libby Islands had been designed by some malevolent force to lure ships to their death, it could not have been more successful. Few other places on the Maine coast were more deserving of the title, "Graveyard of Ships."

R. T. Sterling, in his book *Lighthouses of the Maine Coast* (Stephen Daye Press, 1935), listed sixty-five lighthouses on the coast of Maine. Only seven of these were built prior to 1822, when Libby's tower was constructed. The choice of Libby for a lighthouse during this early period seems to indicate the degree of danger it posed for ships sailing Maine's northeastern coastline.

When Sterling was doing the research for his book, he wrote to each lighthouse keeper and asked that someone be assigned to collect information for him. Father gave me the job. I was fourteen. Sterling suggested that we search for old records, particularly in the attic of our home. This we did, and, to our surprise (no one had ever before climbed through the attic opening), we discovered a box of old records. Among them was a shipwreck journal, its cover half torn off but its contents unimpaired. The record ran from 1856 to 1902 and included accounts of thirty-five shipwrecks during that time—an average of about one every eighteen months. In all of these shipwrecks, only fifteen lives were lost. Many times the crews were saved by the heroic rescue efforts of the lightkeepers. Several years after Sterling's book was published, the Lighthouse Service office in Portland requested that we submit all old records. I have always wondered what became of them, particularly the Libby shipwreck journal.

Most of these ships had made the same tragic mistake. They headed for the passage between Cross Island and the eastern end of Big Libby, which gave them clear access to the protection of Machias Bay. But either due to piloting error or the severity of a storm, they went too far west and attempted to sail between the two Libbys, where they were wrecked on the bar between the islands. The shipwreck journal gave a summary of the weather, how each ship was wrecked, and the number of crew and passengers lost. Any aid given by the lightkeepers was described. It was an unforgettable experience to read these cryptic entries, written in the personal hand of the keeper at the time. It was also frightening to contemplate that each entry meant a large ship with full crew had been destroyed on Libby's ledges, often with lives lost. After reading this journal, I found it hard to look along Libby's southeastern shores without envisioning all of the broken ships strewn along the bar. The wrecks were so frequent that the wave-beaten hulks of several of them must have been visible simultaneously. The only bits of evidence remaining by 1934 were several giant anchors and some old anchor chains.

Sterling's book contains many fascinating accounts, of which I will describe only three. The facts were drawn from Libby's shipwreck journal and submitted in my research report.

In September 1892, Captain John Brown of the *Princeport* was bound from Nova Scotia to Boston. Off Libby he ran into a severe storm, probably a fall hurricane. Mistaking the passage between the two Libby Islands for the Cross Island channel, he ran his ship high on the bar. Shortly after dawn, the keepers saw what was left—a small piece of wreckage to which the crewmen were clinging. After a dangerous trip in their small boat, the keepers were able to take the men off only a few minutes before the last bit of wreckage slipped under the sea.

On a December day in 1878, the *Caledonia* of Windsor, Nova Scotia, was driving down the coast when she encountered a gale. The captain did his best to get into the shelter of Machias Bay, but he miscalculated the passage and ran between the two Libbys. The ship struck with such force that all of the crewmen were thrown into the waves and drowned. When the lightkeepers sighted the wreck, her two passengers were clinging to the rigging. A volunteer rescue crew from Starboard rescued them.

Keeper W.A. Aerman Wood saw the barkentine *Fame* making her way into Machias Bay in a wild sea. She tried to change tacks but did not succeed and was swept onto one of Libby's outlying points. The lightkeepers were able to wade out in the surf and throw ropes to the crew. They then rigged a boatswain's chair and rescued all but three.

Although sailing ships had almost disappeared by the 1920s, two wrecks occurred while we were on Libby: the *F.C. Lockhart* in 1923 and the *John C. Myers* in 1925.

The *Lockhart* was a three-masted schooner built in 1910 at Annapolis Royal, Nova Scotia. She weighed 309 tons, was 125 feet long, 21.4 feet wide, and 11.8 feet in depth. Technically, she was a tern schooner, built to enter shallow harbors. Her keel was extended by a centerboard that could be raised and lowered. Her home port was St. John, New Brunswick.

Here is an account of the wreck of the *Lockhart,* as my brother Irwin remembers it:

> The *F.C. Lockhart* was hauling freight between New England and Nova Scotia. On this trip she was loaded with phosphate rock. It was December and extremely cold. The captain came into Machias Bay for protection from a bad storm and had to wait for more favorable winds. On this particular morning, there was a lot of vapor on the water—it was so thick that the fog signal was blowing. But the wind was favorable, so the captain de-

cided to weigh anchor. He planned to go by the west end of Little Libby, but in the fog he miscalculated and struck the eastern end of Big Libby—an error of at least two miles.

He ran the *Lockhart* directly into the rocks. It being high tide, her jibboom ran almost up to the grassy edge of the island. As the tide went down, she came to rest between two smooth ledges, which supported her in an upright position as if she were in a cradle. Unfortunately, a large rock had broken through her bottom, locking her solidly on the shore.

Father sighted the ship's masts over Big Libby from the whistlehouse, after the vapor had begun to lift. Normally he would have called the Coast Guard on Cross Island, but a previous big storm had broken our telephone cable. The light station powerboat was in Portland being repaired, so all we had was our peapod. After the tide went down, Father, Justin Foss, and I walked across the bar and over the island to where the ship had been wrecked. The captain and one member of the crew came back with us to the boathouse, where we launched the pod. With the two men aboard, Father and Justin rowed them into Starboard against a 25 m.p.h. headwind.

It was a long, hard pull, but they were used to it—just another day's work for them. The captain was able to make phone calls to the Coast Guard, the owners of the vessel, the families of his crew, and, of course, to his own family. They then returned, with Father putting them ashore on Big Libby so they could go back to their ship.

The next day the wind was blowing even harder, but we walked back across Big Libby to the wreck and climbed up the ladder to the deck. I can still remember the wind whistling through the rigging, and how cold it was. The captain invited us down into his cabin and the cook served us vegetable soup. I can still see the yellow carrots and other vegetables. Oh! How good it tasted!

The Coast Guard, having been notified, sent the *Kick-apoo*, an icebreaker, to the island. She had very powerful steam engines. They ran out her anchors, put lines on the *Lockhart*, and tried to pull her off with their steam-powered winches, but it did no good. They were unable to budge her off the rocks. The *F.C. Lockhart* was a total loss.

She stayed there for two months without much further damage, it being a mild winter. But in March, another big storm swept the coast, bringing down her masts. A short time later, another storm came and took off her house. By the end of the next winter, she was a shapeless hulk.

I remember this wreck very clearly. On one of the trips Father took across the bar, I, at age six, was allowed to go along. It was a tiring walk the length of both islands and the slippery bar—probably four miles. I can clearly see Father and Justin trudging along ahead of me through the snow-laden grasses, dragging heavy blocks and tackle that they hoped to use in refloating the *Lockhart*. It was tragic to see this majestic ship wedged on the rocks, and it seemed impossible that she had been mortally wounded.

We salvaged only a few things. Most ships had round wooden balls inserted on the tops of their masts, probably to protect the wood. We got one of these, but I was more impressed by the heavy coffee mugs, which were similar to those used in some restaurants. They were a part of our family's dish supply for many years afterward.

On a bitter early December night in 1925, I made my way out to the barn in gale-force winds to make certain the animals were secure and to close up the henhouse. Darkness was closing in and snow was beginning to swirl. I could hear the heavy surf pounding against the cliffs only a short distance away. It was going to be a bad night. I was only eight, but I realized that I had to be very brave because I was the only "man" in the house. Father and Irwin had gone to the mainland on their annual deer-hunting trip. Nonie had returned from school with a friend, Frances Miller, for the Thanksgiving holidays. With Mother, there were four of us in our big house.

I hurried to finish the chores, not being too anxious to be out after dark. As I returned to the house, I could see that the snow was shadowing the light in the tower and hear that it was muffling the steady booming of the fog signal. I was glad to reach the security of the rainshed, although it was always a scary place at night.

Our bright kitchen and Mother's smile welcomed me back to warmth and security. The evening passed quickly, but the storm did not weaken. Although we did not have to stand watch, out of habit we often glanced at the light reflected in our outside mirror. It continued to burn steadily, although dimmed by the snow. We talked, as we so often did, about ships that might be out in such a bad storm, and we hoped they could find their way into some safe harbor.

Unknown to us, the three-masted barkentine *John C. Myers* was driving her way through the high seas and sixty-knot winds from Nova Scotia to Boston, loaded with six hundred cords of pulpwood. Sometime during the night, when the storm was at its height, her captain decided to seek refuge in Machias Bay. Just when he thought he had almost reached safety, his ship shook violently. She had struck ledges off the western end of Big Libby—another victim of this terribly deceptive place. Hoping to keep his ship from being forced farther into shallow water, he ordered the anchors released. They struck bottom, but the huge waves were pounding with such force that they swung the giant ship around and pushed her toward the island, where her stern grounded high up on Big Libby's shore.

When she struck, the force of the waves catapulted her entire deckload of two hundred cords of pulpwood into the water, forming a pulsating bridge to dry land. Meanwhile, the waves were steadily crushing her bow timbers until her whole forward section was broken off. The nine crewmen, looking out from the aft cabin, saw a chance to escape. Their lifeboat, which had been suspended from davits, was already gone, but the ropes that had held her still dangled there. One by one, they climbed down these ropes, landed on the heaving pulpwood, and made their way across it to shore. Only the mate fell through, breaking his leg, but he was able to reach safety with the help of his mates.

At daybreak, the Coast Guard lookout on Cross Island saw the ship and dispatched a lifeboat to offer help. They could tell that the ship was lost, but they hoped at least to find survivors. They landed, located the crew, and carried them to the mainland, where arrangements were made for them to go home and for the mate to receive medical attention.

Snug in our beds, we, of course, knew nothing about the life-and-death struggle that occurred so close to us. Sometime during the night, the wind subsided. When I took my early morning walk to the outhouse, I tried to search the shoreline, as we always did, but it was obscured by low-lying fog. I could see over the fog, however, and make out the edge of Big Libby. Then I realized I was seeing something strange: several fenceposts along the shore. But these were much higher than usual. I ran into the house and grabbed the spyglass, which always hung on the wall over the kitchen table. Quickly focusing on what I thought were fenceposts, I realized that I was seeing the broken masts of a giant ship. There was no doubt: Big Libby had been the scene of another disastrous shipwreck.

I immediately ran back into the kitchen to tell Mother and then went through the rainshed to tell the other keepers, who called the Coast Guard on Cross Island. They reported that the men had already been taken off the island. As the crewmen set off from Starboard for their homeports, with only salt-sodden clothes on their backs, their hearts must have been filled with relief and thanksgiving that they were safe.

Soon the fog lifted, and I could see much more clearly. Instead of the ocean, I saw cords and cords of pulpwood, which turned the water's surface a pale whitish-brown. I looked through the spyglass again and could see the wreck clearly. The whole forward section of the gigantic hull looked as if some giant sea monster had crushed it between its jaws.

Nonie, her friend Frances, and I could hardly wait until the tide had gone down far enough so we could walk across the bar and reach the wreck. I am surprised that Mother let us go, because there must have been great danger that masts and spars would fall and steel rigging break loose, but on Libby we were given a great deal of latitude to make our own responsible judgments. Checking *The Old Farmer's Almanac* for the time of low tide, we started out so we could cross the gut at the earliest possible moment. Of course we felt sad that such a disaster had taken place on our shores, since we remembered the *F.C. Lockhart* wreck only two years earlier. But this *was* an unusual occurrence, and, like all young people, we enjoyed the excitement, even though it was mingled with sadness.

We walked the length of Libby through the snow-covered fields, and when we reached the bar, the tide had uncovered about two-thirds of it. But a strange sight met our eyes: the usually brown weed-covered bar was a highway of bleached white pulpwood, each piece about four feet long. The *Myers* had been on her way to Boston, where her load of Nova Scotia pulpwood would have been sent to a paper mill somewhere in New England. Unfortunately, it would never reach its destination.

We could have walked almost all the way across the bar on the pulpwood, but we tried to avoid it, because it provided a footing even less secure than the slippery rocks. The tide was still too high when we reached the gut, so we had to wait, but we were within full view of what was left of the once-proud *John C. Myers.* What a heart-sickening sight to see this magnificent vessel totally destroyed. As I recall, two of her masts were still up, but angled weirdly. Her running rigging was blowing in the wind—swinging crazily back and forth—and her shredded sails were hanging from other pieces of rigging.

The ship had been built in Tacoma, Washington, in 1903. She

was 200 feet long, 15.4 feet deep, and had a 40-foot beam. She could carry a load of 794 tons. Her owner was the Boston Ship Brokerage Company.

It was difficult to comprehend that the wind and the seas, combined with the destructive power of Libby's Ledges, could so totally destroy a ship of this size and strength in a few hours.

When the water through the gut was low enough so we could wade across, we drew closer, and the ship, or what was left of her, loomed higher and higher. Feeling like midgets, we stood near the hull and looked up at the largest manmade structure we had ever seen. It was as wide as our rainshed and twice as long.

Desperately wanting to go aboard, we tried to figure out how to scale her high, smooth sides. Finally, we worked our way around to her stern, which still rested on cords of pulpwood. It was not easy to pick our way through this scattered mass of short sticks, but we ended up directly under the davits where the crew had swung overboard to escape. I cannot remember how we climbed to her deck, but we did make it. All was chaos on deck. Lines were everywhere, intertwined with a few sticks of pulpwood left in spite of the waves that had swept her repeatedly from stem to stern.

We were anxious to descend into her captain's and crew's quarters, which, fortunately, were near the stern. The companionway was open and nothing blocked our way. As we climbed down the steps, the sight was appalling: furniture, dishes, everything that made life comfortable aboard this well-constructed ship had been thrown about. What I remember most was the cabin floor covered with slimy water in which were floating large chunks of salt pork. It made me nauseated.

From our experience with the *F.C. Lockhart*, we knew that once a ship was totally wrecked, and this one certainly was, anyone could remove anything that could be pried loose and carried away. So we began a search for souvenirs. I spied an elegant black mahogany box and thought that it must hold a treasure, but it turned out to be empty. It may have held a sextant or a compass, and I hoped the captain had been able to take it with him. But I liked the beautiful velvet-lined box and decided to take it home anyway. For many years I stored money and other treasures in it.

We stayed as long as we dared, then climbed down off the deck to make our way back across the bar. We did not want to get caught by the incoming tide and have to wait in the cold until someone came by boat to rescue us. It had been a unique and exciting adventure. How many other kids ever had a chance to explore a wrecked ship hours after she had struck the rocks? As we headed home with a sense of melancholy, we found the spot where the crew apparently had spent the night. They had made a fire by burning the ends of pulpwood sticks set on the rocks like the spokes of a wheel. Discarded nearby were an empty salmon can and a bloody rag. This confirmed the fact that someone had been hurt. What a miserable night they must have spent huddled under the bank of the island trying to keep out of the wind. We had quite a story to tell Father and Irwin when they returned. I am sure Irwin was quite envious. No hunting trip could have been as exciting as a shipwreck.

We returned to the wreck many times during the winter, usually with Father, to continue our search for treasure. We salvaged several pieces of furniture—chairs, a chest, and a bookcase—and some of them are still in our family. The most valuable items were various fittings of brass and lead. Ships of this era had lead pipes for their plumbing, and we were anxious to find as much of it as possible. We would chop our way through floors and bulkheads until we had removed a pipe right down to where it had gone through the hull. Sometimes, at low tide, we would climb inside the ship, spot pieces of pipe dangling overhead, and try to break them loose. Crawling inside the enormous hull, we could almost imagine how Jonah must have felt in the belly of the whale.

All of the heavy cable in the standing rigging had lead caps to finish off the ends. We found dozens of these and whacked them off with the head of a hatchet. One cold, snowy afternoon we spent several hours sawing through a 2 1/2-inch brass shaft with a small hacksaw to remove a large brass cogwheel used in some of the ship's hoisting apparatus. Even though we suffered with the cold, we took turns sawing until we could knock the wheel free.

The heaviest item we removed was a large capstan, a type of winch used to exert great pulling power on a heavy line. It must have weighed several hundred pounds, and I do not remember how we transported it, but we did. The capstan stayed in the boathouse for many years. I do not remember that we ever sold it.

Another bonus from our salvage operation was several large pieces of canvas from the sails. We later made these into large tents, which gave us a great deal of pleasure.

All of our booty had to be carried home, most of it over the bar. For the lighter items, a crocus sack worked well. We would fill it with our cargo and then drag the bag over the rocks and along the snowy grass until we reached home.

The other big salvage job was pulpwood, which Father and the other keepers spent many hours collecting. They piled it up on the edge of the island, where it would be safe from future storms. Fishermen—and anyone else who had access to the shore—were collecting pulpwood all along the coast for quite some time.

The final item of value that we salvaged from the *John C. Myers* was cable from her rigging. Someone conceived the novel idea that the individual pieces of wire, when unstranded, would make excellent hoops for our lobster traps.

After we had removed everything of value from the wreck, Father brought a junk dealer out to Libby to assess the value of our treasures. I do not know how they arrived at a price, but as I recall, Father received forty dollars, which he shared liberally with Irwin and me. For the work of freeing the brass cogwheels and getting them home, we got about four dollars each. A pulpwood dealer paid a dollar per cord for the eighty cords that Father and the other men had collected, but he never retrieved the wood from the island—it rotted where it had been piled.

All through the remainder of the winter, heavy seas continued the destruction of the *Myers*, until, in an unbelievably short time, she had been reduced to a pile of broken timbers held together by rusty bolts. Father had said she would not last long because she was made of Douglas fir, a West Coast wood that is not as durable as the Maine woods used for shipbuilding. Later, the Coast Guard came out to the island and burned what was left of the hulk so it would not be washed out to sea and create a hazard to some other ship—a sad end to a once-proud barkentine.

At the ages of thirteeen and eight, Irwin and I already were "experienced ship salvage operators." We could go aboard any wrecked sailing vessel and identify all the removable parts of any value. We were even familiar with the plumbing layout. But since most of the great wooden sailing vessels had already been wrecked, it was not likely that we would ever again have a chance to use our new skills.

Having seen the destruction of two of the last sailing vessels wrecked on the coast of Maine, I also experiencd some of the sadness that goes with the loss of objects of such incredible grace and beauty. Whenever we saw a full-rigged ship making her way past Libby, we stopped whatever we were doing to watch her as she "schooned" over the water, white sails set in their curving patterns. And we were glad that two windjammers still frequently entered our waters; the *Lucy Evelyn* and the *Rebecca Douglas* continued to bring freight into Machias during most of the time I was on Libby Island.

One of the last profitable uses of windjammers along the Maine coast during this period was in the rum-running trade, what with Prohibition in full swing. We would often see one of these full-rigged ships make her way past Libby, disappear in the distance, and then return in a short time. The fog nearly always set in early in the afternoon, but we could tell the ship was still there, because the sound waves from the fog signal would strike her hull and reverberate as if they had struck a solid wall. Later in the evening, we would hear the sound of powerboats, which would go back and forth until just before dawn. Then all would be quiet. The ship's cargo had reached the mainland, where land-based rum runners would transport it to their thirsty customers.

The last wreck on Libby of which I am aware took place in

1940. It was reported to me by Julian Colbeth (son of Gleason). A loaded barge broke up on the bar in a northeast snowstorm. Three men and a woman rowed to the station in a rowboat and landed safely. With the treacherous bar between them, the islands still are dangerous, although powered boats and electronic navigation equipment make them less so for today's sailors.

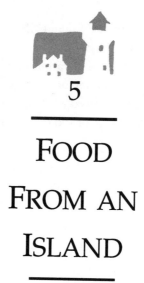

5

FOOD
FROM AN
ISLAND

SURROUNDED by the rich waters of the North Atlantic and with Libby Island's land—all of which was good for pasture or for growing crops—our families shared with Maine's farmer-fishermen the opportunity to be nearly self-sufficient in food.

Dr. Charles McLane, author of books on Maine islands, reports that the Libby Islands were being farmed as early as the 1760s. This was evident in Libby's smooth, rock-free central plain. The two islands together made a farm of approximately 120 acres. There is no way of telling what crops were raised, but charts from the 1880s showing fencing (in squares) indicate that some sheep were being pastured on our island. This was undoubtedly true also of Big Libby; sheep raising was its final agricultural use. During all the years we were on Libby Island, sheep were grazed on the big island. As I recall, the sheep were owned by the Libby family of Starboard, although other sheep owners might have leased the island.

There appear to have been people living on Big Libby into the 1860s, and of course there were lightkeepers and farmers on Little Libby from 1822 on. It is not clear when independent farming ceased, but it is certain that the lightkeepers continued to use the pastureland for raising sheep and cattle and the arable sections for food crops.

Another source of food for these early island dwellers was the "birds of the air and the fishes of the sea." There also were edible wild plants—cranberries, dandelion, goose grass, and probably other species we did not know about.

Wild birds were a major source of meat for us, especially during the fall and winter. We hunted black ducks, mallards, sheldrakes (mergansers), sea ducks (eiders), oldsquaws, and coots (white-winged, black, and surf scoters). We boys began our hunting training early. Our first guns were crossbows—pistol-grip bow guns that Father made. A whittled wooden arrow about three inches long was propelled along a groove (the barrel) by a cord attached to a tough, flexible bow. The cord was pulled back and lodged into a notch at the back end of the groove. A trigger was attached to the side of the gun just below the notch. When the trigger was pulled, the cord was lifted and released, "firing" the arrow. We practiced by shooting these arrows mostly at paper targets, which they hit with considerable force. Our next gun was larger, a full-sized crossbow that operated on the same principle. These guns, 2 1/2 feet long, were powered by a dried spruce limb at least an inch in diameter at the center. As we grew older, we were allowed to insert brads into the ends of these arrows, and they became rather deadly weapons. Although we shot them mostly at wooden targets, I am afraid a few songbirds fell prey to our accuracy.

About the age of seven, I inherited Irwin's Daisy air rifle, since he already had graduated to Father's Stevens, a single-shot, 22-caliber target rifle. This gun weighed about seven pounds, and Irwin had great difficulty holding it up to shoot. Evidence of this was a three-inch groove on the wide porch railing where he had often rested the barrel.

The Daisy air rifle was a dangerous weapon that shot BBs with considerable force. Irwin had pretty well worn it out, so Father sent it back to the factory to be rebuilt. It returned as good as new, and I was quite proud of it. This gun became my constant companion. In spite of Father's admonition against practicing on songbirds, a few succumbed to my increasing skill. And Father did not set a very good example, because he often practiced for his mainland deer hunts by taking long shots with unerring accuracy at gulls sitting on tidal ledges two hundred yards or more from the house.

The year Irwin was twelve, he shot more than twenty small, quick-diving ocean birds we called "water witches" (grebes), which can dive within a fraction of a second. This was done wholly for "fun," but Irwin was learning the skills that would make him an effective hunter for the family. Father was quite proud of his accomplishment. Looking back now, I find it an appalling waste of wildlife.

After many months of saving all the money he earned (Father paid him three cents each for "knitting" bait bags for the lobster traps), Irwin had enough money (twelve dollars) to buy his first shotgun—our main hunting weapon. It was a 12-gauge, single-barreled Iver-Johnson, and it kicked with such a wallop that he had to buy a special leather boot to fit over the stock. This had several layers of sponge rubber to protect his shoulder.

Oldsquaws, perhaps named for their raucous courtship calls, were among our favorite birds. They are ducklike, black and white in color, and move about in flocks. They feed off the ocean bottom on small fish, mollusks, and shrimp and dive to incredible depths, using both their webbed feet and their wings for propulsion. Their strategy for feeding is to move slowly in a series of dives toward a shoreline that they have ascertained to be safe. Irwin, taught by Father, became very skilled at stalking these birds. The hunt began when we spotted a flock heading for the shore. (We often used our spyglass for this purpose.) Then came the stalking. These birds are shy, and, at the slightest sign of danger, they will head offshore or dive and come up out of range. Irwin would hide behind rocks and watch surreptitiously. Then, every time the birds went under, he would dash, accompanied by our dog, to the next hiding place. He had to calculate the exact distance and time so he could hide before the birds surfaced for air. Depending upon the distance and the terrain, this process might take a half dozen or more moves. If he made a mistake, and the birds surfaced before he was safely hidden, they would dive quickly and come up farther away. He would plan his last move to bring him as close as he could get to the edge of the water. This was the most hazardous stage, as the rocks near the water were covered with slippery rockweed. When the birds surfaced, he would fire his one shot, trying to line up as many as possible. If the birds were close together, he might kill several with a single shot. Father, with his automatic, could kill even more, some on the wing as they flew into the air. At the sound of the exploding shell, the dog would hit the water, diligently making as many trips as necessary to bring in the game.

Some types of birds made excellent meals. Sea ducks were hunted in much the same way as oldsquaws, and two of them would make a meal for the whole family. Sheldrakes usually feed singly and were more difficult to kill. Many people refused to eat them because their meat was oily, but Mother soaked them overnight in a soda solution, which counteracted the fishy taste.

Cooting was one of Father's favorite fall hunting activities. Coots fly in flocks, skimming low over the water, and will respond to decoys known as tollers. Father had a set of these that were cut out of inch-thick boards and painted to resemble the silhouette of a coot. Two of them were fastened together by narrow boards of varying lengths, attached at the bottom. The connecting boards were varied just enough so that the tollers could be stacked. Each was fastened to the next with a cord, and the lead one (with the narrowest board) had a long rope with an anchor attached. They could be placed in the water, one set after another; the one with the anchor was set first. These "shadow" birds would bob around on the water, looking exactly like a flock of coots feeding. The tollers were stacked away during the rest of the year, taking up very little space. It was always surprising that these simple crude silhouettes could be so effective.

It was an exciting experience to get up before daybreak on a cool morning during the October migrations, load the tollers into the pod, and row out over the bar to one of the birds' favorite feeding places. A calm morning was necessary for this, because heavy surf often broke over the bar. After the tollers were set, we anchored the pod a short distance away and huddled into our coats to keep warm. We constantly scanned the horizon for flocks of coots flying close to the water in a long, black line. Often several would go by and then one would spy the tollers. It was fascinating to see them suddenly change direction. They would usually make several passes over the tollers, while we kept as low as possible. Then they would turn sharply, come right over the tollers, and stretch their feet down to alight among what they had discerned to be "friends." When their feet were still about four feet above the water (any closer and we would have damaged the tollers), we would stand up and blast away. When the smoke cleared, we would usually see several coots floating on the water.

Some mornings this process could be repeated several times. It was a satisfying feeling to row home, warmed by the rising sun, with enough food for several meals. If we shot more than we could use, we gave them to the other families.

Another way we hunted birds was by hiking down to the bar at low tide, standing behind a high rock, and waiting for them to fly over within range. Shooting them on the wing took a great deal of skill. Sunrise and dusk, when the bar was exposed, were the best hunting times. We could shoot almost any variety of birds this way, because the low bar made a flyway between the high islands. The lowest point in the bar—where there some-times was water going through—was their favorite route.

I shot my first sheldrake this way. Birds flying before the wind over the bar travel at tremendous speeds. One time I had not even reached our usual stand when I looked over my shoulder and saw a bird coming—fast. I crouched low so it would not see me. Father had coached me carefully to lead a fast-moving bird by at least four feet—perhaps even farther, depending on the distance. When the bird passed, it was a considerable distance away, but I raised my gun, led it by much more than four feet, and fired. I could hardly believe it when the bird crumpled, topsy-turvy, into a ball and fell almost at the water's edge. This time I was the proud hunter. Father kidded me, saying that only one shot found its mark and it must have hit the bird in the eye. Actually, this was an advantage; too often we bit down hard on lead shot when we were eating these birds.

In the late 1800s, professional hunters decimated wild bird populations along the coast, killing them for meat to be shipped into the cities and for feathers to decorate ladies' hats. Without refrigeration, thousands of birds spoiled en route. Finally, public sentiment called for game laws to stop the appalling waste.

But the new laws created a dilemma for Maine's farmer-fishermen, who depended upon game year-round to feed their families. They could see nothing wrong with shooting game for their own use as long as it was neither sold nor wasted. But this philosophy brought them into direct conflict with the game wardens hired to enforce the laws. In spite of the enforcement, most rural Mainers continued to hunt, shooting game as needed in and out of season. Father was one of the most honest men I have ever known, and we children were brought up to be scrupulously honest. Lying, stealing, and lawbreaking were absolutely forbidden—except for the game laws. Along with most other Maine men, Father believed there was a "higher law" than the ones that prevented them from shooting game to feed their families. We never saw any contradiction in this view of right and wrong, and we hunted throughout the year, totally disregarding the game laws.

On May 1, 1924, Irwin decided to take his dog and gun and go to the bar to see if any birds were flying over or feeding in the tidal pools. No game appeared, but as he was about to leave, he was startled at the sight of two men crossing the bar from Big Libby. Since he was curious to know who they were, he waited.

The two men greeted Irwin in a friendly fashion and asked if he had had any luck. He said no. They told him they were looking for driftwood to burn in their herring smokehouses, but then they added that they had never been on a lighthouse station before. They asked if he thought his father would be willing to show them around. Irwin, of course, said, "Sure, my dad would be glad to show you the light and the fog signal." As they walked along, the men asked many questions. How long had he been hunting? What kinds of birds did he kill? When did he do most of his hunting? Did his father and the other keepers also hunt? They asked what kind of shells he used and told him what kind they had used the previous week to kill three geese.

One of them finally queried, "Do you have any curlew wings? They make excellent crumb brushes for the table." Irwin gave full and honest answers to all of their questions. He told them that he killed many birds of all the edible varieties, throughout the season, when they were available and meat was needed for the table. He said that the other keepers also hunted to feed their families. No, he did not have curlew wings, but he did occasionally shoot curlews.

His new friends praised him for helping his father hunt to feed the family and then said they were short of food themselves. Since they said they had several more islands to visit, their next question was, "Do you have any birds now that you would sell us?" Irwin replied generously, "No, I wouldn't sell you one, but I have one I'll give you. I was going to give it to one of the other keepers. He sometimes gives me shotgun shells, but I could shoot another one for him."

The men thanked Irwin for his kindness and then followed him to the house. As they walked along, talking about hunting strategies, Irwin was glowing with pride that these visitors had recognized him as a fellow hunter. He quickly found Father, who gave the men a tour of the fog-signal building and light tower. They appeared to enjoy themselves thoroughly, and having company on Libby Island was so rare that Father was delighted to have them show an interest in the station and his work.

When the men returned to the house, Irwin came out of the kitchen entryway with a sheldrake, all dressed, on a platter. The men looked at the bird, identified it, and then turned to Irwin and Father, their friendly expressions gone. Producing his badge, one of them said, "I'm a federal game warden,* and my partner is a state warden. You shot this bird out of season. That is against the law."

That scene is etched indelibly on my mind. I was seven and had been standing close by, enjoying the visitors. But I realized immediately the seriousness of what had happened. I was sure Father and Irwin would be rushed off to Machias and put in jail. I could even imagine them peering out from behind bars. It was the unhappiest day we ever spent on Libby Island.

In tears, I rushed into the house to tell Mother what had happened. Next, the other keepers were summoned. Poor Irwin. In his open, friendly way, he had divulged enough information to convict them all. Even my mother was involved. Stressing how careful we were not to waste anything, Irwin had told his "friends" that she made pillows from bird feathers, and a store in Machias had three of hers for sale—a very serious crime for which she never was charged.

The two wardens fined Father twenty-five dollars, a sizable sum in 1924, when many men worked for a dollar a day. I do not recall the amounts paid by the other two keepers, but the fines were not the worst penalty. As head keeper, Father was required to report everything that happened at the station, so he had to send in a full account of this incident. Since, as part of his duties, he was charged with protecting wildlife, the lighthouse superintendent cut his pay and that of the other keepers. The reduction was large enough to necessitate a family conference to see where expenditures could be trimmed, and such extravagances as our summer shopping-day ice-cream-cone treats were eliminated.

Having entrapped a twelve-year-old "criminal," the wardens confiscated the sheldrake and returned to their so-called smoke-wood boat anchored carefully out of sight. I am sure they had meat for the table that night. Later, they confiscated Mother's pillows in Machias.

Ironically, the following year, the state warden was arrested

* A federal warden was involved because a state warden had no jurisdiction on federal property.

for stealing blueberries. Years later, when Irwin was an adult, one of his friends mentioned that the former state warden was working in a nearby service station, and he urged Irwin to confront the man. But my brother declined, believing no purpose would be served. We have always wondered, however, what the man's reaction would have been.

Father was concerned about Irwin's name being included in the official records of this case. Fortunately, someone with whom Father had grown up held a high position in the state wildlife department. He wrote to this friend, explaining what had happened and taking full responsiblity for the incident, and requested that Irwin's name not be mentioned in the formal report. The friend agreed, so Irwin escaped being branded as a criminal at the age of twelve.

Irwin was never reprimanded for this incident, and I do not believe the other keepers held it against him. Nor did these "friendly" game wardens stop the "poachers" on Libby Island. We continued to believe in the higher law that gave us the right to hunt for the table. Since we had no refrigeration, and there were no meat markets around the corner, we had little choice. From then on, we hunted only when the sea was so rough that nobody could possibly land on either of the islands. And we never carried game directly back to the house. We always returned empty-handed, checked that no visitors had arrived to tour the lighthouse, and then sent our dog Peter (short for Peter Pan) back to where we had hidden the birds. She would make as many trips as necessary to bring them all to the house, delivering each one without a toothmark. (Despite her masculine name, Peter was female.)

It is a shame that when the game laws were passed, lawmakers did not exclude hunting for family use and concentrate on commercial hunters. Had they done this, every Maine farmer-fisherman would have been an ally, and they would have cooperated with the game wardens. Instead, wardens were considered enemies, and most Maine men continued to hunt in spite of the laws.

Although hunting continued to be an important part of the lives of my father and brother, there were aspects of it that troubled me. One was the use of birds, crippled by gunshot, to train our retrievers. Father would take any bird that was unable to fly, let it flap away trying to escape, then send the dog after it. This would continue, time after time, despite my tearful protests, until the bird died. The cruelty of this process deeply disturbed me. After the training session was over, I would pick up the dead bird and try to revive it, but of course my efforts were too late.

I received the same training in gun-handling, marksmanship, stalking, and "gunning" with tollers that Irwin and Arnold received, but it never quite took hold with me. Perhaps it was because I was nearsighted and not quite as successful a hunter. As I grew older, the sport—which it became as we spent more and more time on the mainland—lost its appeal. Father continued to hunt until he was in his eighties, and he killed a deer regularly every fall into his seventies. Mother joined him after he retired. Irwin continues to be an enthusiastic duck and deer hunter, as does Arnold, although he hunts less frequently. I found, as I matured, that hunting came increasingly into conflict with my other values about the preservation of wildlife, although I know that hunters often are ardent conservationists. This is one of the few things upon which Irwin and I disagree. When he goes deer hunting in the fall, I always wish him "bad luck." But, as he says, hunting gives him a chance to enjoy being in the woods in the fall, and in recent years he has not substantially reduced the deer population in New Hampshire.

Despite my reservations about hunting, I have no regrets about my early training. We were taught to have the greatest respect for firearms and to observe every safety precaution. We were not allowed even to point a stick at each other and say, "Bang! Bang!" We did not always follow this rule, because it greatly inhibited our games of Cowboys-and-Indians, but we always knew that Father disapproved.

Because of this safety training, we never had a hunting accident, and only once did we have a near-accident. I was hunting with Father, down on the bar, where the rocks were extremely slippery. Suddenly I saw his feet go out from under him, and his gun went off with a blinding flash. I was petrified until I saw that he was not hurt. The only damage was to his ego. After his many lectures about safety, he was the one who almost shot himself, and possibly me. He asked me to promise that I would never tell Mother. I kept that promise, and afterward, somehow, I always felt closer to him, perhaps because we shared a secret.

Julian Colbeth, the son of Gleason Colbeth (whom I introduced in chapter 2), was not so lucky. While he was hunting on this same slippery bar, his gun discharged accidentally and tore away the inside muscles of his arm. It is difficult to understand how he managed to walk to the house after that. Thanks to our telephone connection via underwater cable, Julian's father was able to call the Coast Guard. They sent a boat that was powerful enough to pick up a doctor at Bucks Harbor in spite of ice blocking the entrance. While the doctor worked on the wound, the Coast Guard carried them farther up the river to Machiasport, where a car and driver were waiting to take Julian to the hospital in Machias. All of this took about four hours, but if we hadn't had a telephone, it would have been impossible, and he probably would have lost his arm. Fortunately, the arm healed well, and I believe he has had nearly full use of it.

Irwin's early mastery of firearms served him well. On his first trip to the rifle range as a Coast Guardsman, he was spotted as an excellent marksman. Later he became a member of the Coast Guard Rifle Team and competed in the National Rifle Matches at Camp Perry, Ohio. He won a Distinguished Marksman's Medal, which required maintaining a high score over a period of three years.

My one "moment of glory" came years later when I won a church-sponsored shooting match organized to raise money. The winning team bought the losing team's supper—served by the ladies of the church—and the individual winners received a fine cake. I was quite proud of mine.

The ocean, which totally surrounded us, was another source of food for the island families. Lobstering, which I will describe in the next chapter, brought us into conflict with the law just as hunting did, but fishing was unencumbered by any conservation regulations. It was regulated only by the tides, the wind, and the seasons.

For a fishing expedition, our first step was to go into Starboard, where there were extensive mud flats for clamming. The fish around our island seemed to be lured only by succulent fresh clams. Irwin and I were assigned this job, while Father and the rest of the family would go to Machias to shop. Our equipment was simple—a short-handled, long-tined hoe that would penetrate the mud; a clam-roller (a rounded box with slats that let water drain out); and a pair of rubber boots. (Clamming with bare feet is dangerous because broken shells are like jagged knife blades.) Little skill was required, but a strong back was essential. Clamming had to be done at low tide, so time was limited, but when our parents returned, we usually had enough for bait and some extras for clam chowder, another special treat from the sea.

Irwin and I often would go fishing by ourselves, but for serious fishing when we needed a winter's supply, we would accompany Father. This was an essential activity, but also fun.

Our fishing equipment was not complex. It consisted of thirty or forty fathoms of $1/8$-inch line, a reel, a three-pound sinker attached to the line, and two hooks suspended several feet below the sinker. These hooks had a shank of about three inches; the distance across the curve at the bottom was three quarters of an inch. The outfit certainly was not intended for casting.

Cod, our most common fish, fed around certain submerged ledges, and Father knew exactly where these were. Most were on the seaward side of the island. To get there, we usually went around the northwest end of Libby, where a reef extended outward. Waves frequently broke over the reef, so it was a long row to get beyond them. We always used our peapod, and Irwin and I did the rowing. Inside several huge ledges, which were above water, was a shortcut that allowed us to stay close to shore, and going by this route saved time and energy, but there was one problem. When a sea was running, small waves would catch us and provide a fast "surfing" ride, sending the boat rushing toward the other end of the channel. On these occasions, when we reached the narrow entrance, Father took over the oars and would row standing up, facing forward, with the oarlocks raised on pipes in typical Maine-lobsterman fashion. Neither my brother nor I was anxious then to be the one in the stern of the boat. This did not seem to bother Father, but Irwin and I always were glad when this part of the "expedition" was over. We never wore, nor carried, life preservers, and I suspect a wrong move by Father might have sent us rolling over, but it never seemed to bother him. Perhaps this was because he had been a surfman in the Coast Guard when they had had to row through breakers to take men off wrecked ships.

Perhaps our fear came from remembering that a drowning had occured on Libby in 1918, just a year before we arrived. Justin Foss and another man, Samuel Holbrook, were fishing in the area when an unexpected sea made up and overturned their boat. Holbrook was drowned, but Foss was rescued by some Naval Reserve men stationed on Libby.

Only recently did I learn more about this story from Justin's daughter Arlona. Ada Foss, having spotted her husband's over-turned boat, tried to alert everybody on the station by ringing a huge bell that was used when the fog signal broke down. She rang until she was exhausted and her hands were badly blistered. Then she tied the bell cord around her five-year-old daughter Millie's waist and told her to run back and forth to keep the bell ringing. Other men on the station finally were alerted, a boat was launched, and Justin was rescued. Few fishermen survive if they fall overboard in eastern Maine's frigid waters, because their temperature rapidly falls below the survival level, and they often die from hypothermia even after being rescued.

Having cleared this dangerous stretch of water, we would load several juicy clams on our hooks and lower them over the side until the sinker struck the bottom. Then we would lift them until we estimated that the hooks were dangling a few feet off the bottom, take a firm grip on our lines, and wait. Father taught us to "saw" the line up and down to attract fish that might be a short distance away. Sometimes we sat for a long time with nothing happening, but at other times the action began immediately. There was no question about a strike when a two-foot-long cod struck your hook, and we wasted no time in "playing" the monster. We pulled in as fast as we could. Sometimes it was an arm-aching process, but soon, if it had not broken loose, the quarry would come flying over the side of the boat, spraying water everywhere and flapping its tail so fast that the coils of cord would soon be in a tangle. This was exciting! I can still hear the whine of the cord coming over the gunwale, which had many grooves worn by our fast-moving lines. The real excitement came when two of us had strikes at the same time. Not all of our fishing trips were exciting, and sometimes we sat for long periods without a single bite, but then we had time to talk and observe the beauty that surrounded us.

We fished on the "slack tide," when the tide was at full flood or lowest ebb—usually the latter. When the tide was running, the current would sweep the hooks up and away from the bottom. By the time we were ready to go home, the tide would have risen sufficiently so we could row back across the bar at the other end of Libby. This was a much safer passage, although even here we had to be careful because seas often broke, running into the channel. Several fishing trips were required to get enough for our winter supply— fish never seemed to be plentiful. At other times of the year, we fished for our immediate use. As Father used to say, "There is nothing like a chowder made from fish within an hour of the time it's caught."

Sometimes we boys fished on our own for harbor pollock—small fish, six to eight inches long, and excellent either fresh or salted and dried. Even these were welcome as part of our winter food supply.

One day, following our usual routine, one of the other keepers' sons and I had launched the peapod without difficulty. And, as I remember, we had good luck bringing in a dozen or more pollock. We always tried to return before the tide was too low on the slip, because that meant a long, hard pull to get the peapod up above the high-water mark. We pulled the pod up a short distance on the side of the slip opposite from the government boat (which had been pulled all the way to the boathouse), and secured its painter to the nearest cleat. We had Father's permission to tie the government boat by its painter, take off the hook and line that ran from the winch, and then use the winch to haul up the pod.

I climbed to the top of the slip and secured the government boat's painter to the frame of the winch, as I had done dozens of times before. Removing the hook from the boat, I released the holding lever on the winch and started pulling the winch line down the length of the boathouse. As I went by the government boat's bow, I thought I detected movement, but I was not too surprised, knowing the slip stringers had just been greased. Then I noticed that the rope I had tied seemed to be twisting. I quickly glanced back to where I had secured it to the winch, and, to my horror, the knot was turning. I watched, paralyzed by fright, as I saw my knot slowly coming untied as if some unseen hands were at work. Suddenly the rope let go with a sharp snap, and the big boat went careening down the slip toward the water, swerving so violently from side to side that I was sure the propeller would strike the rocks. I was numb with fear and shock as I watched this boat, which Father used with such great care, hurtling toward the peapod. There was no room for the two to pass. My friend leaped out of the way as the big boat's transom struck the pod's bow, and then, with a giant white cascade, they both hit the water and went plowing offshore. I still do not know why the big boat's rudder did not turn sideways and send the boat crashing into the rocks.

My next thought was for the government boat's hull. I figured it was holed and she would sink in minutes. I stood there transfixed, expecting to see her start settling into the water. To my relief, she did not, so I thought there might be time to save her.

I knew I had to run to the house and tell Father. That was one of the hardest things I have ever done. I ran up the steep hill, through the pasture gate, and along the path to the house. I found Father and the other keepers painting one of the buildings. I was totally out of breath, but I managed to gasp out my story. The men immediately started running to the boathouse. I tried to keep up but was too exhausted, and I was not sure I wanted to go back to find that our boat, upon which we depended so much, had disappeared. But when I finally reached the crest of the hill, I could still see her.

The only boat left was the government pod, which was tied up in the top of the boathouse. Getting the pod down took several minutes. Luckily, oars had been left in it. Soon Father and one of the other men had the pod in the water and were headed out to where the two runaway boats seemed to be stationary. Luckily, the wind was not blowing and the tide was not taking them in toward the shore.

I stared, still in a state of near-shock, as Father looked the boat over thoroughly and then stooped to start the motor. I was convinced the propeller and shaft were bent. But, to my relief, the motor started and they were soon headed back with the two pods in tow. One of the other keepers had pulled down the winch hook and line, and the government boat was hooked on. She began to ascend the slip at a pace far slower than her recent descent. When she was secure at the top, we pulled up the two peapods. The only damage seemed to be some dents in the big boat's transom and a broken painter on the peapod.

Now that all was in order, my next problem was handling the great shame I felt. I was distraught. How could I have made such a terrible error? I still could not understand how my knot came untied, but it had. Perhaps I had not tied it securely enough. I would never know, but I hated to face anyone. I cannot remember precisely what happened next, but I think I headed for the house to avoid walking with the others. Father had always taught us to take meticulous care of all government property. That boat was our vital link to the mainland. Without it, we could have been marooned. Replacing it could have taken several months, and what excuse could Father give for what had happened? If a giant wave had crushed the boat on the slip, or if a miscalculation during launching or landing had wrecked her on the rocks, that would have been excusable. But how could Father report to the lighthouse superintendent that his young son had been allowed to untie the government boat and she had crashed due to his carelessness?

I am sure I ran immediately into the house to tell my mother what had happened, expecting to be given a severe punishment. I thought that nothing could be severe enough to punish me for this terrible carelessness.

I shall be grateful forever to Father for the way he handled the situation. He never punished me, but I did receive some good instruction in how to tie the boat. My mother later told me that he thought I had been punished enough through my anguish over what I had done, and he was so right. Father was a kind, understanding man. It was a long time, however, before I got up enough courage to tie up the big boat to release the winch. And never again did I tie a sloppy knot.

Throughout the fall, we fished often until we had a good supply. In preparation for drying, we removed the head and discarded it (a great waste, since many people make fish-head chowder), split the fish on the underside to the tail, then cut out the backbone. This left each fish flat and ready to be put in a tub for salting. We applied only enough salt to penetrate the flesh thoroughly and prevent spoiling. This was called "slack salting." Father built fish flakes for drying the catch. These racks were about four by eight feet, four feet off the ground. They were made of stakes with wood strapping and then chicken fence wire was fastened across the tops. The wire supported the fish and allowed the air to circulate freely. After the fish had been soaked thoroughly in the brine, we would spread them on the racks to dry. The only hazard at this point was what we called "blowflies." To discourage them from laying their eggs, which would hatch into maggots, Father sprinkled liberal amounts of pepper on the fish. I am not sure whether this kept the flies away or merely disguised the fly specks. At least we could think we were eating pepper.

After the fish were dried (the time it took depended on the weather), they would be stored in whatever containers were handy. They kept perfectly and no maggots ever appeared. During the long winter months, one of our favorite meals was creamed salt cod. The fish would be washed thoroughly, soaked, then mixed with cream sauce and spread over potatoes. This made a tasty, nutritious meal with cream-of-tartar biscuits. Some of the smaller dried fish, especially pollock, were great for snacks even without careful washing.

One saltwater food item that we completely ignored was mussels. They grew in abundance all along the shore and we could have gathered them by the bushel. They would have made a tasty addition to our diet, but in our part of Maine they were considered inedible. What a waste!

I am sure that the way we fed ourselves was not much different from the way the Indians who inhabited Maine's shores for many years obtained their food. We were not only hunters but also food gatherers. One of our favorite foods on Libby was cranberries—not the commercial variety but a close relation, highland cranberries. They were smaller than bog cranberries and grew in high, dry areas, particularly around ledges, which broke through the surface of our fields in many areas. August was the time to pick cranberries, and the whole family participated—even Father came when he could get time off from his work. This wild crop was always shared among all the families according to an honor system. The three families reported how many quarts they picked each day so that each family would get its share.

Picking cranberries was a pleasant task on a dry, sunny day. Although we were plagued throughout the summer by fog, there were more clear days as fall approached. Each of us had a pick-ing dish that held about a quart of berries. When it was full, we would dump the contents into larger containers. We children kept careful track of how many quarts we picked, because we were paid a few cents for each quart.

These berry-picking times are among my happiest memories of Libby. The whole family worked together as we spread out over the grassy knolls looking for patches of berries. These were scat-tered, but often they were close enough to allow conversation. As we knelt in the soft grass, picking the cranberries one by one, they looked like bright red jewels in the setting of gray-green moss around the lichen-covered ledges. It was easy to pick without concentrating, making it a good time for daydreaming to the ac-companiment of the rhythmic beat of surf on the shore a short distance away. This was also a time for sharing thoughts not otherwise easily revealed. I had one of my most intimate conver-sations with Mother one day while we were picking side by side on adjoining ledges. I can remember exactly where we were, but I cannot recall what we shared. But whatever it was, the conver-sation was so different that I still remember and treasure that special occasion.

When the containers were all filled, we would make our way carefully back to the house. Some of the island was rough terrain, and we did not want to spill our precious ruby-red cargo.

The next step in the cranberry-gathering process was winnow-ing. Usually there was a brisk wind blowing from the southwest in the afternoon, and Mother would lay an old white sheet on the grass in a windy area near the light tower. Holding a bucket high, we would pour the berries slowly onto the sheet, the fruit making a crimson waterfall. The wind would then blow away most of the leaves as well as the green berries. After supper, the family would gather around the kitchen table to continue the cleaning process. In the center would be two large containers—one for the winnowed berries, the other for those we had given the final cleaning. Each person had a dinner plate. We scooped a handful of berries onto our plates and then painstakingly pushed out all the leaves, sticks, and green berries still left after winnowing. Again, this was a wonderful time for conversation, since the task was repetitive and rather mindless. I only wish I had a tape recording of what we shared. All I remember is the closeness we all felt, with Father, Mother, and the children working together for the good of the family.

The next step in the berrying process was canning, which Mother would do. She would boil jars full of these tiny red gems and cap them while they were still sterilized. Only one other ingredient was added—lots and lots of sugar. Highland cranberries are very tart. I do not remember how many quarts and pints Mother canned, but I remember dozens of jars making a brilliant display on the shelves. There was always enough not only for Thanksgiving and Christmas but also for nearly every meal, except breakfast, throughout the year. At the table, whenever we would inquire about some additional treat, Father would remind us of some legendary character who admonished his children, "Eat what's set before you and say nothing." Five minutes later, he would ask, "Maybelle, where's the cranberry sauce?"

Another treat Mother made with the cranberries was conserve, a tasty relish that contained sliced orange peel, walnuts, and other ingredients. This was served only on special occasions.

In addition to harvesting our island's highland cranberries, we often hiked across the bar to Big Libby for bog cranberries. High on the island was a swale that made an ideal habitat for them. The picking and winnowing process was the same, but our honor sharing system did not extend to Big Libby. We probably should have shared them with the island's owners. These berries were kept fresh in paper sacks in a cool place and cooked as needed.

Greatly prized berries that did not grow on Libby were raspberries. For them we went to Stone Island, about two miles closer to the mainland. Since this was on the way to Starboard, sometimes Father would land several of us there on a shingle beach and we would pick the berries until he returned. Although the island was almost totally covered by a spruce jungle, Father had discovered a clearing on its western head that had been claimed by raspberry bushes. It was a tough climb from the landing place to the clearing, and a great relief to break out into the open.

We would spend the day, picking, talking, and eating. This would include a picnic lunch high on the head, where the view was best and the breezes cooling. We also would take time to explore the head of the island. We could see Libby, lying south of us, resembling a giant green whale, the tower looking like white water rising from the whale's spout. Directly westward, we could see dozens of low-lying islands that looked mysterious in the distance. Although we yearned to explore all of them, the only one we ever reached to the westward was Ram. I do not think we knew who owned Big Libby and Stone island, and we never asked permission to harvest their berries or to cut their spruce limbs, which we used in making lobster traps. We must have considered uninhabited islands part of the public domain.

By the time Father returned, we would have filled several buckets. Again we would go through the cleaning and canning process, and another long line of red jars then would adorn our larder shelves.

Wild blueberries were another favorite. These we picked on the mainland. Most forest land cleared by lumbering and burned by fire grows up in blueberries. Thousands of acres now are kept cleared by cutting all brush and periodically burning the vegetation. Father would get permission from a commercial grower near Machias for us to glean berries after the fields had been picked. He seemed to know exactly where the pickers would not bother to go. They were paid by the bushel, so there was no point in picking where berries were scarce. But in two hours—about all the time we ever had—our whole family could collect enough for blueberry sauce, blueberry muffins, and blueberry pies for a whole winter. Another row of jars, this time dark purplish-blue, lined our shelves.

One more food treat that we could gather on our island was dandelion greens. Amid the lush growth on Libby, dandelions were plentiful. Their leaves were young and tender in the spring, and they were a welcome change from the canned vegetables and greens that we had eaten all winter. As soon as the dandelions attained sufficient size, we went out with our knives and dug them up. We also had many ferns, and undoubtedly some of the tops would have made excellent food, but no one seemed to know then about fiddleheads. We did know that if we pulled them up by the roots and peeled away the stems, at the very bottom we would find a tiny core of pure white "cheese."

During some earlier time, Libby had been heavily wooded, so the soil was rich in humus. In fact, some areas of the island still were covered with what we referred to, for some unknown reason, as "nigger knolls." These were small, sharp hillocks that looked like grass-covered tree stumps. If broken into, they revealed decaying wood. Apparently the first settlers had cleared some of the land and dug out the roots. On the rest, they probably cut trees for firewood, leaving short stumps. When Father burned the island each spring to stimulate a richer growth of grasses, the fire sometimes would get into the soil, which was almost pure decayed wood, and burn for days. For no known reason, we called this type of soil "mink dirt."

The climate was ideal for most crops that flourish in a moist atmosphere, and the growing season was several weeks longer than on the mainland because it was warmer. Moderated by the ocean that surrounded us, the temperature was always warmer on the island in the early spring, late fall, and winter than in Machias. We also were free from most insect pests. Three miles offshore was a little too far for them to fly, although we did have potato bugs.

There was, however, one severe handicap: exposure to the salt-laden winds, which damaged some plants. We could grow no corn, peas, beans, squash, pumpkins, cucumbers, or tomatoes. No crop that bore fruit above ground could flourish. We grew mostly beets, turnips, carrots, radishes, potatoes, swiss chard, and lettuce. There probably were other crops that could have survived, but apparently they were not familiar to Father. There was no way to shelter the gardens with a grove of trees because trees would not grow either. Occasionally we would find tiny seedlings pushing up through the grass. We would treasure and nurture them, but within a few years they would turn yellow and die. We also tried to bring trees from the mainland—with the same result. This was all very strange for an island that once was heavily wooded.

Father's cultivation practices were similar to those used on many seacoast farms. The previous keeper, Albion Faulkingham, had sold him some simple farm implements—a plow, a harrow (made from two-by-fours in the shape of a triangle with huge spikes driven through it), a cart, a hayrack—plus a horse (Tim) and a cow (Blacky). We never used commercial fertilizer; cow manure was our only means of enriching the soil. I do not think we used lime, either, so the soil must have been quite "sweet."

Father loved farming. He could hardly wait for spring to come so he could harness the horse to the plow and start breaking up the soil. He rotated the fields, so he often was plowing new turf. I can visualize him now with the reins around his neck, trudging behind the plow, cutting straight, neat furrows. At the end of each row, he would tip the plow on its side and let it slither onto the grass. At intervals he would wipe the perspiration from his face with a big red bandanna and give himself and the horse a rest.

After harrowing, which broke up the soil further, the field was ready to be spread with manure, a smelly job that Father never seemed to mind. When the soil was ready, he would sow the seeds. He always planted more radishes than we could possibly use, probably because they came up first and quickly. After a week or so, Father would walk down to the garden every night to see if the seeds had sprouted, and I liked to accompany him. He would point out each tiny sprout, but he seemed to be most excited by the hairlike shoots of the beets. They were his greatest pride. He would exclaim over things that I could not even see.

After a few weeks, weeding and hoeing would begin. This was work we boys could do. We might not have had many pests on

Libby, but we had plenty of weeds, and these seemed to grow at double the rate of the tiny seedlings. I spent hours clearing weeds and loosening the dirt around the plants to stimulate their growth. Although the task was not pleasant, there was satisfaction in seeing weed-free rows of freshly cultivated plants. The potatoes were the hardest to weed, perhaps because there were more of them.

Our first harvest was radishes, which seldom appeared on the table. More often, we pulled them from the soil, wiped them on the grass, and ate them on the spot. We also did this with a small, sweet variety of turnip that we called egg-turnip. The next fresh treat came when Father thinned the beets—a task not to be trusted to the boys. Mother cooked the surplus beets and tops and what we did not eat, she canned. All summer we had all the fresh vegetables we wanted. In the fall, we harvested the beets and canned them. Some were made into pickles. Turnips and carrots we merely pulled from the ground and stored in our cool basement, but potatoes were different. As an old Maine story goes, someone asked a farmer how his potatoes were turning out and he replied, "Sonny, they don't turn out. You have to dig them out." Digging potatoes was one of my jobs, and a truly satisfying one. Both red and white potatoes were stored in bins in the cellar.

By the time all of the crops had been harvested, we had added considerably to our food supply for the long winter ahead. Father bought other kinds of vegetables from mainland farmers and Mother made many quarts of cucumber and tomato pickles, which were served with nearly every meal.

With all this early exposure to farming, I never became an enthusiastic gardener. The work often was very pleasant—working down a row of vegetables, pulling out the weeds, stopping often to look at the bright sky (unless it was foggy) and the whitecapped sea stretching out in all directions. As an adult, I tried for many years to live where I had a small piece of land or could rent a small plot from a neighbor. But, year after year, I went on vacation in August, only to have my neighbors tell me upon my return how great my tomatoes and cucumbers had been. Then I also realized that what I had labored so hard to produce I could buy from nearby farmers for a few dollars. Finally, I asked myself why I was doing this, and the answer came to me. I was doing it because every time my father came to visit, his first question was, "Philmore, where's your garden?" The next year I turned my garden into lawn. But this was not the end of my agricultural career, for I later married a gardener as enthusiastic as my father. Again I was back working in the soil, but now I have the plot reduced to about ten feet square, not including the flowers.

It was always difficult to get fresh fruit other than berries, but one fruit we always had in abundance was apples. Lobster smacks, which carry lobsters to shipping points, served not only the eastern Maine lobstermen but also those in Nova Scotia. While they were in Canada, they loaded their decks and all other available space with apples from the Annapolis Valley. When they arrived at Libby, Father sold his lobsters and used the money to buy apples—several barrels of different varieties. Through such arrangements, we had enough apples to last us all winter. Some were for immediate eating and others were to be savored during the long winter evenings. Favorite varieties were red Astrachans (for early eating) and Baldwins and Northern Spies (hard as rocks in the fall but ripe and mellow by midwinter). To me, there is nothing as sweet as the aroma of apples. We stored ours in one room in the house and I loved to enter that room just to sniff the air. I always associate their rich scent with Christmas, because for many years we erected our Christmas tree in that room.

Father also bought crabapples from mainland farmers. These were always preserved in a rich, sweet sauce, stems and all. We would hold them by the stem and pull them through our teeth so that the skin and sweet meat of the apple remained in our mouths, leaving the core and stem to be discarded.

Thanks to the animals we raised on the island, our supply of meat was adequate (in the cold months when it would stay frozen). Our cow kept us well supplied with dairy products. Each spring, Father bought a piglet and brought it back to Libby, where it was assigned to a pen and fed mostly scraps from the table, sour milk left from making butter, and almost anything else edible for which we had no use. On this diet it would grow round and fat. Although most of these pigs were Chester Whites, they were seldom white as they rooted about in the muck and mire.

The pigs would continue to grow until December. They could not be slaughtered until after the temperatures remained below freezing because natural freezing was our only way of preserving the meat (except for the fat pork, which we salted down in wooden barrels to be used for cooking such savory dishes as baked beans).

We children all looked forward with great anticipation to the day of the pig butchering. Father had a special technique for killing the animal. With his equipment for making lead balls, he would cast one, trim off the excess lead, and insert it into a shotgun shell from which the regular shot had been removed. He then would replace the wadding and load it into his shotgun. We never were allowed to witness the "execution," so we would wait in the Fosses' entryway, which had a window facing the barn. It was too high for us to look out, but we could hear. We would stand there in absolute silence until we heard the roar of Father's gun. Then we would rush pell-mell for the barn, where the pig would still be writhing on the floor, blood gushing from its wound. Father would be circling about, waiting for the carcass to stop twitching so he could insert his knife to drain out the blood. This was truly a gory sight, and since we were allowed to see this shocking part, I never could understand why we could not witness the whole episode.

When the pig was dead, Father would insert a stout stick under its hamstrings and hoist its huge bulk clear of the barn floor. I can still hear the creak of the blocks and the snapping of the rope as it stretched under the animal's dead weight. It was an awesome sight to watch this several-hundred-pound creature slowly lifted off the floor to hang in midair.

The next step was to remove the bristles. Mother would have a wash boiler and other containers full of steaming hot water ready on the kitchen stove. These would be carried to the barn and dumped into a huge barrel. Father then would lower the pig into the near-boiling water. When the carcass was hot enough, Father applied pitch to "clump" the bristles so they could be scraped off to leave a clean, well-shaved pig.

The entrails, which Father previously had removed, were left to steam in the cold December air. The odor was not pleasant. In spite of the odor, many Maine farmers made sausages, using the intestines for casing, but we did not. However, we prized the heart and liver and would have them as a rare treat for our dinner the next day. Another part of the pig's entrails highly prized by us children was the bladder. We would get this as soon as it was cut loose, wash it, blow it up like a balloon, and then let it dry. It made a great ball for kicking and tossing. We would also retrieve the pig's kinky tail, and someone was likely to get it (as a joke) for a Christmas present, tied up with a bright red ribbon.

The pig supplied us with fresh pork throughout the winter months. We sawed the meat free as needed, since it would be frozen hard.

Libby Island was an ideal place for keeping cows, which were brought out from the mainland in a seine boat borrowed from herring fishermen. (More about cow transportation appears in chapter 9.) Since the island was one large pasture (although we fenced off an area for the buildings, garden plots, and for growing hay), the cows were left free to graze.

We cut hay and stored it in our barn to feed the cows during the winter. This process always began with the sharpening of Father's scythe. We had a grindstone that was turned by hand, and one of us boys had that job. It was tiring work, although satisfying to see the blade become bright and keen. Water in a trough under the stone kept the wheel constantly wet to improve its cutting power.

Selecting the area of the hayfield to cut first, Father would adopt his mowing stance and cut a swath of hay in a wide arc, leaving only about an inch of stubble on the ground. Swinging and walking forward steadily, he soon could cover a large section. This task took great stamina, and he would stop often to wipe away the perspiration and to restore the cutting edge to his blade with a scythe stone. This stone was about eight inches long and three quarters of an inch in diameter. He would place the base of the scythe handle on the ground, lean it against his body, holding the top with his right hand, and with his left hand (he was left-handed) stroke both sides of the blade at a fast pace, letting the stone go around the end of the blade. This made a clear, metallic sound that was pleasant on a warm July day. But this was a skill that had to be mastered thoroughly, because the slightest error meant a sliced hand.

Watching Father demolish a field of standing grass was an aesthetic experience. His even, rhythmic strokes, the swish of the blade through the grass, and the twisting of his body from the waist made it seem like he was performing a strange ritual dance as he advanced across a field. Once he had cut a section, he would stop for refreshment. He liked a mower's drink (which I assume other Maine farmers used) we called "twitchel." It was made from cool water with molasses, oatmeal, and ginger added to give it substance and flavor. At the appropriate time, one of us boys would take a jug of this out to Father and join him in a glass or two. We never drank this beverage at any other time—it was reserved strictly for the haying season.

After the hay was cut, it had to be spread with a pitchfork to dry. Sometimes, in the middle of the day, Father would ask Irwin and me to go out and turn over the hay so it would dry on the other side. At night we used a wide wooden rake to pull the hay into rows to protect it from the fog that usually descended. Making hay was difficult, because we had fog for some part of nearly every day in summer.

Father finally would declare that the hay was made and we

could rake it into haystacks to make it easier to pitch into the hayrack, a framework made of round posts held together at the top and bottom by two-by-fours and attached to the wagon base.

Of all the farm tasks, this was the one that we youngsters enjoyed the most, because work could be combined with play. Our job was to tread down the hay after the men pitched it into the hayrack. There was some danger involved, as there was in many of our tasks—we had to be sure to step back when the sharp-tined pitchfork pitched in the hay—but the men were careful and so were we. Performing this service, we felt proud. Thanks to our efforts, the hayrack could carry a tremendous load. After it was declared full, we got a ride to the barn, where we would help stow the hay after it had been pitched onto the haymow—another exciting activity. Although the rides were short, we usually had time to burrow in the sweet-smelling hay. Apparently Libby had no ragweed, because none of us had sneezing fits.

We were always sorry when haying season was over, the hayrack was taken off the wagon, and the scythes, pitchforks, and hay rakes were stored for another year. Even after haying season was over, we sometimes returned to the barn to play in the hay. This apparently did not damage it in any way, and we greatly enjoyed making slides and tunnels.

Keeping a cow imposes a certain discipline. Twice a day, the cows had to be fetched from the pasture and milked. Sometimes retrieving the cows was a disagreeable task that required wading through fog-dampened grass. In the winter, when the cows were confined to the barn for long periods, there was a more odious task: cleaning out the manure. I was called upon frequently to fetch the cows and to clean out the manure, but not to do the milking. I observed early that as soon as Irwin had learned how to squeeze our cow's teats to extract the milk, he got the job. I was determined to avoid that, so I never learned how. And as long as Irwin was available, Father never insisted. Apparently I was not destined to become a farmer.

From our one cow we got milk, cream, and butter. When I was very young, I followed a strict ritual at bedtime. I waited until whoever was milking the cow returned so I could have a glass of "cow-warmed" milk. To me, this was a great treat and also postponed the bedtime hour. I doubt that I would enjoy cow-warmed milk today.

Our "refrigeration" consisted of a cool cupboard in the kitchen entryway and a cool closet in the dining room. This is where Mother placed the milk so the cream could rise. After a few days, she would skim the cream off the top, leaving a thick, white substance called "bonnie-clabber." About once a week, we made butter with an old-fashioned churn that had an internal paddle and an external crank. The task of hand cranking the churn usually was assigned to the youngsters. Sometimes it seemed that the cream would never "make," and when it did, it happened suddenly, with a loud swishing as the globs of butter separated from the milk. With what joy we greeted that sound! Mother had wooden molds into which she pressed the butter to make attractive flowerlike designs.

One of the staples of our diet was eggs, and we always kept a flock of hens, mostly Rhode Island Reds and Plymouth Rocks. We had a henhouse with laying boxes and a fenced-in area to keep the hens from wandering around the lighthouse grounds. The hens supplied us not only with eggs but also with meat. I frequently got the job of decapitating a rooster and preparing it for the pot—an assignment I did not like. I particularly disliked making a decision as to which bird was to be executed. Eventually, I worked out what I considered to be a fair way of meting out this injustice. Since roosters are notorious runaways and it was always exhausting to catch them, the last one to have led me on a merry chase was the next one to get the ax. I hope I did not make too many mistakes in identification.

Some of the hens also were adventurous and liked to go exploring. One summer, Mother thought that Irwin was too thin, so she decided to fatten him up by feeding him a large glass of nonalcoholic eggnog every afternoon. After one taste of this treat, I decided that it was delicious, and I asked if I could also have eggnog. I was denied, however, on the grounds that I was not thin and the hens were not producing enough eggs. One day I saw a runaway hen pushing her way through the deep grass near the edge of a steep cliff. She was clucking loudly—the "I-just-laid-an-egg" cackle. Squeezing under the fence, and being careful not to go too near the edge of the cliff, I searched through the long grass and soon found a secret nest containing not just one egg but several. I was suspicious of the others, but I knew the warm one was fresh. I ran to the house with it, told Mother it had been laid in the grass by a stray hen, and asked if I, too, could have an eggnog. How could she refuse? After that, throughout the summer, I watched for cackling stray hens and often was able to join my brother in his eggnog treat.

There was little wasted on our lighthouse farm. Scraps that did not go to the pig went to the hens and the dog. Although we did not eat mussels, we dug them to provide the hens with grit. On Franklin Island Light Station, my brother-in-law, George Woodward, decided to add a new ingredient to his hens' diet. After finishing churning one day, he took the pans full of bonnie-clabber to the hens. They went for it with gusto. A few hours later, he happened to walk by and saw his hens staggering about, "spurting" clabber "from both ends." In a short time, many of them were dead, and he claims that those which survived stopped laying eggs.

Irwin also had a traumatic experience with poultry. This episode occurred on Whitehead Light Station, before we moved to Libby. Soon after the head keeper's hens hatched out a large flock of baby chicks, Irwin, then five, heard Father discussing the danger the maturing chickens might pose to his newly planted garden. This worried Irwin, so the next day he decided to take preventive action. Enlisting the aid of one of his friends, he led the way behind the buildings to the edge of the woods, where the henyard was located. Here they carefully planned their attack. Irwin's friend would catch the chickens and pass them to Irwin.

Irwin, armed with a stout stick, would hold a chicken in one hand, break its head with one swift blow, and throw it into the woods. The two boys continued this assembly-line process of destruction until the entire flock of chickens was gone. Then, to be sure the threat to Father's garden was totally eliminated, they drove a setting hen off her nest and destroyed all twenty-six of her eggs.

With great pride, Irwin revealed the action he had taken and told Father that his garden was safe. Father, of course, was shocked. He rushed to the keeper's house to tell him what had happened and to arrange suitable recompense. But the keeper was understanding when he learned the boys' motives. Irwin escaped punishment because he said he was coming down with a cold, but his friend's mother was not as lenient. Irwin recalls that shortly after the story was out, he saw his friend heading for the woods. His mother, with stick in hand, was only a few steps behind him and gaining fast.

In spite of the fruitfulness of Libby Island and the sea around us, we could not be quite self-sufficient. We still were dependent upon mainland sources for many staples. In the fall, before the weather became too severe, we would buy barrels of flour, large bags of sugar, molasses, salt, and canned fruit and vegetables to add variety to what we raised and gathered. We also bought great quantities of beans for baked beans. Grains for the horse, cow, and chickens also had to be imported.

We always accompanied Mother and Father on these shopping trips, helping to carry the supplies to the car. At the end of shopping, we made sure that Father stopped by the penny-candy counter. We would indicate a few choices and then Father would say, "Give me a quarter's worth and mix the rest of them up." One of my childhood ambitions was to reach a stage of affluence in my life where I, too, could step up to a candy counter and address the clerk, "Sir, give me a quarter's worth—one of those and one of those and mix them up." Now that I have reached the stage of sufficient affluence, my diet does not allow sweets, there is no longer any penny candy, and few stores have behind-the-counter clerks.

As the groceries were stored away in the car, we would always watch to see where the candy bag was packed. Once the government boat was underway for Libby, we could no longer stand the wait and would urgently request a piece of candy. Our wishes usually were granted, unless the spray was flying and it was impossible to get out the bag. In that case, we each would get a piece soon after reaching home. Mother would dole out the candy each day, as long as the supply lasted. When it was gone, we even coveted the bag. By this time, some of the chocolate would have melted onto the bag, and licks of chocolate-covered paper were not too bad for a treat.

With our shelves full of jars of fruits and vegetables; the bins full of flour and sugar; food stored for the animals; our closet full of Nova Scotia apples; and a pig, plus possibly a steer or a deer, hanging frozen in the barn, we were ready for a long, cold winter. With a continuing supply of wild birds, and several good hunters in the family, the winds could howl and the waves could roar— we knew we would not go hungry.

By mainland standards, our diet was rich and varied. We had not only the usual cuts of beef and pork and poultry but also a wide variety of game birds. While most families in our area had blueberries, few had cranberries. Fish was available at the markets in town, but not the fresh fish we so often consumed. And lobsters, even then an expensive luxury, were staples for us. As I look back on what our island environment provided us, I realize that not even wealthy families could have had a more abundant or varied supply of food and delicacies.

For breakfast, we children usually had cornflakes, shredded wheat (Father called them "mattresses"), or cooked cereals. I loved oatmeal, especially when it had been allowed to "set" a while on the back of the stove and become a little dry.

I often read in fairy tales about people eating porridge and always wondered what it was. Goldilocks ate the porridge belonging to the three bears; a woman had a pot that made porridge when addressed by a magic word, but she forgot how to turn off the pot and she went floating out her cabin door with her three-legged stool on a river of porridge. I was very curious about this magic food, because these fairy-tale people seemed to eat little else. They seemed to have porridge not only for breakfast but also for lunch and dinner. Many years later, on a visit to London, I saw porridge listed on a menu. I decided to order some—to satisfy not only my hunger but also my curiosity. What a surprise when the waiter served me oatmeal! I had been eating porridge myself all the time that I was reading and wondering about this fairy-tale food.

Father frequently had fried potatoes and leftover meat for breakfast. He did a hard day's work every day and needed the sustenance. We also ate eggs prepared in a variety of ways.

Our main meal came in the middle of the day, as with nearly all Maine farm families. We had meat in the usual ways— baked, fried, and made into soups and stews. Except for black ducks and mallards, which were always baked, all the other wild birds were made into stews with dumplings and lots of gravy. Fish was fried in batter or made into chowder (my favorite) with potatoes and onions.

During the spring and fall lobstering season in our area (summer was a closed season), lobster was a staple of our diet. We had lobster then at least three or four times a week. It came as quite a surprise to me, later, to discover that lobster was a luxury most people could not afford.

Mother prepared lobsters in a variety of ways. The simplest method was to boil them and eat them fresh from the pot. We often went out on the cliff near the house with a dishpan full of lobsters, freshly boiled, and had an impromptu picnic. Father loved to do this. We dipped the lobster meat in vinegar but never in melted butter. Another favorite dish was lobster stew. Mother would first boil the lobster, then remove the meat from the shell, cut it into small pieces, and simmer it in a broth of milk and butter. This was often an evening supper dish. Mother also served lobster salad, arranged decoratively on a platter and flavored with her own special salad dressing. Sometimes we even had fried lobster for breakfast!

Beans! Beans! Beans! Our other dietary staple was baked beans. Historically, in Maine and some other New England areas, baked beans always were served for Saturday night supper, sometimes supplemented with brown bread (made from flour and molasses), and frankfurters. Our family did not merely eat beans on Saturday might; we also had them Monday noon for dinner (lunch). Monday was a busy day—wash day—and the beans made a quick meal. We would finally finish the batch Wednesday night for supper. On Friday night, the cycle would begin again, when Mother would soak the beans that would be baked with lots of molasses, brown sugar, and salt pork all day Saturday.

The practice of having beans on Saturday night began in colonial times, when baking was done on Saturdays in large brick ovens. There was room in the back of the oven for a pot of beans, and by the time the baking was done, so were the beans. This provided not only a Saturday night meal but also food for the Sabbath, when Puritans were not supposed to work.

For desserts, Mother sometimes made pies, cakes, and puddings, but our standby was cookies and sauce (canned fruits and berries). Mother made two varieties of cookies: molasses and sugar. The molasses cookies were simple. The main ingredients were flour, sugar, molasses, ginger, nutmeg, and cinnamon. The dough was rolled out on a bread board and cut into rounds about three inches in diameter, but before Mother cut them, she took a fork and ran it lightly over the surface of the dough, making decorative diagonal lines. While one batch was baking, Mother would be in the pantry preparing the next batch. This process went on until she had two heaping pans full, one of molasses cookies and the other of sugar cookies. If they had raisins, we called them hermits. I do not have her recipe for the sugar cookies, but they were equally delicious.

Cookies were our favorite snack as well. When we would come

in to get warm (both winter and summer) after playing outdoors, we would reach high up on a shelf where the cookies were kept and help ourselves to one or two. We washed them down with a ladle full of water from the kitchen pump. Mother sometimes complained about how fast her cookies disappeared, and Father threatened to put them under lock and key. The only security measure ever taken, however, was to move them to the dining-room closet where the cream was kept (in similar pans). After that, getting the cookies required a little more effort, but we did not mind. Our only problem was that we could not tell which pans contained the cookies and which the cream, so we often had cookies flavored with cream from our fingers.

For bread we depended mostly on buttermilk biscuits. During our years on Libby, Mother did not make any yeast bread. Perhaps raised bread was not a part of her family's food patterns. Father was also an excellent cook and frequently baked the biscuits. The first step was to build a very hot fire with driftwood or with edgings provided for kindling when we had the steam fog signal. The wood ignited quickly and rapidly brought the oven to a very high temperature. When the biscuits came out of the oven, they were served hot for supper with lots of butter. As they cooled, they developed a different texture and were good with butter and jam.

Looking back on our island diet, I marvel at its richness, variety, and wholesomeness. It is little wonder that we Wasses have lived long and healthy lives.

THE LOBSTERMAN

He rose and glowing red from dawn he strode
    the length of his island home.
At land's end he launched his boat into the hollow caves
    of waves that crushed the shore.

The wind toyed his craft first high then low
    blowing him by its will to familiar shoals.
Slowly his winged oars steered to where the red
    tipped buoys taunted him from each wave's crest.

Casting out he caught fast a rope and coiled
    hands full of hope aboard.
Ten, twenty, thirty fathoms rose from the ocean, then
    came the wooden frame.

A quick glance, and one more chance was burst into
    somber champagne as the trap fell below.

Once, twice, one hundred times his arms plunged
    into the icy brine, but only regret swept his face
and laced his body into a statue bowed against the wind.

He slowly rowed toward shore, a hollowed shadow from the sun.
    His day's work done, he walked again the
back of his granite home.

Beyond sleep he lays now in the sun's last rays—

Who knows what catch he may haul from this red deep?

P.B.W.

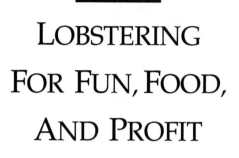

6

LOBSTERING
FOR FUN, FOOD,
AND PROFIT

"PHILMORE, time to get up if you want to go haul with me!" It was still dark. When I arrived downstairs, a bowl of hot-out-of-the-pot oatmeal and a cup of cocoa were ready for me on the kitchen table. While I ate, if Father had had the last watch, he climbed the tower stairs to put out the light. This could be done a half hour before sunrise, but when the fog signal was blowing, he had to wait until six to call the next keeper on watch.

Lobster-fishing season ran from September to December and mid-April through June, and the early mornings in the spring and fall were cold. I wore a heavy sweater, a wool cap, and rubber boots, yet I shivered as we left the shelter of the rainshed. In spite of the cold, I would never miss the first haul of the season. As Father and I trudged off toward the boathouse the sun would just be breaking free from the water in the east. As we swished through the wet grass, Peter would run ahead, scaring up sparrows as she went. She would wake the cow by barking vigorously and nipping at her heels, then moving swiftly away to dodge the flying hooves. As we went through the pasture gate, we could see the inside shores of the island stretching before us. The bright lobster buoys made the ocean almost as colorful as the fields of flowers through which we were walking, and the colors were even more varied.

We had to stop by the baitshed to pick up a tub full of baited pockets, which I had stuffed with near-rotten herring the night before—one for each of our forty-five traps. Irwin and I shared this odorous task, and it was the one lobstering job I did not like. The baitshed was old, dark, and smelly, with years of fish oil soaked into the floorboards. The place was always full of flies. As soon as I immersed both hands in the bait, a fly would light on my face and I was quite defenseless—unless I wanted to smear my face with fish gurry, which would make me even more attractive to the flies.

After loading the bait tub into the boat, Father would tell Peter to get in. Then we would lower the pod down the slip. Peter would move onto the stern seat just as the aft end hit the water, but never until the boat was level. I would follow Father, giving the boat a shove, then take my place on the rowing seat toward the bow, fit our newly painted oars into the oarlocks, and start rowing. Father had taught me to row well, turning the blades so they would slice through the tops of waves on the back stroke, and pulling the full blade through the water on the power stroke. We also kept the blades close to the surface of the water to cut down on wind resistance. But this morning was perfectly calm, and the oars cut evenly into the water, making tiny whirlpools as we moved rapidly forward. Rowing is excellent exercise, and I developed strong back and arm muscles. Later, I met few boys my own age who could beat me at arm wrestling.

Father directed me, from time to time, until I brought him abreast of the first buoy. He would reach out with his gaff, catch the warp of a lobster trap, and start pulling. The boat would move rapidly in the direction of the trap, which lay on the bottom. After a few minutes of vigorous hand-over-hand hauling, the trap would come to the surface. I could feel my heart pound a little faster with both fear and excitement as I peered down into the water, trying to see what might be inside. Sometimes Father would have to lean over and right it with his gaff so its flat surface would sit on the side of the boat. I was often concerned when he did this, because the gunwale would be only inches above the water and sometimes waves would slop in.

Often a trap would be empty, but at other times it would contain what we wanted—lobsters. Of those in the trap, only a few would be legal size. The law then required that, to be taken, a lobster had to measure approximately 3 1/4 inches from its eye socket to the back of its carapace. (The legal length is changed from time to time.) Fishermen were supposed to throw back the short lobsters, but Father and most lobster fishermen sold the legal lobsters and kept enough short ones to feed their families. In this illegal activity, we never were caught. If we had been, the penalty was quite severe.* But again, to Father, the right to feed one's family from what nature and hard work provided was above the state's laws.

Many other forms of sea life also liked the bait in our traps. A small cod was a real prize and would appear that night on our table in a creamy fish chowder. The traps also snared crabs, which we sometimes cooked. There were always many periwinkles, which were tasty when boiled. Crabs, when they were plentiful, ate too much bait, so, almost by habit, Father would smash them on the side of the boat when he threw them out. An occasional toad sculpin provided entertainment. These small, bright orange-red fish would blow themselves up like red balloons when brought into the air. We threw the inflated fish overboard, and try as they might, they could not get under the

*My only close brush with this law came much later, when I was a teenager working in a store in Machias. My boss sent me to Kennebec one evening to pick up a package. He mentioned that I could take along my girlfriend. I was happy to go—anything to get away from the store, where I was putting in about fourteen hours a day. I picked up my girlfriend and drove to Kennebec, following my employer's directions to a house at the end of a nearly deserted narrow road. A man came to the door and I told him who had sent me. He said he did not have the package and directed me to another house. The second man said he did not have it but he knew where it was. He took a lantern and disappeared into the bushes. By this time I was becoming suspicious and concerned, and when

water again. Our last sight of them would be their tails flapping back and forth like tiny red flags. I suppose it was a form of cruelty to dumb animals, but I always liked to think that they eventually managed to deflate and return to the bottom.

The suspense in wondering what might be in any trap, as it broke the surface, was perhaps one of the prime reasons Father, the other keepers, and even many full-time lobster fishermen, enjoyed this "trade." An old fisherman from Addison who retired after fifty-five years of lobstering, when asked how he felt about quitting, said, "I sure hated to haul that last trap because you never knew what you were going to find."

Occasionally, we would catch a real giant that would nearly fill the trap, and Father would exercise extreme care in extricating it. A lobster could be handled safely only by putting thumb and forefinger astride its back beside where the claws were attached. Catching a lobster of this size, we first felt elation, followed by tension. Often these were female and would be carrying eggs under their tails. As fertile specimens, they had to be thrown back, and as gently as possible. But before we did that, the law required that a hole be punched in one of the small sections at the end of the tail, so if the female were caught while not carrying eggs, she could be recognized. Even though she would shed her shell many times, the hole (which we punched with a nail and hammer) was permanent. How we hated to throw these beauties back, but we knew it was necessary to preserve the lobster population, which even then seemed to be dwindling.

he finally emerged and tossed a burlap bag into the back seat, I was glad to pay the agreed-upon sum and get away.

In a few minutes, we knew what was in the mysterious package: short lobsters. We could hear them hissing and snapping. Now I knew I really had a problem—my girlfriend was the daughter of the local game warden.

Since she had not actually seen the lobsters and did not know *for certain* what was in the bag, she said she would not mention our cargo to her father. Luckily there were no wardens out checking cars that night.

My boss was understandably upset when he found out who my girlfriend was. I was quite upset myself at being sent on such an errand, and I left the job a short time later.

After we hauled a few traps, the bottom of the boat became a lively place, with fish splashing in the water that came in with each trap and the lobsters and crabs crawling about trying to find something to bite. Peter would watch all this activity with great interest, making sure to stay secure on the stern seat, away from the snapping claws. We also had to be careful. Lobsters have specialized claws, one for crushing and the other for cutting. The cutting claw of a large lobster can easily slice through a rubber boot and into the wearer's foot.

Hauling all forty-five traps required rowing the length of the island and back. On a windy day, this distance sometimes was greatly increased, especially if Father had set some traps in deep water—perhaps thirty fathoms (180 feet). The minute the trap was lifted off the bottom, the boat would drift with the wind and current while we cleaned out the trap and installed a new bait bag. By this time, it might be several hundred feet or even yards back to where the trap had been on the bottom. So rowing to pick up traps required a series of overlapping loops. Lobstering from a pod was a lot harder work than from a well-equipped lobsterboat with hoisting gear to pull up the traps and a motor to hold the boat in place or move it to any location desired.

In spite of the hard work, hauling was a satisfying process, especially when the catch was good. And on a beautiful spring or fall day, as the sun rose and warmed us, few activities were more pleasant. When the last trap was hauled, we would swing around and head for the slip. Father would begin to wash out the boat, scooping up fresh sea water in his bailing dish and throwing it against the sides. His aim was not too accurate, and often I got rinsed at the same time. After the boat was thoroughly clean, he would bail her dry. Then he would gather up the lobsters from the stern of the boat, where he had placed them, and after capturing those that had gone exploring, he would plug their claws with wooden plugs to keep them from attacking each other. When he was finished, sometimes he gave me a break from rowing and I would snuggle up to Peter on the stern seat.

Before landing at the slip, we would stop at the mooring where our lobster car was tied. This was a heavily built crate in which we stored lobsters between visits from the buyer. Father would drop them into the crate and then securely tie the covers. Early in the season, he might have forty or more lobsters from a single haul, but as the season progressed, he would catch only four or five. After closing the crate, we would head for the slip, haul up the pod, take whatever fish, crabs, and short lobsters we had saved, and begin the climb up the hill to the house, where Mother would have a hearty meal or generous snack ready, depending on the time of day.

This first haul of the season was always an enjoyable event, but the preparation for that day was a process that had begun many months before and involved the whole family.

Today, many lobster fishermen buy traps manufactured of plastic-covered wire, but we always built our own. The base of our traps had two sills, two inches by two inches and approximately three feet eight inches long, with four smaller connecting sills approximately two feet in length. The upper frames of the traps were made of natural tree limbs, one inch in diameter. They were bent from one sill to the other, driven into holes, and nailed. Two end bows and one in the center gave the trap its basic curved structure. Once the framing was done, the trap was covered with laths nailed the width of a hammer handle apart. A hinged section of laths at the top of the trap allowed us to put in the bait and to remove our catch.

The traps had two basic designs, old-fashioned and "patent." The old-fashioned traps were open at each end, with two funnel-shaped nets, called heads, extending into the trap. The openings in these heads were formed by small hoops of wood or wire. The bait bag was hung in the middle inside the trap. Lobsters would climb up into the head to reach the bait and then fall down into the bottom of the trap. It was very difficult for them to crawl out, since the head angled upward. Lobsters did escape from these traps, however, often when the trap was being hauled. Many a disappointed fisherman has watched a large lobster slip through the bottom hoop and propel itself backward to the bottom, flipping its powerful tail. The patent trap (someone must have invented it and applied for a patent) was quite different in design. It had two small heads on each side of one end of the trap and one large one inside that led into what we called the "bedroom," or "parlor." The bait was hung in this inner chamber. When lobsters fell into the bedroom, escape was practically impossible.

We used a variety of wood for making the frames of the traps. Often we were able to pick up long poles along the shore. Originally these were the stakes used to hold nets in fish weirs, but storms had ripped them out and reduced them to driftwood. These poles were well cured, and if we got to them before the sea worms did, they made excellent trap sills. More often, we sawed out sills from two-inch planks. Sometimes these were from driftwood or were left over from building projects on the island. The laths, and occasionally planks for sills, were bought from sawmills on the mainland.

Most of the bows we cut (without permission) on Stone Island. This always made an exciting "explore." That was how we first discovered that raspberries grew there. Usually we cut branches from the plentiful island spruce, but we also experimented with birch. Black birch had a pleasant minty smell, and the spruce always reminded us of Christmas. Once the bows were cut, we tied them into bundles and floated them in the well-house, which provided a supplemental water supply for the fog signal. This kept them supple for bending.

We set up our lobster-trap shop in the far end of the rainshed, and in our spare time Father, Irwin, and I built traps. I can remember spending hours ripping planks into sills. It was an arm-busting, backbreaking job, but each cut had its reward when the new sills were set in place to make the base of a new trap. The doors for the traps were made separately and hinged with leather cut from old shoes. Whittled wooden buttons (made of a small piece of lath turned on a nail in the center) held the door closed. Another button, nailed in the center of the trap, was used to hang the bait pocket. When our lobster traps were completed, we wheeled them to the boathouse on our wheelbarrow. Until they had soaked up water, they were not very heavy. We could carry three in one trip. We seldom called our traps "pots," but this is a common name for them. I never could understand why until we visited the little Cornish village of Mousehole, where we saw circular lobster traps made out of what appeared to be reeds with a hole in the top. These did indeed look like pots.

Another time-consuming process was knitting the heads and bait pockets, which were made of 1/16 -inch cotton twine. Both the pockets and heads were "knitted" with a "needle" (more like a shuttle) and a mesh board. The pocket needle was made from a small piece of oak 1/8 inch thick, 3/4 inch wide, and about nine inches long. The needle was loaded by looping the twine over the center tongue, down through the end notch, up the other side, around the tongue again, down to the notched end, and so on.

Father made the needles with his jackknife. The needles for knitting heads were made the same way, only they were about one-third larger. The pocket mesh board had an ellipse shape and was an inch wide, a half-inch in diameter, and about six inches long. The mesh board for the heads was larger.

Everybody in the family learned to knit heads and pockets. We spent many evenings in this activity, but it was also something we did at odd moments. Each of us had a work station—a hook screwed into a kitchen window frame. It was an enjoyable way to spend time, because you could both work and talk. Sometimes we had exciting races to see who could complete a pocket or head first. We kept count of our production, because Father would pay us for each one we completed. We also found a ready market for them in mainland stores. Apparently some fishermen's families were not skilled netmakers. I still have my two needles and mesh boards and I have retained this skill. The basic knot we used goes into the making of every kind of net (including tennis nets) I have ever seen, and although I have no historical evidence, I feel certain that the nets Peter, James, and John cast into the sea were of the same construction.

We also made the hoops that spread the inner openings of the heads. These could be made of small boughs bent into a circle and tied securely, but many of ours were made of $1/8$-inch wire. As I mentioned in chapter 4, we salvaged some of the wire rigging from the 1925 wreck of the *John C. Myers* and dragged it home across the bar. When we unstranded the steel cable, we had long pieces of wire that were ideal for trap hoops. We sawed this into the right lengths, but then the real work began, since each piece was spiraled. These spirals had to be pounded out on an anvil to straighten the wire. I can almost hear the metallic clink of Irwin's hammer as he spent many hours straightening this wire. Once it was straightened, he bent it around a form, pounded the ends into hooks, and fastened them together, making near-perfect circles and near-perfect hoops for our trap heads.

From local merchants we bought large quantities of rope, which joined the buoy floating on top of the water to the trap on the bottom. But we had to make the buoys ourselves. Father hewed these from cedar poles with his ax. They were tapered to a point on one end, with a hole drilled to run the warp through. At the other end, a spindle was inserted so the buoy was more visible and could be picked up easily. Closer to the trap was tied a toggle, a second float to take up the slack in the line at low tide, making it less likely to become entangled in bottom growth or rocks. A favorite toggle was a whiskey bottle with a rubber stopper. In spite of Prohibition, these always seemed to be in plentiful supply. At low tide, both the toggle and the buoy might be floating on top of the water, but with eleven-foot tides, only the buoy would be showing at high tide. And where there was a strong current, even the buoy might be submerged.

For identification, and to protect the wood, the buoys had to be painted, and every lobster fisherman has his own special colors. Father's buoys were painted black on the lower (tapered) half and white on the upper, and we spent many hours painting them.

By doing this, I learned to cut a line between two colors without the benefit of masking tape, which, of course, was unknown at the time. A backup identification system was a name and a number. All of Father's traps and buoys had to carry his number, 5631, and his name, H.H. Wass. We had a small gouge for doing this, and I always felt quite proud to see Father's name on his buoys and traps.

Most fishermen spent many winter hours making plugs. To keep lobsters from injuring each other (they were capable of disconnecting a claw in a skirmish), their claws must be held closed. Now heavy rubber bands often are used to hold the claws closed, but we used small pieces of wood about $1^1/2$ inch long and $3/8$ inch in diameter, tapered to a point. Inserted into the "thumb joint," these prevented the lobster from opening its claw. Father used to whittle plugs during his whistlehouse watches and store them in jars on the kitchen shelf. Many were taken on each haul, since two were required for every lobster. (Father ran out of plugs on one haul and substituted trap nails. The lobsters all died.)

It was not necessary to build all new traps every year, because most of them would last for several seasons. But inevitably, storms would break up some and traps would be lost when warps were severed, so each season we built some new ones and, of course, checked and repaired all the old ones.

Since the lightkeepers were only part-time lobster fishermen, they did not have regular lobsterboats, but instead used the traditional Washington County peapods. Before the season began, the pod had to be repaired and painted. The pods had floorboards to keep pressure off the planking. We made sure these were in good condition and then removed them temporarily so we could paint the bottom. On the outside was an extra layer of planking where the boats rested while coming along the slip. These planks, too, were checked carefully.

Painting the pod down at the boathouse was a pleasant task. We tried to choose a clear day so the paint would dry quickly. Although putting on a coat of paint consumed several hours, we often paused to watch the gulls soar along the edge of the island.

When the wind was blowing from the land, it would hit the island bluffs, creating updrafts. Not understanding this, I always used to wonder what carried the gulls along so effortlessly.

One of the best parts of getting ready for lobstering was the day we tarred the lobster warps and sometimes the heads and pockets. This process began with a hot fire of driftwood that we kids had gathered. Father always located the fire on the rocks and sand near the boathouse, far enough toward the bluff to be above the high-tide line. We always had an ample supply of five-gallon cans, because they were used to bring out oil for the signal light. Father would cut the top out of one of these, put tar in it, and place it on the fire. The thick, viscous substance would melt as it heated, giving off what to me was a delectable aroma. Whenever I go by a crew of men tarring a roof or repairing a road, I can always recall this scene.

The warps would have already been cut into proper lengths and coiled, ready for tarring. Father would have made a wooden fork about thirty inches long, notched at one end. Standing amid the sparks and smoke, he would drop a section of line into the tar and place the crotch of his stick over it, retaining a hold on one end of the line. Then he would slowly pull the warp through, leaving it just long enough for the tar to permeate it thoroughly. Standing near the flames with smoke wreathing about him, his face gleaming with sweat, and his hands and arms growing blacker by the minute, Father looked like some demonic figure soaking his nets in an evil black brew.

Tarring the warps was a long, hot job for Father, but we all thought it was fun. After the warps were done, Father dunked batches of bait pockets and heads. When the thoroughly blackened warps were coiled neatly on planks high on the bank for drying, Father doused the fire, which emitted a great hissing cloud of steam, and dumped the tar on the rocks.

Next came the cleanup. All of us children, although we were not involved directly in the tarring process, somehow or other always seemed to acquire some tar. The best removal agent was ordinary lard, which we used in quantities before we were clean enough to sit down to the supper table.

Mother had her part to play in the preparation for lobstering. She liked to knit heads and pockets, but her major task was making oilskins for Father and knitting heavy woolen mittens for him. He wore the mittens for hauling to protect his hands from the rough, splintery rope. In spite of this protection, though, as the season continued, his hands grew hard with calluses and then cracked. This was extremely painful, and I remember him complaining often about his sore hands. Mutton tallow seemed to be the best remedy, but this did not completely heal the deepest wounds. The salt of the water not only caused some of the problem but also aggravated the condition.

Mother made foul-weather gear for all of us. Our coats, jackets, and Father's lobstering aprons (called barvels) were made out of unbleached sheeting. After she had completed them, they were immersed for several hours in linseed oil and then hung on a clothesline to dry. Multiple coats of the oil made the cloth totally impervious to water. These garments would last several seasons, remaining quite waterproof. Although the barvel did not keep Father completely dry when hauling, it and his rubber boots gave him a good deal of protection from the icy-cold water.

Another project that preceded the lobstering season was collecting flat rocks that could be strapped into the bottom of a trap with laths nailed over them. The section between the middle two sills of a trap was filled with these rocks to give the trap enough weight to hold it in place, right-side-up, on the bottom. When the traps were first set, they were dry and light, so until they soaked up water, adding to their weight, additional small rocks had to be placed loose in each trap. For no known reason, these were called "dug rocks." Father would send us scouting along the inner shores of Libby to find suitable stones—smooth, flattish, and not too large. We would gather these in places where he could land the peapod to pick them up. Although carrying rocks down over slippery rockweed to a landing place was strenuous, we always looked forward to this assignment.

Once Father decided he had enough rocks to weight down all his traps, he would row his heavily laden boat back to the slip, where he would dump the rocks so that they would be handy to reload into his boat when he was ready to set his traps. After a few weeks, when the traps had absorbed sea water and were heavy enough, Father would toss our carefully selected stones into the sea. We collected them year after year, but we always seemed to be able to find enough new rocks along the shore.

The final job before traps could be set was obtaining lobster bait, which Father usually purchased from the sardine factories in Machiasport. Some of the bait came from cuttings left over from the canning process, and the factories saved some herring for the lobster fishermen.

We seldom ever went farther than Starboard in the government boat, so the trip was a real adventure, and we youngsters usually got to go along. Of course, we had to get all spruced up for the trip, even though we might not be able to go ashore. The only way to get onto a sardine factory wharf was by climbing a slimy green ladder, and when the tide was low, the climb would be a long one. Father usually planned to go there as the tide was flooding and return on the ebb. A current as fast as two knots, in a boat that in calm water only went five, could greatly lengthen the approximately seven-mile trip. With a fair tide, we were swept along at a good speed. If the trip were well timed, the tide would turn while the bait was being loaded, so we would have a fair tide homeward bound as well. Another reason for going while the tide was high was the depth of the water. Machiasport is located at the mouth of the Machias River. Beyond the town, the bay opens up, but large parts of it are dry at low tide, leaving mudflats with only a rather narrow channel up to the factories.

On the way up the river, we always passed Avery's Rock. It was the lighthouse nearest to us, although we could see it only from the center of our island. Its light was red and the station was quite different from Libby. The tower and the house were combined in one building because it was built on a very small, rocky island. While we were on Libby, the Avery Rock station was nearly lost in a severe storm. Although it is situated far up Machias Bay, there is no protection from the open sea. During that storm, the waves produced by high winds swept over the whole island, and if the keeper had not opened the lower part of the building, allowing the seas to flow through, the entire structure might have been demolished.

We always tried to pick a clear day for the trip, but even if we had gone in the fog we could have located the factories without the aid of our compass. The odor from the cooking fish and the refuse permeated the atmosphere for miles around. We would tie up at the wharf, and Father would go looking for the baitman, leaving us to sit in the boat and watch all the activity going on around us. Other lobster fishermen would be coming and going, most buying large quantities of bait. What I enjoyed most was watching the sixty- to seventy-five-foot-long boats that brought in the sardines. These would go out to buy herring wherever the owners of fish weirs had made a catch. Fish weirs were the most common method for catching herring. Most Maine coastal towns of any size had sardine factories, and there once were hundreds of fish weirs. These were barricades of poles and brush extending about two hundred feet out from the land into a small bay where herring came to feed. At the end of the barricade would be a circle, making the entire structure look like a giant question mark with just enough room for a boat to enter the circle. The herring, swimming in large schools, would strike the barricade and follow it into the circle, in which a net would have been strung. Lead weights on the bottom of the net kept it close to the bottom of the bay so the fish could not escape. The fishermen, of course, would keep their weirs under observation, and when they saw the water inside "boiling" with fish, they would close the opening. Then, as if they were using a giant purse string, they would draw in the net, imprisoning thousands of fish. They could continue drawing in the net until the fish were squeezed into a small area. The herring then were transferred into the sardine boats, which came alongside the weir.

Some fishermen used a different technique. They would cruise along the coast until they spotted a large school of herring. By careful "herding," they would drive the fish into a small bay and close it off with nets. Sometimes, in a single night, fishermen could catch a small fortune in these silvery fish. One of my uncles, after years of merely making a good living, in one night trapped a giant school of herring. By the time all the shiny fish had been dipped out and sold, he was a wealthy man. Since he was close to retirement age, he decided to take his fortune, sell his boats and gear, and enjoy a life of leisure. He did that for one whole winter. But when the sardine factories began to blow their whistles in the spring, calling their workers to pack fresh catches of fish, he could not bear to sit on the sidelines while others were playing his lifelong game. So he purchased all new equipment, making a sizable dent in his nest egg, and returned to fishing.

I often wonder why Father did not become a full-time lobster or herring fisherman. With his skills in boatbuilding, his great physical strength and endurance, his knowledge of the sea and all its ways, and his courage and persistence, I have no doubt that he would have been successful. But perhaps he had a different philosophy. He always advised us to get good, steady jobs and never to leave one until we had something better. During the Depression, we were glad that he followed his own advice. Lobstermen and herring fishermen fell on hard times then, while he continued to enjoy a good income. And when it came time for him to retire, his income continued, while fishermen could rely only on their often-scanty savings.

But my early ambition, perhaps before my father had given me his advice, was someday to become captain of a sardine boat. I spent many hours watching sardine boats ply the waters around Libby. One boat I especially liked was named *El Placita*. She had the sleek lines of a pleasure yacht, which she previously had been. The owner, having apparently fallen on hard times, had sold her, and the buyer converted her into a workboat. But she never looked like a workboat. I especially enjoyed seeing her running by Libby Island in a stiff breeze and a steep chop, throwing spray her entire length as she drove her sharp, elongated bow proudly through the waves.

Finally, as we waited in our government boat at the sardine factory, the bait would be loaded into several barrels and lowered with a net into our boat. We tried to be careful not to spill any of this greasy, smelly load, since the lighthouse ladies might be going to Starboard for shopping on the next trip.

When we arrived back at Libby, the bait was shared with the other lobster-fishing keepers. This bait trip had to be made about every three weeks during the fishing season, and each keeper took his turn and shared the costs. The trip usually was combined with a stop at Starboard to pick up the mail and to get supplies.

Now all was in readiness for trap-setting day in September. The months of hard work finally culminated in one hectic day when, with all three keepers fishing, nearly 150 traps were set. All hands were on deck early to start work. Mother would prepare an especially hearty breakfast, because we would expend a lot of energy before the day was over.

The first job was to get the traps down from the high bank where they had been stored during the off-season. (We also repaired them in that location.) After sliding the traps down the bank, we would lift them onto one stringer of the slip and then slide them down with little effort to where we would help Father load them on his peapod. He would load two traps on the stern crosswise and two more on top of those in the opposite direction. A single trap placed on top of those four completed the stern pile. Then he would stack three on the bow, making a total of eight. Any higher piles would have made the sixteen-footer too top-heavy. With the traps piled on and a tub of bait pockets loaded aboard, Father had about six feet of working space in the middle of the boat. Peter would look on, appearing greatly disappointed but seeming to sense that on these trips there was no room for her on the stern seat. As we gave the pod a gentle shove into the water, I always watched with some concern, hardly believing that this heavily loaded, top-heavy boat could remain upright, but I was reassured when Father fitted his oars into the oarlocks and, with a few swift strokes, headed off along the shore.*

Knowing where to set traps is the skill of a lobster fisherman. Anyone can dump traps into the water and haul them again a day later, but understanding the ways of *Homarus americanus* determines the success of a fisherman—and some are far more successful than others. Lobsters seem to like feeding around the edges of rocks, so although it meant setting traps close to the shore, Father often selected these places. This always worried me, because sometimes waves would be breaking in these areas and we would have to go in fast, hook out a trap, and pull away during a calm spell. But the intent on the first day was to get the traps into the water. Later they could be moved to other locations if they continually came up empty.

As soon as Father left, we would start sliding traps down the slip for the next load. This would continue until the last trap was set late in the afternoon. We paused only long enough to grab something to eat and drink. September was a pleasant month, with little of the fog of earlier months. The "fallish" tinge in the air would quickly dry the perspiration from our faces, leaving us cool and refreshed.

Although September was a mild month, it also was the month of the "line storms," as we called them. (Now they have human names in alphabetical order and are called hurricanes.) If one of these storms struck before the traps had soaked up enough water to weight them firmly on the bottom, it could wreak havoc. The

---

*Before the invention of the gasoline engine, the only other source of power was wind in a sail. My mother recalled that her father once had instructed her to write to a boatyard in Friendship, placing an order for a Friendship sloop, the sailing workboat of much of the Maine coast. He gave her the precise dimensions he wanted, and a few months later he was notified that his sloop was completed. Her only "auxiliary" power was a pair of large oars.

On the Maine coast, the morning breezes are off the land and the afternoon wind blows onshore. This provided a perfect system for getting out to the fishing grounds and back, but there were still those dead calm days when oars were the only power.

first notice of a storm's approach usually would be in a call from the Coast Guard station on Cross Island. A telephone call signaled by a single very long ring always meant a storm warning.

After getting the report, Father would tell us, with a serious expression on his face, what we could expect. He often spoke in terms of "the glass falling." I did not understand then what a falling glass could have to do with weather, but later I learned that this referred to the column of mercury in an upright barometer, which does "fall" when bad weather is imminent. The warning would come only about twenty-four hours before the storm.

It was a helpless feeling to realize that little could be done to prevent storm damage to the lobster traps strung around our island and all along the nearby mainland shores. Along with the threatening black skies and heavy rains came winds so strong that you could almost lean against them and not fall over. The men were particularly careful to be sure the light and the fog signal were in good order, even though this was part of their daily routine. If fishermen had been hauling that day, the station would receive calls from their wives, asking if we had seen them and if they had left for home. When there was time, Father, the other keepers, and fishermen all along the storm-threatened coast would haul as many of their traps as possible and set them farther offshore, away from the rocks. One fisherman seemed to be fearless about bad weather or threats of bad weather, and he had the smallest powerboat that fished around Libby. As I recall, his name was Guy Clark, and his tiny green boat had a one-cylinder engine with a putt-putt-putt exhaust. On the roughest days we would hear the putt-putt-putt—and there would be Guy, hauling his traps. Sometimes he would go very near the rocks when the waves were so high his boat would disappear between their crests. After all the other boats had left before a storm, Guy still would be calmly finishing his haul.

With a storm approaching, a few of us would go to the boathouse to bring in the government boat, close the huge protecting doors, and secure any boats left outside on the slip. When everything was as secure as we could make it, we would return home to watch the gathering violence. With the wind came a sudden increase in the size and power of the waves. The sound of their fury beating against our protecting cliffs, combined with the howling wind, sometimes nearly drowned out conversation. Most of the time we would stand at the windows, watching the waves grow higher and higher. Finally, they would be high enough so their hungry, frothing tongues would rise over the cliffs and reach in beside our outhouse, leaving a salty, foam-filled pond only a few feet from our door. The spray would splatter our windows with a salty scum.

By this time visibility would be so low that Father or one of the other keepers would start the fog signal, which could hardly be heard above the wind and the surging of the water. The keepers had to be careful when going back and forth between the house and the whistlehouse, because occasionally the top of a wave, with the full force of the wind behind it, would sweep across the path. No one ever was swept away on this passage, but there always was the chance of a freak wave.

Inside our kitchen, when not watching the waves, we did our usual chores. Darkness came early on these days, so Mother would light the cheery Aladdin lamp that always sat in the middle of the kitchen table. Its warm glow increased our feeling of security, but we never felt really frightened by these storms. It never occurred to us that the tall crest of a wave might come crashing through our house, as had happened at Avery's Rock. Although we did not know it at the time, there seems to be no record of the houses, tower, or whistlehouse on Libby ever being damaged by a storm. In spite of our being only a short distance from the water, the rocks sloped away from the cliffs in front of our house, diminishing the full force of the waves. Another factor in our security was our height above the water, which apparently put us just beyond the reach of the most powerful waves. But ships at sea had no such protection, and as we sat around our kitchen table during these storms, we often expressed concern for anyone who might be at sea on such a night.

Some fifty years later, I was helping to deliver a thirty-nine-foot sloop from Portsmouth, New Hampshire, to the British Virgin Islands. We were caught by two severe North Atlantic storms only two days apart, and I learned, for the first time, what is was like to be at sea under such conditions. It made me think about our warm, secure, Libby Island kitchen, and I wished I were there.

We were quite safe on Libby Island, but our lobster traps and those of other fishermen were not. We always had to wait for a few days after a storm before the waves would moderate enough to allow us to launch the peapod. If a brisk wind sprang up after a storm, blowing in the opposite direction, it would level the waves quickly.

The first hauling trip after such a storm was a sad experience. Many times we found several buoys and warps totally entangled, and it might take nearly an hour to clear them. With several wound together, it was impossible to haul the traps off the bottom. When we did get the lines clear and could haul a trap to the surface, often it was partially or totally destroyed, particularly if it was one of the older ones. Also, traps often were filled with seaweed, sand, and other debris. It would take a week or more to get our gear back to fishing readiness, and there were always several traps missing. They might be on the bottom where we had set them, but with their warps chafed through on sharp stones. Or they might be caught under heavy stones that had moved about on the bottom, leaving the warps too short for the buoys to reach the surface, where we could find them. Others would be "caught down," and no matter how hard Father pulled, they would not budge. He would fasten the warp to a seat in the peapod and row as hard as he could, first in one direction and then in another. If this did not work, he would row in a circle. If all else failed, he would leave the trap and hope that further shifting of rocks on the bottom would free it.

Pulling on caught-down traps could also be dangerous. One cold fall day, when Father was fishing around Whitehead Island, he pulled hard on a trap that he did not want to lose. The warp broke free and Father went over backward into the icy waters. He did not know how he did it, but despite his heavy clothes, he managed to swim to the boat and climb back in. This would have been impossible had the day not been calm. Fortunately, Father, unlike most Maine fishermen, knew how to swim. That he could save himself under these conditions was almost a miracle, since hypothermia can quickly disable a person.

One September there was a storm before we had set our traps, and this caused an even greater disaster. When we received the warning, we followed our usual procedure of putting the government boat in the boathouse and hauling our peapod to the top end of the slip, where we tied it down securely. The storm was severe, and the winds howled about our house all night, rattling the windows in the bedrooms facing southwest—the direction of most of our bad storms. I slept in a room on the other side of the house, which was much more protected, but still I could hear the windows making a hollow, spooky, rumbling sound. (I was not afraid of high waves, but "spooks" were another matter.)

When we arose in the morning, the windows were covered with salt spray, seaweed was strewn about the yard, the low area beside our outhouse was filled with water, and brownish sea foam was blowing about in the air. The air itself had the acrid odor that always accompanied gale-force winds and high waves. Broken bodies of migrating songbirds lay scattered at the base of the light tower, a sad aftermath to these fall storms. Apparently, the light attracted them, and they would crash against the heavy glass windows. Some of the storm's fury had struck the mainland side of the island, so right after breakfast we decided to go to the boathouse to check for damage. As we got to the rise above the slip, we could see that the sea was still white with wind-whipped foam. We entered the boathouse from the back door and could see no evidence of damage, but when we opened the big doors facing the ocean (we had braced them with heavy iron crowbars), a scene of chaos lay before us. The first thing we saw was the wreck of our peapod. All that remained was the stem, still tied securely to the slip (a testament to the strength of good manila hemp rope). A six-foot-long piece of one side was still attached to the stem, but the rest of the boat had disappeared as if a giant shark, in one crushing bite, had swallowed it. Then we looked up on the bank where our lobster traps had been piled neatly, ready for setting, and saw only a mess of broken laths and buoys and a tangle of warp. Parts of the traps were scattered about, but some traps appeared whole. The work of months was almost totally destroyed, and our boat, upon which we depended so much, was smashed to smithereens. It was an ugly and depressing scene. The bank where our traps were stored was at least thirty feet above high-water mark—and that was on the protected side of the island. We felt fortunate that at least the slip, the government boat, and the boathouse were not damaged.

This was the worst disaster we ever suffered on Libby, and although it took us several days to comprehend its full impact, we knew immediately that our fall lobster fishing would be very limited. There was no place to buy a new gang of traps, and even if we could have afforded that, we had no boat. Fortunately, Father was not one to be discouraged easily. Soon we were all at work repairing the traps that were left and rebuilding others that we had considered not worth salvaging during the summer when we had had time to build new ones. We all began knitting new pockets and heads. Within a few weeks, we had about fifteen traps ready to be set. In the meantime, Father had been able to locate and buy another peapod. She was a scrubby-looking craft, without the clean, easy-rowing lines of our previous boat, which Father had built according to his own design. She was sound and stable, however, and she served us well for a number of years.

The skeleton of our former peapod allowed us to be among the first to try water skiing, though of a rather unusual style. We took the beautifully curved side of our pod to the Big Pond, near the house, and invented a new game. First we lengthened the painter so it could stretch across the pond. One person would stand on the "water ski" while the others tried to pull him (or her) across so fast that the ski would not sink. We played this game for many weeks after our disaster, salvaging at least something from our great loss.

From storm disasters we also learned to appreciate how fortunate we were not to be wholly dependent upon lobster fishing for a livelihood. For us it was a part-time effort largely for food, fun, and a small profit. Our real support came from Father's regular monthly check, which never failed to arrive during his many years of lighthouse service. When bad gales came, smashing lobster traps up and down the coast, the full-time fishermen might lose a large percentage of their traps, and, although they could replace a few during the fall, their earnings would be cut sharply. This meant real privation for them and their families during the long winter months.

Another great loss caused by storms—and this happened to us a few times—was damage to the car where we stored our lobsters. It did not take too much force to break open a door or to loosen a side plank. Since we had to tie the cars by a line to a tall wooden mooring off the boat slip, there was always the danger that a wave would crash them into it. After a storm, it was a disheartening shock to row out to the mooring and find the car gone or totally empty—weeks of work would be lost. This meant that when the buyer arrived in his smack, Father would have no lobsters to sell him.

We always looked forward with great enthusiasm to the coming of the lobster smack. We often could spot her in the distance, plowing through the waves toward Libby. All work was immediately suspended while keepers and kids all headed for the boathouse and rowed out in their pods to be ready for the buyer. The smacks were large boats, approximately fifty feet long, that carried lobsters in a well: a section of the boat walled off by watertight bulkheads and with large holes in the bottom to let in sea water. I always wondered why the boat did not sink, but the water rose only as high as it was on the outside. This well made a perfect environment for lobsters until they were taken to large lobster pounds on the mainland to await shipment to market.

Each keeper would unload his lobsters onto the smack so his catch could be weighed. The buyers always scrutinized the lobsters carefully to make sure they were all legal size. Father often included what he called "fuzz-touchers," hoping they might just pass inspection. The lobster's shell, at the rear edge, has tiny hairlike projections. The metal measure might just touch these, meaning the lobsters were a tiny bit too short. Father made his own measures and felt they might be a bit inaccurate. There was never any negotiating about price—the price was whatever the buyer said it was.

When we saw all the bills and silver being placed in Father's hands, we were sure he was rich. He always was very generous in sharing his wealth with us. I can still remember some of the shiny coins Father gave me, which I saved sometimes for long-range objectives like buying a bicycle (but I'm sure I also set apart some to buy my own private supply of penny candy on the next trip ashore).

As I mentioned in chapter 5, sometimes Father took apples instead of money for his lobsters. The enterprising buyers had loaded their decks with Nova Scotia apples, and these were our fresh fruit all winter.

I do not know what Father's annual lobstering income was, but it was not a large amount. The money was not needed for our basic living expenses, but it did subsidize a few extras that we all enjoyed. During the Depression, the price went below ten cents a pound, and it seemed that even the lobsters were insulted; they nearly disappeared. Irwin, fishing on his own, managed to accumulate one hundred pounds over several weeks, and he sold them all for only ten dollars.

In all the excitement of the lobster-fishing season the ongoing work of running the lighthouse station had to continue. Long watches had to be stood (both day and night when it was foggy), equipment maintained in topnotch condition, the activities of the station carefully recorded, and monthly reports submitted to lighthouse district headquarters. But the men always took time to haul the traps, weather permitting, and the lighthouse superintendents did not object so long as the lightkeeping work was done. Sometimes, when watches interfered with hauling, the keepers would relieve each other so they could haul and rebait their traps.

Lobstering was important in our lives for several reasons. The obvious advantages, of course, were the added income and the delicious food supplied for our table. But in addition, the entire lobstering project added a wholly different dimension to our lives. As a family enterprise, it was something to which every member could make a contribution. Of course, we all played a role in the running of the light station to make Father's work less burdensome, and we helped with planting and harvesting the garden, but lobstering had its own special appeal. I never really enjoyed gardening, but all the activities related to lobstering were fun. We thoroughly enjoyed knitting the heads and pockets, and our speed contests added an element of excitement. This activity filled many hours, particularly in the long winter evenings. And building the traps was quite satisfying, perhaps because it was "grown-up" work. I always enjoyed painting—and still do. It was a joy to see buoys and the boat, which had looked gray and beaten after a season's use, appear almost like new. Going to haul with Father was pure excitement.

To Father, lobstering was his recreation. I think he would have done it even if it had not provided him with extra money. From the first haul of the season, he went eagerly every day to see what he would find in his traps. Other men might be baseball fans, play golf, or go fly fishing, but Father was a recreational lobster fisherman. The activity broke up the routine of light maintenance, record-keeping, and watch-standing. I think that in some ways it served the same purpose for the rest of us. We had no entertainment except what we made for ourselves, so lobstering filled many voids in our lives.

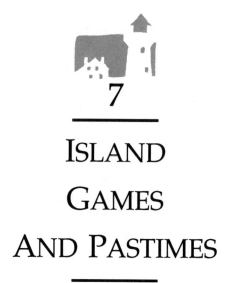

7

ISLAND

GAMES

AND PASTIMES

"JUNIE, what's that? Look over there behind that ledge. See those four things sticking up? They look like stakes. I've never seen them before."

"You're right, Phil, I ain't never seen them either."

"Let's go take a look."

"I dunno if I want to," Junie Foss quickly replied, drawing back. "Remember we saw something else about there last week, and it moved. I was scared."

I admitted to myself that I had been a little scared too. But the stakes didn't move. They appeared to be coming up out of something round, like a big balloon. I hunched down low, so whatever it was couldn't see me, and moved in a little closer.

Junie reluctantly followed me. We crept closer, always looking over our shoulders to make sure we could make a fast retreat. "Junie, did you ever see anything like that before? It looks like a big animal lying down flat with his legs in the air."

"I don't like it. Suppose it got up and started chasing us. I'm going back," Junie whispered.

"Come on. Let's just keep low and see if it moves." I edged a little closer. "I can see its head. I think it's a dead horse. It ain't moving. Maybe it's a seahorse that got grounded out when the tide went down." I had been reading about seahorses in one of my books. By this time I was losing some of my fear, and my curiosity was growing. I finally stood up where I could get a full view. "Junie, come on," I said. "It's really a big dead horse." We went closer but still with great caution, just in case.

By this time, we were quite sure of what we were seeing, but during the previous few weeks, we had had some real frights. A strange figure had appeared from behind rocks and knolls when we were on our exploring expeditions. And although we began to suspect that it was one of the keepers dressed up in old foul-weather gear with discarded lobster warps strung over his head, we were not quite sure—and never quite dared challenge the spectre.

We kept moving closer until we could see the strange figure stretched out on the rocks. It was a horse, and there was no doubt it was dead, but we still approached cautiously. Never had we seen a horse with such a large, round belly. Finally we stood up and could look down at the poor creature—its mouth agape so we could see its greenish, grass-stained teeth. Entangled in its mane and tail were bits of seaweed. Its legs were angled in the air as if it were still galloping. Since it wasn't our horse, it had to have come from the mainland. "We better go tell Father," I said.

"You're right," Junie replied, holding his nose. "He don't smell so good, and by the looks of those flies, he's going to smell worse."

We struck off for the house, still glancing over our shoulders to make sure we had not seen another apparition. En route, we approached cautiously any knolls where the "Old Scratcha" (our name for the devil) might be hiding.

We made our report to Father and he and the other keepers were immediately intrigued, so we all set off at a brisk pace for the Tip-End of Libby. When we reached the horse and Father saw its condition, he said, "I think he's bloated. Must have gotten into a grain barrel and then drunk a lot of water to blow him up." The others agreed with this hypothesis. The men decided that immediate action was necessary. The rising tide would float the horse free, but there was no way to tell where it might next run aground. A few more landings in the hot sun with the wind just right and our fresh air might become foul with unpleasant odors. They decided that as soon as the body floated, it had to be towed out to the southwest head of Libby. From there, they hoped, the ebb tide would take the carcass out to sea.

Back we all went to the house to collect ropes for towing our unwelcome visitor. Father consulted The Old Farmer's Almanac to see when the tide would turn. It was already rising. When the tide was high enough to allow approaching our "seahorse" but still not so high that it would float away, Father rowed his pod over the bar and took the horse in tow. Pulling this bloated creature along the shores of Libby to the west end was a long, hard row, but with two men working at the oars, they finally made it. When Father untied his strange cargo, we could already see signs that the tide had turned. The water was rippling by the lobster buoys. The horse began to turn slowly, like some grotesque sea creature, and then seemed to set a course clear of Libby's outlying ledges.

Immediately I went out onto the headland, beyond the whistlehouse. With the spyglass, I quickly picked up the horse, slowly spinning, feet erect, looking like some strange sailing craft—two masts forward and two aft. Although we looked along the shore and tested the air for several weeks, this was the last we ever saw or smelled of our seahorse.

Being curious to know where our drifting visitor had come from, Father asked "Uncle" Jim Sprague about it the next time we went to Starboard. It was his horse, and Father had guessed right about the grain barrel. "That horse," he related, "was one of the smartest horses I ever had. He was always getting out of the pasture. Somehow he broke out of his stall a few nights ago, lifted up the grain barrel cover with his teeth, I suppose, and ate till he couldn't hold no more. Then he went to the back of the barn and drank his fill from the water barrel. Well, when that dry grain started sloshing around in that water, it began to swell. His next move was to try to get out the door. By this time I reckon he'd swelled up nearly twice his normal size. When I found him, he was jammed in the doorway, not able to go forward or backward. I'll tell you, he was the smartest but also the greediest horse I ever had."

"Uncle" Jim, shifting his tobacco cud to the other side, went on, "I didn't have time to dig a hole to bury him—it would have been enormous—so I borrowed another horse and dragged the doggoned creature to the shore, where the tide would pick him up. I was sure he would clear the islands and I'm sorry he struck on Libby going by."

"That's all right," Father said. "Things like that break up the monotony."

Thus was born the legend of "The Greedy Horse," which has been told and retold in our family for several generations.

"Taking a walk around the shore" was one of our favorite pastimes. We usually went on the ocean side of the island because here were the beaches caused by the high waves that almost constantly beat upon the shores. The first part of our walk was along the edge of extensive rock formations, and there was no sand. These rocky shores were near the house, so we explored them frequently, but they were too high for any debris to be deposited by the waves, and we usually were beachcombing. We could reach the first beach in about five minutes. The cliff here was about twenty feet high, but a sloping ledge led down to the sand. Our sand, unlike that of most of the Maine coast, was a very dark gray—black when wet. The beaches were not wide and their outer edges were weed-covered rocks with many tidal pools. At low tide, these rocks extended about a hundred yards toward the sea ledge, a large formation just off our southern coast. We watched during storms as waves swept over this small rocky island, sending jets of white spray high in the air. We could imagine how this cruel rock had destroyed many ships during the 1800s.

There were often loons or flocks of eiders feeding in this cove. If we spotted loons, we would play one of our favorite games with them. They are innately curious. We would get down behind a rock and wave our caps in the air, making a call that we thought resembled a loon's. They must have thought so too, because they would immediately begin to swim toward us. Before they dove and swam away under water, they would come close enough that we could see every detail of their glistening white throats, black heads, and backs sprinkled with silver gray.

To get to the next larger beach, we had to climb over a ledge apparently made of harder rock, for it had not broken down to sand. One of our favorite games on this second beach was dam building. Water constantly ran down off the island bank and made small rivulets. Erecting dams of sand, we could capture this water, making sizable pools. Then we could run water off in several directions, creating miniature irrigation canals. We had to repair our systems constantly, because the sand dams quickly gave way to the flowing of water. And, of course, when the waves came in, all our engineering works were leveled smooth.

At high tide, the waves ran up onto these beaches, flooding most of them, but at half-tide, there was some clear space around the ends of each small dividing promontory. Another of our favorite games was to watch for a wave to recede and then dash around the end of the rocky point to safety on the other side. We did not do this when the waves were high, so our greatest danger was getting wet. That was penalty enough, since the water, even in midsummer, was numbingly cold. A variation on this game was to use a jumping pole made from one of the small weir stakes that we picked up around the shore. With a little trimming, they were excellent for vaulting. We would back off to where the sand was dry, then run, plant the pole in the sand, and, if we were lucky, propel ourselves high and far enough to clear the water. We felt as if we were flying.

The second beach was one of our choice places for summer outings. Father loved picnics, and at mid-morning on any clear day in summer, he might come in from his work and say, "Maybelle, this is a good day for a picnic lunch," to which Mother would readily agree. Lobsters were our favorite picnic meal, and we often had cooked ones stored in a cool cupboard for just such an occasion. With cream-of-tartar biscuits, salad, a jug of cold homemade root beer (which we kept suspended in the cistern for cooling), and molasses cookies, apples, oranges, and perhaps bananas for dessert, we had a sumptuous meal. All of this went into a large gray-enameled dishpan, which two of us carried along the grassy path. Bluebells, buttercups, daisies, blue flags, and many other varieties of flowers bordered our walkway. We had to walk with care as we neared the edge of the bank where we could get down to the beach, because each year pieces of the island's edge broke away during storms. When this happened, we had to tread down a new path a few feet farther inland. Erosion was slowly making Libby smaller.

It was a steep, rocky climb down, but, living on an island with only grassy and rocky pathways, all of us were surefooted. Soon we would be seated on the black sand, cracking lobsters and enjoying our feast. Here in the shelter of the island, with the sun shining on us, we were quite warm. The sea was bluish-green until it became clear as the waves surged over the beach, turning the sand to a shiny black. Some days, when it was very warm (by island standards), we would attempt to go swimming. But all we did was briefly splash about, because the water was paralyzing. We would soon come out, red and shivering. The water was so frigid that our skin felt as though it were burning.

These impromptu picnics were some of our happiest times, with simple yet delicious food and a chance for the family closeness we all enjoyed. When Father and Mother did not have time for a picnic, which was seldom, we had our own. Packing a simple lunch, we would find a sheltered spot down over the rocks, pick up driftwood, and build a fire to cook our main course: baked potatoes. When the fire was hot, we just dumped the potatoes into the coals. They came out black, covered with ashes. But after brushing off the soot and breaking open the crispy skins, we thought the insides were tasty even without butter or sour cream.

We spent many hours doing this. Whenever we ran out of things to do, someone would always suggest, "Let's go down around the shore, build a fire, and roast potatoes."

Following along the shore after leaving the two beaches, we had to traverse an area of rough, jagged rocks, but nestled among these ledges was a unique tidal pool. We loved it because it contained tiny fish with bright red scales. We called them "minnie fish." This was the only pond around the shore where we could find these fish. The water in the pond was kept salty by frequent flooding when the waves were high. Using nets that we had made, we would catch several of the fish and keep them in a jar like goldfish, but they had to be handled with care, because they had tiny thorns that could inflict painful jabs.

Beyond the "minnie fish" pond was the mystery beach. This beach had little sand; instead it had magnificent rocks, six to eight inches in diameter and rounded into smooth ellipses. The mystery was that they were unlike Libby's usual bedrock. On stormy days, when the waves crashed into this area, the rolling of these stones made a deep rumbling sound that could be heard from a considerable distance. The constant rolling, of course, had given them their rounded shape. They were obviously granite and of several different colors. We loved these smooth stones and often carried some home. Later, I believe I came to a logical explanation of the mystery. Many ships were wrecked along this shore during the 1800s, and some of them carried granite blocks for ballast or cargo. Years of being jostled against the natural ledges and each other must have broken the ballast rocks and gradually shaped them so that they looked like giant eggs. (I suppose there may be a geological explanation for these unusal granite cobbles, but I like my ships' ballast theory best.)

Beyond the mystery beach was a stretch of ledges with tiny beaches and other secret crannies where we liked to play. When we reached the Tip-End, we again found a beach, which stretched away to the bar leading to Big Libby. Here, at high tide, waves converged from both sides of the island. When the sea was rough, these waves would crash into each other and send giant spumes of sea-green water into the air. Nearly every day, winter and summer, waves broke along the outer edges of the bar. They marched like horses with silvery manes flying in the wind, one following another in endless procession. These waves usually were large enough that we could see them from the house, more than half a mile away, and also hear their roar, especially at night. They were the powerful force that destroyed all the ships unfortunate enough to run aground in this area.

The inner, or mainland, side of the island was quite different from the outer side, with fewer beaches and more precipitous cliffs. It was evident that the erosion of giant waves striking the outer side of the island had created the black sand beaches. Beyond the boathouse, about two-thirds of the way toward the southwest end of the island, there were no beaches, just steep cliffs, so there was no way to get down to the water. Because we seldom frequented this part of the island, it always had an aura of mystery about it, but that did not keep us from exploring the area inch by inch. We always were looking for caves to hide in when playing hide-and-seek games, but we never found any until one of the other keepers' kids and I discovered a place where a huge slab of rock had broken off and slipped down, coming to rest on a flat shelf. There were two entrances just barely large enough for us to crawl through. We spent hours playing in this cave, pretending we were pirates. In one end we could build a fire, and the smoke seemed to escape through a natural chimney. Although it was not large enough for us to stand up in, we could be quite comfortable sitting down. I do not think our parents ever knew about our secret retreat. If they had, I am sure we would have been forbidden to enter it lest other rocks slip down and block the entrances, which could well have happened. We also kept our hideaway a secret from the other kids for several months.

Toward the southwestern end of the island, the cliffs grew increasingly steeper until at the Big Pond, behind our barn, there was a sheer drop of approximately fifty feet, with only the breakers below. Nearer our home, in front of the duplex house, was a deep indentation in the shoreline with nearly sheer cliffs on each side. This was the area we called "Aunt Gelia's Gulch," after Angelia Clark, the wife of Willis Clark, the second assistant keeper who was on Libby when we arrived from Whitehead. The next gulch was west of our house, but it had no name. (Maybe the other keepers called it "Mabel's Gulch.") Beyond that was the high head where the tower and the whistlehouse stood. There was no way we could walk close to the water in this section of the island, so the shoreline went quite unexplored.

One of our favorite games was "Grass is Poison," in which the object was to go around the island, except for the southwest head area, without walking on any grass. We would start at the tower on the seaward side of the island and climb straight down to the Salt Water Pond, where we played lobster-fishing games. This was an almost vertical descent of about fifty feet over rough, sharp rocks. We often traveled up and down here without our parents knowing it. I can still remember how my fingers tingled from hanging onto tiny projections in the rock face. From here to the Tip-End, the walking and climbing were quite easy, but when we reached the point and turned back up to the inside, the cliffs rose ever more steeply from the water. Beyond the boathouse was a sheer cliff that was not very high but it was almost vertical. It had us stopped for a long time—until we discovered that it had a sloping crack running across it. One day, when the tide was out far enough so there was "land" beneath us, we decided to try traversing it. By hugging the rock, holding onto any tiny outcroppings above our heads with our fingers, and carefully placing our toes in the crack, we inched our way across. With legs and arms aching and fingertips showing tiny pinpricks of blood, we reached the other side. We did not do this many times, but overcoming this last obstacle meant we finally could go around the island without touching the "poison grass." We were quite proud of our accomplishment, but sometimes I had nightmares, and still do, about getting caught on a rock face and not being able to move either up or down.

One time, on an "explore" we had a different kind of nightmare: an attack from the sea. On this particular day, we walked down on the inside of the island, through the boathouse, and out onto the slip. Much to our amazement and horror, we saw what looked like a small monster—with a gigantic mouth full of jagged teeth—heading right for us. Not knowing what it was, we armed ourselves with rocks in case it attacked. The creature seemed in no way afraid of us and kept coming right for the slip. So we started zinging rocks at the gaping mouth, which made a good target. Soon small rocks had collected in its mouth. We continued our fusillade until the creature expired. Then we pulled it out with a boathook to get a good look. Years later, I learned that our monster was a monkfish. It was one of the ugliest creatures I had ever seen. Certainly it did not deserve to die that way, but small boys are not noted for being merciful.

Our many hours spent climbing on the rocks proved hard on both clothes and shoes. I remember that one year Mother bought me a new pair of sneakers and within a month I literally wore them out. She was quite annoyed at the poor quality, and I went with her when she confronted the storekeeper. He looked at the shoes and shook his head, saying, "I don't see how anyone could wear out a pair of shoes in just a month." He gave us a new pair, but I felt a little guilty, because not even my mother knew what those shoes had been through, climbing on razor-sharp rocks.

Roger Beal was the son of John and Katie Beal. He was about my own age, and we had some great adventures together.

"Roger, how would you like to go over to Big Libby to see what's over there?" He readily agreed, so I checked *The Old Farmer's Almanac* and found out that it would be dead low water in about two hours. This would give us plenty of time to walk along the shore and across the bar. We should have taken something to eat, but we were too anxious to get started. I rousted out Peter from behind the stove, where she slept a good deal of the time. After she was awake, she seemed quite eager for a romp, so we started off. Had we known the trouble she would get us into, we would have left her sleeping.

We followed our usual path along the shore, always keeping

our eyes open for anything useful that might have drifted in. Many valuable things came ashore. We picked up buoys and bottles that could be used with our lobster traps. Some of the pieces of lumber we collected were used in building the trap frames. Weir stakes were a prize because they could be used for jumping poles. Sometimes good-sized logs came ashore. These we would haul up clear of the tide so Father could retrieve them with the horse and wagon. We depended partially upon driftwood as fuel for our kitchen stove when we needed to make a hot fire for baking, and to use for kindling to ignite the coal. If we could carry or drag it up clear of the tide, no piece of wood ever was allowed to escape.

As we moved on toward Big Libby, we kept to the inside of the bar, where there was more sand and fewer weed-covered rocks. We had taken many bad falls clambering over these slippery rocks, but on this day we made good progress. Peter always went on ahead, scaring up plovers and sandpipers. We carried our air rifles with us "for protection" and in case any strange birds appeared. Our consciences finally had persuaded us not to target practice by shooting at sparrows, but sandpipers were considered game as long as we ate them. And we were death on cowbirds, because it was obvious that they were annoying the cows. (Not until later did I learn that the birds were catching flies, actually helping the cows.)

When we got to the lowest part of the bar, waves were still flowing through the gut. We knew the water soon would be low enough to walk across if we took off our shoes and stockings and rolled up our pant legs. So we spent the time poking around in the tidal pools and found some tiny pink "flowers" that closed when we approached them. (We later learned that they were sea anemones.) There were also tiny periwinkles as well as hermit crabs, which appropriate abandoned periwinkle shells for their homes. In a half hour we noticed that the tide was lower and so were the waves. Finally, we decided that if we watched our chances, we could reach the other side. Looking carefully and seeing no waves coming, we made our way quickly across the shallows. By the time we reached the other side, our legs were stinging from the cold water, and our feet were "burning" from both the cold and the coarse sand and ground-up shells over which we had walked.

Being on Big Libby was always exciting. It was twice as big as our island and equally treeless, except for a few scraggly specimens growing in sheltered places. We were intrigued by trees, probably because we had none. As we walked up the beach, we saw driftwood everywhere—these beaches were not kept clean by small beachcombers. On the right was all that was left of the *John C. Myers*. We stood and looked at this mute evidence of a captain's mistake and hoped that if we ever became captains, we would do better.

We climbed up over the bank and at last were on Big Libby's land. The island stretched away ahead of us, and in the distance we could see the sheep that grazed regularly there. They looked like puffy white dots on the green grass.

Suddenly Roger shouted, "Phil, look at Peter!" I looked. She had gone rigid, sinking into a crouching position, and she was staring directly at the sheep. Gone was the relaxed, easygoing dog we all loved so much. In an instant she had become a predator. I grabbed her by the scruff of her neck, gave her a cuff, and shouted, "No! No! No!" She straightened up, looking ashamed, and reverted to her normal personality. But her marked change frightened me. I had never seen her do that before. When she chased the cow, she always acted mischievous, and it was obvious that she was playing a game. But this was no game.

I kept my eye on her as we continued our "explore," following the shore as we did on Libby. We scanned the sea and looked across to heavily wooded Cross Island, where the Coast Guard station was located. A few lobsterboats were working their way along the shore, making looping turns as they headed in toward the ledges to pick up their buoys. We finally stood on the edge of a large bay—on a black sand beach much larger than any at Libby —with high cliffs on each side. We wished we had a beach this size on our island; perhaps with such a wide expanse of sun-warmed sand to flow across, the water would actually be warm enough for comfortable swimming.

On one side of the bay, a low promontory, level at the top with the surrounding land, extended out toward the sea. It stood free except for one small strip of grass-covered rock still tying it to the solid land. The bridge was about six feet long and two feet wide, suspended over an abyss at least fifty feet deep. I knew that someday I was going to have to walk across this natural bridge. Irwin had met that challenge, and I did not want him to get ahead of me. Maybe this was the day. But I stood and stared at it. Roger had no intention of taking the daring step. I studied it a long time but could not quite get up my courage. Next year, I figured, I would be a year older and maybe braver. (I did cross the bridge later—probably a foolhardy thing to do. During my 1980 visit to Libby, when I sailed by this bay and saw the bridge crumbled to a mass of rubble at the foot of the cliff, I could not repress a shudder.)

Just as I turned away from the bridge, I caught a flash of white on top of a nearby hill—and, to my horror, a flash of brown by my side. Peter had gone after a sheep. We ran as fast as we could, but both sheep and dog were too fast for us. We shouted as loud as we could, but she still paid us no heed. Fortunately, the sheep were almost as fast as Peter, and there was a lot of space in which to escape. She caught up with one but it broke away. By this time, she was very tired, so we were able to catch up with her. I grabbed the loose skin around Peter's neck and to my horror saw blood on her teeth and muzzle. I cuffed her several times and scolded her. She put her tail between her legs and hung her head down, giving every evidence of guilt. I was in a state of shock. I could not believe that this kind, peaceful animal could suddenly revert to a wild state. Her primitive emotions had risen to the surface suddenly, and she was hunting for her food on some wild, primeval plain.

Since the sheep Peter had caught had broken away, we hoped its wound was superficial. Guarding the dog closely, we hurried back toward the bar, knowing that in all the excitement, more than two hours had elapsed and the tide would be flooding fast. We ran as quickly as we could, but, being tired, we found it hard to follow the narrow sheep paths, which did not always lead in the direction we wanted to go. When we reached a high point of land, we could see waves going through the gut. Arriving at the water's edge, we realized that there was no way of getting across. We thought of swimming, but we knew that the water was frigid and the current strong. We were cut off!

Struggling back over the slippery rocks, we walked through the sand, our feet feeling like lead, until we reached the bank where we could sit in the grass. There we sat a long time, a little stunned and very tired. Peter stretched out beside us and promptly fell alseep. I gazed at her with a mixture of sadness and compassion, wondering if I could ever feel quite the same toward her again. It was like having a person with whom you were very close unexpectedly exhibit character traits that frighten you. Peter had never revealed the least signs of anger or viciousness. She had always shown nothing but affection to her own family as well as to anyone who approached her. I found this new behavior hard to accept, and I knew I would never bring her on another trip to Big Libby. After all, one of the reasons that islands were used for sheep pasture was to eliminate the dangers from wild animals and dogs.

Roger and I did not talk much. We just kept looking down at the bar, which was now rapidly being covered with water deep enough for high waves to rush across. We felt certain we did not have to worry about being marooned on Big Libby. I had told Mother when we left that we might take a hike across the bar, but I did not tell her we would be away this long. I knew that Father had gone to Starboard and Machias for supplies, and when he got home, surely he would start looking for us. Still, being totally isolated gave us a scary feeling. And there was another feeling—embarrassment at allowing ourselves to be trapped. This had never happened before. Somehow, we always seemed to have a built-in sense of how much time we could spend exploring Big Libby and still get back across the bar, although we often waded through quite deep water.

As our weariness began to recede, another thought came to the fore. "Roger, are you hungry?"

"Ayuh," came a quick reply, "and we ain't got nothing to eat, either. And no water. I'm starved."

"What are we going to do?" I asked. Roger glanced down at his air rifle. "Maybe we could shoot something?"

I agreed, so we started looking for some plovers or sandpipers. We spotted a flock and began crawling toward them, trying to keep behind rocks so they could not see us. As we got closer, we could see them running about, looking for tiny shellfish. When we were close enough, I said, "Roger, you pick one out and I'll pick one out. We'll shoot at the same time. I'll say, 'One, two, three, fire!'" We drew our beads on two of the plumpest birds, trying to follow them through our gun sights, which wasn't easy. I whispered, "One, two, three. . . ." At that moment, Peter must have raised her head, because the birds flew up, wheeled about, flashed their white wings in the sun, and settled down again a little farther away, but this time in a much more open area. The next time, we both fired, but the birds kept carefully out of range.

"Roger," I said, "all that work didn't get us even a mouthful, did it?"

"Nope, and I'm still famished," Roger answered, looking downcast.

"You know," I said, "we promised we wouldn't shoot ground sparrows any more, but do you suppose it would be all right to shoot one to eat?"

"A man can't starve, can he?" was his quick rejoinder.

About that time, a plump-looking sparrow lighted on a piece of driftwood not too far from us. I took careful aim and fired, and it toppled over. Fortunately, we had brought matches, so while Roger kindled a "sparrow-sized" fire, I got out my jackknife and dressed our game. We found a small, wet-looking stick to use as a skewer, and I held the tiny piece of meat over the flaming wood.

It would make about half a mouthful for each of us. As I was slowly turning the skewer, I glanced at Peter, now peacefully sleeping and all signs of viciousness gone. Even the blood on her muzzle had disappeared. As I looked at her, a thought occurred to me: hadn't I just reverted to a "primitive" state by killing game for food? And didn't my father do this all the time? Wasn't this what Peter had done? In a wild state, she would have had to hunt for her food. This was just a part of her nature, and it was never revealed before because we always fed her. The sheep had triggered a primitive instinct. My distrust of her began to fade as my understanding grew.

About this time, Roger let out a whoop. "They're coming! See? There's the government boat coming around Stone Island. I think they are coming this way!"

Sure enough, I could see the familiar gray hull blasting through the chop with the spray flying over the bow. Suddenly, roasted sparrow lost its appeal. I laid our meal down on some rocks and buried the fire. Then we started running for a nearby beach, where we knew Father would come to pick us up. I was not worried that we had wasted a sparrow, knowing that our mouthful soon would make a meal for the huge raven that had been flying around us. But I have always wondered how roasted sparrow would have tasted.

We quickly arrived at the beach, and soon the government boat pulled into the cove. Father headed toward us in the peapod. The minute she touched the sand, we jumped in.

"What are you two doing over here?" Father queried, a half smile on his face. Of course, he knew the answer. Mother had reached him by telephone.

I quickly told him what had happened and said how disappointed I was in Peter. But I assured him that I thought the one sheep she had caught had not been seriously injured. He did not seem surprised. He said, "That's her nature. Just be careful. Don't take her with you again unless you put a leash on her." I agreed to this wholeheartedly. Peter had gone directly to her stern seat in the boat. Now I wrapped my arms around her, happy that our adventure was over. I did not tell Father that in our "extreme hunger" we also had reverted to primitive hunters and killed a ground sparrow.

Roger and I made many more trips to Big Libby, because we loved exploring this large island and going there gave us a sense of freedom. One of our favorite "explores" was a large cave on the mainland side of the island. Since we often went to Big Libby in the peapod, we could reach the cave easily from the sea. At high tide the water nearly filled the cave, but at low tide we could walk in. The opening was about twenty-five feet high. This probably was an ancient volcano tube, which the waves had continued to shape into a room nearly fifty feet deep. In our imaginations we could populate this huge cavern with all kinds of strange creatures, but in reality the creatures on the inside were about the same as those on the outside. Of course, there was always the possibility that we might find pirate treasure.

At one end of the island were the remains of an old house. The sides had caved in and the attic was on the ground. Nearby, to our surprise, was a clear, fresh, bubbling spring. We often wondered how fresh water could come up through an island located in the ocean. Near this building was the swale where we harvested bog cranberries. The swale also provided another kind of food: Father occasionally would surprise a flock of brant geese feeding here. I understand that this area has become one of the largest nesting areas for eider on the Maine coast, but it was not the case when we lived on Libby.

There was one section of land on Big Libby that we scrupulously avoided. Legend had it that several large piles of stones marked the graves of some shipwrecked sailors, and we were quite sure their ghosts still inhabited the area.

The highest part of Big Libby afforded a view of the ocean with islands and the mainland intermingled. To the northeast were Cross Island and the town of Cutler. To the north we could see Avery's Rock Light Station, its squat tower appearing to rest nearly on the sea. Northwest was Stone Island, with its crown of island spruce, and beyond that were Starboard and Howard Cove, where Jasper Beach is built up with many jasper stones. (Oddly enough, a family named Jasper once owned the house nearby. This beach has now been bought and preserved as a public park by the town of Machiasport.) For many years, there was a fish weir in this cove. It may still be there.

To the west of Stone were Ingalls (Starboard), Foster, Ram, and many other islands stretching toward Jonesport. Then, to the southwest, was our own Libby Island, which we often referred to as Little Libby. We could see the white tower with its black dome reaching into the sky and the houses snuggled together beneath it. In the summer, Libby always looked like a giant piece of granite covered with a brilliant green rug sprinkled with colors. We loved our island and always looked forward to going home after an exploring trip, but the trek to Big Libby was a welcome change and it added a new dimension to our lives. Without Big Libby, we would have felt much more confined.

The only other island I ever tried to explore by myself was Ram, which lay west of Libby. One clear, calm day, Junie Foss and I were down at the boathouse fishing for pollock. We did not have many days like this, and we both agreed that it called for something special. Looking across the open bay, we became intrigued by one of the distant islands—which, because of the clarity of the atmosphere, did not look too far away. Probably it was about a mile. I think we both had the idea at the same time: "Let's row over there and explore that island." Soon we were rowing across the tidal current toward our destination. Being careful to skirt areas where there was surf, we found a small beach and landed. We scampered over the rocks and climbed to the top of the island. It was not very large, so it was not long before we had seen most of it. Libby began to look farther and farther away. Also, I began to worry that the fog might come in, as it did nearly every afternoon, so we pulled the pod down over the beach and out over some rocks that had emerged with the ebbing tide. Just as we were both ready to jump in and start rowing, Junie said, "I've gotta go! I can never make it back if I don't."

He took off, back to the beach, splashing through the water as he went, leaving me holding the boat. Since we had pulled the boat out past a lot of rocky areas, he had to go quite a distance. I watched as he disappeared beyond a knoll, seeking "privacy." After about ten minutes, I began to get impatient and concerned. The tide was rising and the waves were beginning to build with the increasing southwest wind, making it harder and harder to hold onto the boat. I shouted to Junie to hurry but got no response. Then I saw him scurrying about the beach, for no apparent reason—until I glimpsed a small, shadowy figure running in front of him. He was chasing a baby mink. As my panic rose, I began to scream even louder. Finally, he must have sensed my desperation, and he started wading out to the boat. I took only enough time to tell him just what I thought of his escapade. Then we jumped into the pod, got our oars in place, and picked our way out through the mounting waves. It was a stiff row back to Libby, because the wind had picked up, as always in the afternoon, and it was blowing against us.

When I got home, I discovered that we had been under surveillance during the whole episode. Our family had a habit of scanning the ocean frequently, and someone had spotted us. With the spyglass, they could also tell quite accurately what we were doing. After this, all of the nearby islands were strictly off limits, except for Big Libby. But I can still remember how thrilling it was to run about on one of those islands that were only silhouettes in the distance. We had actually explored a "desert" island.

The center for many of our activities on Libby Island was the Salt Water Pond. It was located on the south side of our house at the bottom of the relatively gentle cliffs, so we could reach it by climbing carefully. On the outside, it was sheltered from the ocean by a huge rock formation, but a break in this bastion allowed the sea water to flow in when the tide was at full flood or the waves were high. This kept the water renewed.

The Salt Water Pond was not much of a pond, but it was the only warm salt water we had. Most of it was only about six to eight inches deep, but in the center was a curved gouge with a depth of about thirty inches. We called this the "deep hole." We tried to swim in this hole, but it was so narrow that we usually skinned our knees. So most of our in-the-water activity was crawling about, using our hands to propel ourselves—and on hot days getting as much of our bodies under water as possible. We could get all under the water in the "deep hole" if we treated it like a bathtub, but of course, none of us realized this, since we had never seen a bathtub.

Bathing suits were primitive: the boys wore old cut-off pants and the girls old dresses. Later, Mother bought us wool bathing suits, which were a great improvement, because they were warm even when wet. Our definition of a real summer day was one on which we went swimming both in the morning and in the afternoon. But this happened seldom, because the southwest wind blew most afternoons, bringing in the chilling fog.

Our other major activity in the Salt Water Pond was our version of lobstering. Father was an expert with his knife and ax and enjoyed making miniature boats for us. The lobsterboats were exact replicas of the big boats used by the full-time lobster fishermen. For "gear," Father made us tiny buoys, until we learned to make these ourselves. From each buoy we strung enough cord to reach the bottom and tied on a small rock to hold it in place. We had great powers of imagination to create lobsters out of the green plant life that would collect around the "warp." We set these traps and hauled them conscientiously, storing the "lobsters" in our "boats." We made the sounds of our favorite Kermath engines by trilling our tongues. This undoubtedly developed our lung power, because we did it unceasingly.

Father also built a boat slip for me. It had two four-foot-long "stringers" about six inches apart, with legs at one end to give it the proper slant. At the top he installed a drum with a handle to make a winch, so I could haul my boat up out of the water the way we did with the government boat.

As we got older, we began to build boats for ourselves, and I built a scow that was about a foot wide and two and a half feet long. We had seen these being used to construct wharves as well as in other building projects. We used ours mostly to carry rocks (our imaginary cargo) from place to place and to store our imaginary lobsters.

Father also built me a two-foot-long sailboat that looked much like a Friendship sloop, a traditional sailing workboat. It had a cutter rig, with jibboom and two jibs forward, a single mast, and a large mainsail. She was complete in every detail. Father hollowed out her one-piece hull from a cedar log and decked her over, so she was very buoyant. He cast a lead keel for her, which provided excellent stability, and a lead anchor. Mother made the sails in panels, like real sails. Since the boat was gaff-rigged, she had a boom not only at the foot of the sail but also at its head. For raising and lowering sails, there were blocks (metal grommets cut from shoes).

I played for many hours with this "ship," and no doubt she started my lifelong interest in sailing. I learned many sailing skills with her, because she reacted to the winds and waves exactly like a real sailboat—which, in fact, she was. I can see her now in a stiff breeze, heeling over and clawing her way to windward across a pond. Whenever the rudder setting let go, she would head into the wind with all sails luffing and be stuck "in irons," unable to move, until we could rescue her. I still have this boat, and soon she will be teaching my grandson some of the sailing skills she taught me.

We had many ideas about how to deepen the Salt Water Pond to provide a real swimming pool. One was to dam up the entrance. A dam no more than three feet high would have been adequate. The water would have come over this at extreme high tides or when the surf was up and then be kept inside by the dam. Father and the other keepers said they would build the dam if we kids would collect enough rocks. We dragged, rolled, pushed, and threw rocks into this spot all one summer, but for some reason the men never carried out their promise. This was unfortunate, because, if they had, all of us could have learned to swim—an essential safety skill for island kids. Everyone in our family learned to swim during visits to the mainland, where the fresh water was warm.

I suppose every youngster dreams of having his own "private residence," especially when he is about twelve years old. When Father announced that he was going to tear down our old hen-house, I decided immediately that, with his permission and co-operation, I would salvage enough of the lumber to build a camp. This set in motion a project that would bring great joy to both children and adults—Father in particular.

At the time, Howard Colbeth, a government carpenter, was on the island to make building repairs. I immediately "hired" him as my consultant—an assignment that he accepted readily. That first night, we had a conference and discussed how to lay a foundation, build floor sills, and erect uprights. We decided that a shed roof would be the simplest to build with the materials we had, and probably the least likely to leak. The size of our camp was determined by the amount of good lumber we could salvage. The building would be six feet square with a six-foot roof at the highest point, sloping to five. This would provide enough of a pitch so the rain would run off.

I could hardly sleep that night, so anxious was I to get started. I also needed a partner, and when I told Roger about my plans, he was excited about joining the project. I knew he would be a real help.

The next job was to select a site for our new "home." We surveyed the island, looking for a place far enough from the houses to ensure privacy but not so far that we could not run back home quickly if we needed "protection." Also, we wanted a sheltered spot facing south for warmth and out of the wind if possible. We finally located it behind a ledge that jutted directly up from the field about halfway toward the Tip-End. The area was relatively flat, another requirement, and it was just behind the pasture fence, located so it would be a good resting place (particularly in cold weather) during walks around the shore. Also, it was just off the path that ran to the Tip-End, so it would be easy to transport our materials. Father approved, his only concern being that it be out of the purview of the inspector, who might be curious about unauthorized buildings on federal property.

Father agreed to supply us with a simple tool kit if we would take good care of the tools—which, of course, we promised. As each board and timber was removed from the henhouse, we examined it closely. All that were sound (and reasonably clean), we carted, wheeled, or carried to the building site—hard work for kids, but we were determined. We also removed all the nails and straightened any that were still serviceable.

When our materials were on site, we were ready to start building. We could hardly wait. When we announced that we had everything we needed—including some flat stones to serve as a foundation for the floor timbers—Mr. Colbeth agreed to help us. After supper one night, we all trooped down to the site and had our first lesson in building. First we selected our heaviest "timbers," which turned out to be planks. Our consultant helped us measure these, saw them into proper lengths, and set them in place. We set our stones at each corner and at midpoints and leveled the timbers. The first night we finished the foundation and put several floor joists in place. Once we understood how to place them, we decided to quit, since it was almost dark, and continue the next day.

This work was very satisfying for us, and we greatly appreciated Mr. Colbeth's help. He taught us a great deal and always treated us with the respect due to beginning construction workers.

The second night, with a lot of help, we put the uprights in place. For some of these, we used good weir stakes that we had picked up around the shore, since they appeared to be stronger than the joists from the henhouse. On the following nights, we put up the rafters and framed the door. Now we were ready for boarding over the roof and the sides, and this we could do ourselves. We worked long hours, and a real building began to take shape. Father also gave us a hand from time to time.

Our first problem was deciding what to use for a window. We did not want a very big one and there were no suitable ones in the henhouse. Finally, Father remembered that he had some old windows stored away from a remodeling job. We got out one of these and, with his help, were able to saw it in two, leaving us with three panes side by side. It made a perfect window, and Father helped us frame it in. He also scrounged some tarpaper for the roof and the walls. Then we had our first lesson in shingling. After the first two courses were laid, we caught on and laid the rest of the shingles. Perhaps the courses were not all perfectly straight, but the roof did not leak, which was all that mattered. On another night, Mr. Colbeth helped us hang the door, which we had salvaged from the henhouse.

How proud we were to see our own "home" taking shape. We immediately made plans to move in. Father helped us to design lower and upper bunks, and we stuffed crocus sacks with hay for mattresses (two for each bunk). They served well, except for the "joint" in the middle.

When we announced that we planned to spend our nights at the camp, some of the adults and the older brothers and sisters scoffed. "That won't last long," they said. "You'll soon get sick of going down there every night." And one remark that really stung was, "I don't believe you'll dare go down there in the dark all by yourselves." This made us all the more determined to move in.

Our first night was exciting. We equipped ourselves with a lantern and flashlights, and Mother let us have a small kerosene lamp. We took all our gear down in the afternoon. Just before dark, we struck out. By this time, the fog had swept across the island, bringing its chill and dampness. We persuaded Peter to come with us, which greatly increased our courage. She wouldn't be scared of any "thing." Mother had packed my breakfast: dry cereal and milk in an empty vanilla bottle. (I shall always remember the taste of that milk with just a hint of vanilla flavoring.) Reaching the camp, we opened the door to a gloomy interior, but the bright flame in the kerosene lamp soon shed a warm orange-yellow light.

We quickly crawled into our bunks, locking the door carefully before doing so. Our air rifles, fully loaded, were within easy reach. Our joy at being under our own roof quickly dispelled any fears of being away from the security of home. As we cuddled under our warm blankets and smelled the fragrance of our hay-filled mattresses, we began to feel quite secure. We could hear the seas breaking over the bar, creating their incessant roar. They were louder here because we were closer. And, although perhaps we did not realize it, we were closer to being two independent young men.

Just as we were falling asleep, we both bolted awake with fear. What was that scratching noise? The older kids and adults frequently spoke of the devil as the "Old Scratcha," so we were ever aware of his potential presence. And that noise was definitely scratching! I grabbed my air rifle, cocked it, and turned on my flashlight. To our amazement, Peter was turning around and around in the middle of the floor, scratching at the newly tacked-down carpet. Apparently there were a few wrinkles in it—not to her liking. She looked up, blinking, with an expression that said, "What's the matter? Doesn't a dog have a right to smooth out her bed?" Greatly relieved, Roger and I had a good laugh, which relaxed our tension. We soon dropped off to sleep, the reassuring boom of the fog signal echoing in our ears. Every night that Peter slept with us in the camp, she always went through this same routine.

We were awakened just before sunrise with more scratching—this time on our roof. In the daylight, our courage increased greatly. Roger, in the lower bunk, grabbed his gun. Without donning his pants, he unlocked the door and stepped outside. I could hear him laughing. Soon he called back, "That noise was ground sparrows on the roof."

"Don't shoot them," I cautioned. "Remember our promise that we wouldn't shoot sparrows."

It was chilly inside the camp, but soon we were seated on some stools around a makeshift table, chomping away on our cereal. A small amount of cream had risen from my milk, and it made a dish of dry corn flakes into a gourmet breakfast. We decided that the first night in our new house had been a great success.

Through the summer, we continued to make improvements. A friend on the mainland heard about our enterprise and donated a real prize: a tiny coal stove. Father bought us some stovepipe and helped us cut out and insulate a hole in the roof. Now, at night, we could build a fire, and our little room was quite comfortable, regardless of how cold and windy it was outside.

We also did a lot of decorating. We searched old magazines for pictures we liked and pasted them on the walls. My major contribution was a stuffed bat. Bats often came around our houses at night, and we would strike at them with brooms as they swooped by us. One night, I made a connection, and we had a dead bat on our hands (and consciences). I had been reading about taxidermy, so I skinned this little creature carefully, filled its body cavities with cotton well impregnated with salt, and mounted it on a board. We hung this trophy quite proudly on a wall in our camp.

Our older brothers and sisters had said all along that we would soon tire of sleeping every night in our new house. We figured that they were just jealous. We even put a padlock on our door to keep them—and the younger kids—out. We had no key for this lock, but we had discovered that a sharp rap at the point of closure would open it. No one else knew our secret, so our private domicile was quite secure, and we never unlocked the padlock when anyone else was around.

But as the weeks went by and the nights became cooler, our enthusiasm began to wane. Leaving our mothers and fathers and the other kids sitting in a warm, well-lighted room made it increasingly difficult to break away for the trek to the camp. The walk was not far, but part of it was through grass always wet with heavy dew. As we left the house, sometimes the fog was so dense that the buildings faded into the mist and even the light in the tower, which we depended upon to illuminate our way, gave off only an eerie glow. Still, we were determined that we would not give up our nightly sojourn.

Our fears at being away from the house alone in the dark and fog had gradually receded—until one night they were quickly rekindled. We had set out later than usual, having been reluctant to leave the warmth of home, so it was quite dark and the fog had so diminished the light that we had to make our way slowly, trying to keep our feet on the path. Even the flashlights did not seem to help much, and the four-times-a-minute blasts from the fog signal sounded muffled. On this particular night, as I recall, Peter refused to join us. Perhaps she was getting tired of these nightly jaunts.

Just as we were crawling over the pasture fence, we heard a terrifying noise from down near the boathouse. This was frightening enough in itself, but a story we always carried in the backs of our minds made it seem even worse. Legend had it that years before, a ship had been wrecked on Big Libby and all the officers and crew were drowned except the captain. He reached the light station, but a few nights later, besieged by guilt over the tragedy for which he felt responsible, had gone down to the boathouse and hanged himself. The thought of this quickly turned our fear into panic. With lantern and lunch pails swinging, we ran from the pasture fence to the house in record time. I can imagine what we must have looked like as we burst into our respective kitchens—thoroughly drenched from running through the wet grass and our faces revealing stark horror. There was no question about our going back to camp that night. How good it felt to be safe in our own beds, with mothers and fathers close by.

With the bright sun of a new day burning away the fog, revealing the brilliance of a blue-and-white sea around us, the fears of the night before also burned away. Roger and I decided to go down to the boathouse to see if we could find out what had made the terrifying noise. Our parents had insisted that there had to be some logical explanation for it. With our air rifles in hand, we approached—admittedly with some caution—the building from which the dreaded sound had come. Sure enough, we quickly saw what had happened. Workmen had been repairing the boathouse the day before and had left a ladder standing. Our cow often went exploring at night, and obviously she had bumped into the bottom of the ladder and sent it crashing to the ground, scraping its way down over the clapboards and creating our mysterious sound. This simple, logical explanation was reassuring, and we began to see how ridiculous our fears had been. That night we went back to the camp—determined that no one, particularly our older brothers and sisters, would be proven right in their prediction that we would tire of our new lifestyle.

During several successive summers, we remodeled and enlarged our camp. The first year, as another building project on the station made lumber available, we tore down the back side and built an addition, much larger than the original. Another year, we decided that we wanted a home with a view, so we tore down the original building, turned the addition around, and added a front section with a pitched roof and a piazza.

We made two innovative additions to the furnishings of this latest version of the dwelling. Our coal stove had by this time rusted away, so we had to devise a new way of heating the camp. Fortunately, Mother's copper wash boiler had just developed leaks, so Father suggested we make it into a wood stove. Putting the cover in place, we turned the boiler upside-down and rested it on bricks to hold it steady at a safe distance above the floor. With Father's help, we cut a section out of the front and hinged it to make a door. We also cut a small hole below this for a draft. Cutting an X in the back end of the top and bending the sections upward, we could hold a stovepipe securely in place. Father always was quite willing to buy us new stovepipe, which rusted away quickly—as did everything else on the island that was made of iron or steel.

We thoroughly enjoyed our commodious retreat, but one day I conceived an idea for a more comfortable chair, like Father's big rocker. So I decided to build one. It was not beautiful, but it was comfortable and strong.

When Gleason Colbeth and his family moved to Libby, the two older sons decided that they were "underprivileged" without a camp, so, with their father's help, they erected a second home a short distance from ours.

ISLAND GAMES AND PASTIMES

157

We used the camp both summer and winter. During the cold, snowy months, when our outdoor activities often were limited by weather, nothing gave us more joy than to go down to the camp with apples or other snacks and build up a fire. In spite of its simple board walls, the camp was quite comfortable as long as the stove was roaring. It was a great place for a quiet "read." We always had an ample supply of wood, which we scrounged from along the shoreline.

The camp also became a welcome halfway station for Father, Irwin, and me when we were returning from hunting trips to the bar. A quick fire would warm us up for the rest of the icy hike home. After Irwin's brush with the law, recounted in chapter 5, we always left our game birds here, well hidden. After reaching the house and checking to see that there were no suspicious visitors, someone would return from the house with a small box of "kindling." If the coast was clear, we would then use that box to carry our game to the house. Once my younger brother, Arnie, was sent to the house to obtain such a box. He had not yet comprehended the system, so he returned with a box adequate only for a brace of sandpipers. Father thought this was a great joke, and this event haunted Arnie for several years as it was told and retold, being embellished with each telling.

In later years, after we kids and our mothers had all left the island to live in Machias for schooling, the station became a lonely place for the three keepers. To break the monotony, Father and Gleason Colbeth would prepare a sumptuous meal, haul it on a sled to our camp, build up a fire, and have a winter picnic. As Gleason would say, "This took our minds off our attention." To mainland adults, this might seem like a rather immature activity for two grown men, but mature recreational opportunities were in short supply on these island outposts. There were many hours to be filled, including long night watches. Under similar circumstances, many men would have become habitual daytime nappers, but I never knew Father to take a nap. He always objected to any suggestion that it might be nice to have a place to stretch out in the kitchen. His comment always was, "I've known many a good man to be ruined by having a couch in the kitchen."

Cold and snow did not prevent us from playing outside in winter, although often it limited the time we stayed out. We seemed to have as much snow on Libby as on the mainland, and we looked forward to snowstorms because of the variety they created in our lives. It set our minds racing to see the sky become overcast, to feel the northeast wind increase in intensity and to watch the first snowflakes begin to fall. Almost immediately, one of the keepers would go to the whistlehouse to start the fog signal. Snow meant thick weather. One of us would be sent out to drive the horse and cow into the barn, if they had been let out for the day. As the wind picked up, we would all return to the house, and we kids would watch through the kitchen windows as the seas grew higher, urged on by the wind. Sometimes we would see a ship clawing her way to windward, trying to make shelter in Machias Bay before the full fury of the storm struck.

If the larder was low, and Father was not on watch, he and Irwin might put on their warmest clothes, load up their shotguns, and head for the bar, provided the tide was right. Duck hunting was great in weather like this, because the ducks' vision was limited by the snow. They would return soon after dark—which always came early on such a night—often with a brace of ducks to throw on the carpet in front of the stove. Peter would strut about, looking proud at her part in the successful hunt, her coat white with snow and frozen salt water. She would quickly slide behind the stove to dry off, and soon the steam would start rising from her fur.

After the supper dishes were done, Father would spread out papers on the kitchen table and begin to "pick" the birds. Their feathers were light, thick, and sometimes very colorful. The mallards, with their bright green heads and wings decorated with dark-blue epaulets, seemed too elegant merely to be used for food. After the feathers were all removed, Mother would pack them into a flour bag, to be saved for making pillows. I still sleep on a feather pillow that Mother made for me.

When there were many birds, others in the family, including Mother, would join in the picking. Afterward, Father would take them to the pantry for dressing. There, by the dim light of a kerosene lamp, he would eviscerate them and put them in water to soak overnight. The next noon, some of them would likely appear, filled with one of Mother's tasty stuffings, on our table.

On other winter evenings, if Father had the second watch (ten until two), he would say goodnight and go to bed for a couple of hours. The rest of us then would knit bait pockets and heads for our lobster traps—or, if they were not needed, we would play games and read. Mother always did knitting, usually mittens or "fancy work," crocheting and embroidery.

Because of their "evil connotation" (they were used for gambling), we were not allowed to play games with traditional playing cards, but we had a substitute called Rook. We also played other card games, such as Flinch and Authors. But one of our favorite games was played with carroms on a carrom board. This board was about thirty inches square, with different designs on each side. Carroms were small wooden rings, an inch in diameter, painted different colors. The game we liked best on this board was like Eight Ball played on a pool table; the carroms, propelled by a snap of the finger, were used instead of balls. Father loved this game, and he and Irwin had some "hot" contests. They would even file their fingernails to try to improve the accuracy of their shots.

During these evenings, I was likely to be reading—if I could find something to read, which was often difficult, unless it was after Christmas and I had received books as gifts. Sometimes I would lie on the floor, using Peter as a pillow, and drop off to sleep. Mother would urge me several times to get undressed and go upstairs, but often I would ignore her. Finally, one night, tired of having to remind me constantly that it was bedtime (and after several threats), she turned down the kerosene lamp and left me alone. A few hours later I woke up, cramped from lying on the hard floor and chilled because the fire had burned low. I did not like the scary feeling of being all by myself, nor did I like having to find my way alone along the dark corridor and up the stairs. It was a great relief to get undressed and into bed, which was already warmed by Irwin, with whom I slept. I do not think that Mother ever had to remind me a second time after that.

Some of our storms came from the southwest, and often these would come during warmer periods. They would begin with snow, sometimes quite heavy, and end with freezing rain. By the time we heard the sleet striking on the windows, we could hardly wait for the storm to end so we could go outdoors. There we would see a new, snow- and ice-covered world. From one end to the other, our brown-and-white island would be pure white. Before our dreams of the night before could come true, however, we had to make one vital test: how strong was the crust? Sometimes we were disappointed to find it would not hold us, but other times it would be solid and strong. We then knew how we would spend our day.

First we would make ice picks, if we had not made them before. Any short, sturdy piece of wood would do, if it was strong enough to hold a headless nail driven into one end. Sitting on our sleds, we could propel ourselves over the fields and pasture. But these were no longer fields and pasture—they became an ocean dotted with bays, harbors, and small towns. We would spend the day, if the sun did not soften the crust too rapidly, "sailing" from one port to another. I always think of this simple game when my wife and I are sailing our boat in Maine from one port to another, and the feeling of sheer pleasure is much the same.

Snow did not accumulate on Libby, because strong winds blew it over the cliffs as soon as it fell. Only when it was damp and heavy did it freeze in place. In this way, our island was "extended" out over the beaches and rocks below. Incoming waves would undermine these huge banks, making it possible to walk or crawl underneath them. This provided the source of a number of winter games—not all of them totally safe.

Our parents did not supervise our games too closely, and I suspect that if they had, many activities would have been forbidden. One of our games was making "body shoots," jumping down through the snow overhang to land on the sand. For this, we dressed in all the clothes we could get on and still walk. We made sure not to choose a bank that was too high or to make the shoot too steep.

Another game involved having one person walk underneath the overhang and push a pole up through so a person at the top could find it and push it down through in another spot. After one winter ice storm, when we were playing this game, I was on the top, peering out over the edge for the pole. Unexpectedly, it appeared right under my nose. Even though my nose was cold, it was not numb enough to ease the pain. Not waiting to pull up the pole, I ran home as fast as my overwrapped legs could carry me. My whole upper lip oozed from the bruising blow. Mother undressed me, washed my wound, and tried to ease the hurt with comforting words. My lip stung for a long time, and I wore a tremendous scab a lot longer.

Another day, when Junie and I were having fun exploring these same giant snowbanks, I said something to him and got no answer. He had been standing beside me a few moments earlier and now he had disappeared without a trace! Then I detected muffled screams coming from deep in the snow. I approached cautiously and solved the mystery. Junie had fallen through the uppermost crust of the bank, but the ice at the bottom was so solid that he had not broken through onto the sand. He was deep in a snow prison, and there was no way I could get him out. Standing at the bottom of the vertical white tunnel, he was screaming for me to rescue him, and my reassuring words did little to ease his alarm. I raced to the house and breathlessly told Father what had happened. He gathered some ropes, called the other men, and we all made our way back to Junie's icy cell. The men rigged a sling, urged Junie to slip it under his arms, and hauled him quickly to safety. I think it was a while before we played these games again—or at least we played them with far greater caution.

I imagine that men on ships going close to our light station examined our island closely to see if they could detect any signs of life. When they saw a huge figure all dressed in white standing in front of our house, no doubt it made them very curious. And they must have been quite surprised, when looking through their binoculars, to see a giant snowman. We built many such figures and also engaged in other traditional winter games—sliding, which was excellent when we had periods of hard crust, and skating on the Big Pond. One game that I am sure was not played on the mainland was related to saltwater ice.

This ice, unlike ice on freshwater ponds, has a high degree of elasticity, evident only after we had run and bounced on it. We usually played this risky game at the Salt Water Pond. At first, the ice would barely move, but with each run across it, its "bounce" would become more pronounced. We played this game in our rubber boots, because there was predictably only one ending— the ice gave way and we fell through. If we were lucky, we came up dry, but more often either the water was deep enough to go over our boots or we fell in and got a thorough soaking. The inevitable result was that we would spend the rest of the day in the house allowing our warm clothes to dry out. For us, the fun was worth it, but I am not sure that Mother agreed.

During the winter, we had a large variety of birds on Libby. Here the seedeaters could always find grass seeds, which usually were not available on the mainland, where the ground would be covered with several feet of snow. Stale bread crumbs also made good food for them. We made bird feeding a game that perhaps was somewhat cruel. Snow buntings were among our most common winter birds. That was what Father called them, but since they had a red flush on their breasts, perhaps they were redpolls. However, the description in Roger Tory Peterson's *A Field Guide to the Birds* tells of snow buntings traveling in large flocks and "drifting over a field like snowflakes." This aptly describes our birds, which could be seen flying about the island like small snow squalls.

I guess all kids like to get close to nature, and we tried it with these birds. They were quite shy and flew away if we approached too close, so we devised a way of getting nearer to them. Wooden boxes were used for many things on Libby, so we had no difficulty finding one for the trap we planned. Putting papers on top of the snow, we spread bread crumbs to attract the birds. Then we put the box over some of the crumbs, tilted it back, and propped it up with a small stick about six inches long. Fastening a cord to this stick, we ran the cord into the entryway of the house. When a sufficient number of birds had assembled under our trap, we pulled out the prop, catching many of them inside the box. Then we could peer in through the cracks and get a good look at them. I do not remember that the birds panicked, and after we had satisfied our curiosity, we lifted the box and off they flew to join their friends. Although our game could have injured some birds, I do not remember that it ever did. But I do remember how awed we were at the beauty of these tiny creatures. We marveled that they could withstand the bleak wintry climate.

March brought high winds to our island, just as on the mainland, but Libby was a better place for flying kites—no trees and no utility wires to catch a kite's tail or its leash cord. We built kites of all shapes and sizes. Father and Irwin bought and assembled a huge box kite. Of course it eventually came down in a crash, but it flew magnificently. We made some kites of the simplest materials. We would split laths with a fine-toothed saw to make frames, string cord around the ends, and cover them with brown paper held in place with flour paste, which Mother taught us how to make. One of my greatest ambitions was to build a kite that would stay up all night. I do not know where I got the idea, but I built one with a round top, using a small section of barrel stave for the frame. This kite turned out to be very slack, and perhaps that improved its aerodynamics. I balanced it well with a long tail. One night, when a good breeze was blowing, I left it flying. Many nights I had done this, only to find in the morning that my kite had crashed. But when I awoke after leaving up my innovative new kite and looked out the window, it was still soaring in the sky. I was quite proud of my accomplishment.

Another game we played utilizing the wind required the shiny pages of mail-order catalogs after they were no longer needed in our outhouse as toilet paper. On a day when there was a strong north wind blowing, we would take the sheets high on the head near the tower and toss them into the air. Then, of course, we watched to see how far they would go. Sometimes they went out of sight, still flying high. We always wondered what faraway places they might reach.

Spring was a time when the ice began to melt and water began to appear in all the ponds. These made excellent places to sail either our big boats or some simple ones that we made out of shingles. As the remaining snow cover and ice melted away, green shoots appeared. As mentioned in chapter 5, to ensure good pasturage, Father used to burn a part of the island that was well away from the houses. This was a highlight of spring. All of us equipped ourselves with brooms, buckets of water, and wet crocus sacks. Father generally did the burning on a day when the wind was blowing away from the houses. The fire spread amazingly fast as the dead grass ignited quickly. We followed its progress, interfering only if it appeared to be moving in the wrong direction—toward the boathouse, the camps, or the fences, where it would burn the posts. One aftermath of the great spring burn was that, although the grass fire went out quickly, some places continued to burn due to the topsoil of decomposed wood. Several days afterward, we would find fires still smoldering. We carried many gallons of water to make sure these lingering fires would not spread toward the buildings on windy nights, although they usually were a long way off.

A good rain after our burn did two things: it put out any remaining underground fires and stimulated the spring growth of grass and flowers. Soon new shoots were coming up everywhere. We were fond of wildflowers and knew where each patch of white and blue violets would appear.

Although most of us had never seen a baseball game, either professional or amateur, we played a modifed version that required only three participants. But first we had to make a ball. All of us kids, during these years, wore long, black, cotton stockings. When the feet were beyond darning, these were available for making balls. The first step was to cut half-inch-wide strips in a spiral fashion. One stocking yielded a considerable amount of material. We next had to find something for a core—large cork stoppers or a rolled-up piece of rubber from an old boot top worked well. Then we started winding the strip of black stocking material tightly around the core until we had a ball of sufficient size. With a darning needle threaded with "Aunt Lydia's" black thread, we sewed the layers of stocking in place until we had our version of a baseball.

Our game was simple. We had only one base, so every hit had to be a home run. There were two ways to put players out: touching them with the ball, directly, or throwing it at them. An accurate aim was essential, as was the ability to duck and dodge. We spent many hours playing this game, and sometimes were able to persuade adults to join us. Then we added more bases and a few more rules. This was usually an after-supper game, and all of us youngsters liked nothing better than to have the grown-ups join in our games.

Croquet was another favorite after-supper game in which our parents often joined. If Father had the second watch, though, we had to cut the game short, because we played on some relatively flat ground right under his bedroom window. When we got a lawnmower, we kept the grass mowed around the houses, and this natural lawn made a farly good surface for croquet, although we had to become skilled at playing around the ledges that protruded here and there on the course. There was nothing more pleasant than playing croquet high on Libby's northwest head with a warm breeze blowing from the mainland and bringing all the scents of every tree and flower. This same aroma always reached us as we approached the mainland, but it seemed to disappear as we made our way inland.

Our sunsets were spectacular on the spring evenings when the weather was clear. We had a view of many islands and the mainland in the distance, and at sunset not only the sky but also the islands and the ocean glowed in many colors. I never knew why, but sunset always was a time of loneliness for me. I tried to describe my feelings to my mother, but my words were not quite adequate; she often gave me something for my stomach, which was where I told her I felt a dull ache.

Sunset was also the time when Father would make his predictions for the next day's weather. I remember distinctly one night, when we all listened intently to what he had to say. Ordinarily, we accepted the weather as it occurred, but this particular night was special. The previous week we had been in Machias and had seen giant billboards advertising a circus — with pictures of clowns, camels, and elephants, plus the announcement that there would be a special parade. All this fired our imaginations, and Father promised that he would take us—with his usual proviso: "if the weather is good." We were used to living with unpredictable weather, but this time we wanted some assurance that circus day would not be marked by rough seas or high winds. The elements, of course, would be of no concern to the townsfolk. The sunset was glorious. Father merely repeated our version of the old saying, "Red at night, sailor's delight." He also assured us that when he had put the light out in the morning, the sky was not too red. We were happy about this, because the rest of the saying is, "Red in the morning, sailors take warning." We had also checked the tide table, and it was right for a long day, allowing us to leave just as the tide reached the end of the slip and to return before it dropped off again. I am sure that when we went to bed that night we all prayed for God to intervene on our behalf.

Father's predictions were accurate, and circus day dawned calm, bright, and clear. We were off to an early start and arrived in plenty of time to see the parade. I am sure it was meager— with one or two camels, an elephant, and a few clowns—but since we had nothing with which to compare it, we thought it was a marvelous spectacle, as was the performance that followed. We were intrigued by the trapeze artists, the galloping ponies with girls on their backs, and all the other acts in this "one-ring" circus.

For weeks afterward, we relived this day full of new experiences. We tried our best to imitate the trapeze artists, hanging upside-down by our toes from Mother's clothes rack and doing "aerial" somersaults around the pipe that ran from the rainshed to the well-house. The circus had been a great event in our lives, and I doubt that Father was reprimanded by the inspector when he had to report being away more than six hours to take his family to the circus.

The nearest we ever came to real aerial feats was when someone introduced us to pole-vaulting. We built ourselves stands, cut thin strips of board for a bar, and used our own favorite weir stakes for jumping poles. The real thrill came when John Beal, recently arrived as second assistant keeper, decided to try this new game. He was a large man, so we must have found an especially sturdy weir stake for him. Our stands were not very high— perhaps seven feet—but after a few trial jumps, he said, "Put the bar on the top!" With several giant strides, he gained full momentum and, planting his pole (which began to bend perilously), went sailing through the air, topping our stands by at least a foot. He landed on the other side in a catlike stance and began laughing as hard as he could, while we all cheered. What a grand sight to see this huge man eight feet in the air, arms and legs flying out in all directions. And he had remembered to let go of the jumping pole, so when he looked back, the bar was still resting undisturbed on the top of the stands.

We practiced many hours after this, but no one could surpass John's record. His jump had equaled, in sheer excitement, any stunt we had seen at the circus.

Although the circus was a once-in-a-lifetime experience, our annual Fourth of July celebrations provided us with enough excitement to keep us going all year. The week before the Fourth, we would go to town to get "supplies." Father was generous in buying us firecrackers in a variety of types and sizes—caps (and pistols if we needed new ones), cherry bombs, Roman candles, sparklers, skyrockets, and any new explosive devices that had come on the market.

Occasionally there were Fourth of July celebrations in Machias, but we preferred to stay on Libby. That day always began when Father came into the hall at the bottom of the stairs and shouted, "Hip, hip, hooray for the Fourth of July!" I'm sure none of us had the slightest idea what we were celebrating, but it was a special day for all of us. The first time I was away from home on the Fourth, I wrote to Father and told him how much I had missed his Fourth of July early-morning salute.

It did not take us long to be out of bed and downstairs at the breakfast table. We could hardly wait to get started blowing up things. One of our favorite blasting jobs was on anthills. We would embed several large firecrackers around the base of one. After lighting the fuses, we would jump back quickly and watch the whole hill go into the air. I do not know what the casualty rate was, but it must have been high. We seemed to have little sympathy for these tiny insects. We also loved to plant firecrackers under cans and old buckets to hear the big booms they made.

We were so busy with our antics that picnic time came almost too early. We usually ate down at the second beach, where our favorite fare of lobsters would be enhanced with coconuts and watermelon for dessert. After dinner, if it was warm enough, we would go "swimming"—actually, only wading and splashing in the frigid waves. We always had our "explosives" with us, so we would continue our demolition in a new setting.

Evening could not come fast enough for us to try out all our fireworks. To pass the time more quickly, we often got a baseball game going. But as twilight began, we were prepared for the evening show. Father usually helped with the more complicated apparatus. Soon the sky over Libby was filled with exploding missiles that rivaled the tower light in intensity. We loved to "fire" the sparklers. I can still see their Z-shaped sparks and hear the exciting hiss that they made. Roman candles, several going at once, illumined the whole yard. When we had shot off everything, it was well past bedtime, and nobody ever had difficulty going to sleep. As we drifted off to the soft sounds of the waves surging around our island home, we were sure that no one could possibly have had a more glorious Fourth of July.

As I relived our island games in writing this, I realized that in many ways they were similar to those played by mainland children, but there were some key differences. Most of our games were related to the ocean or greatly influenced by it. We spent many hours searching our shores for interesting objects that might be useful to Father or for play equipment for ourselves. Our almost total isolation also markedly influenced our play activities. We were entirely dependent upon our own imaginations to create games, and, as a result, our imaginations were well developed.

Being largely cut off from other adults, we were much more dependent upon our parents for any help we needed in our games, so we were fortunate, indeed, that Father had retained his sense of play. He created many of our toys and entered into many of our activities with enthusiasm. And Mother was always there to lend a hand by teaching us how to decorate May baskets, making fudge, and sewing sails for the boats Father made for us.

Perhaps our greatest loss was in contacts with other children our own ages. I do not think any of us quite overcame this, perhaps tending to be loners rather than joiners. Then, of course, we missed the wide variety of experiences provided in nearly every mainland community by churches, youth clubs, Boy and Girl Scouts, 4-H clubs, and the myriad other organizations that bring young people together in constructive social activity. On balance, perhaps in many ways we were deprived, but we certainly never realized it, and certainly our island environment produced other valuable characteristics that compensated for any losses we may have had.

8

ISLAND-TO-ISLAND
VACATIONS

UNTIL about the mid-1930s, Father had thirty days of vacation
each year, some of which he always saved for his Thanksgiving
hunting trip. (Later the leave policy allowed eight days a month
ashore.) Some vacation times were spent visiting "the folks."
This began when we were living on Whitehead Light Station.
The folks (Father's and Mother's relatives) all lived in Addison,
about a hundred miles from Whitehead. Automobiles were not
yet available and the trains were expensive and not easily
accessible, so Father solved the problem of travel by building
himself a twenty-eight-foot cabin cruiser.

One of the men with whom Father had served in the Coast
Guard on Whitehead (then the Life-Saving Service), Forrest
Snow, was an excellent boatbuilder and built boats in his spare
time. He agreed to help Father build his boat.* Father knew
what he wanted—a fast, able craft that could make the trip to

---

*Father often told us how much he had appreciated Forrest Snow's
help and about the very large Snow Family. One of the sons I would encounter three decades later, in a very unexpected place. I was serving as
an editor for American Education Publications, owned by Wesleyan University, of Middletown, Connecticut. I heard that there was a professor
Snow from Maine on the faculty. At one of our social functions I introduced
myself to him and we soon were launched into animated conversation. We

Addison in two days safely and with a degree of comfort for his wife and children. He designed his boat with these objectives in mind. To get more speed, he sacrificed some width. For comfort, he built a flush cabin, which extended about two-thirds of her length.

There is no way you can build a boat in secret on a small island, and Father's radically designed boat soon became a topic of conversation on Whitehead as well as in the mainland village of Spruce Head. Word got around that she was so narrow she would topple over and sink when she hit the water. Apparently, Father was not worried, having first built a carefully designed scale model.

When Father's boat was launched, not only did she not sink, but she was easily the most beautiful boat in the harbor. Of course, there were few boats like her, since most of the others were workboats for lobstering and fishing.

Father used his new boat to go to Spruce Head and other nearby towns for supplies. He loved to tell the story about the day when the fastest boat on the bay pulled up beside him and roared a challenge, the owner opening up his engine's throttle. Father had been waiting for a chance like that, and he accepted. Quickly his new boat proved her worth—it was no contest. She was light and fast and went streaking away, leaving the challenger rocking about in her wake. No more derogatory remarks were made about "Hervey's folly."

I have no memory of family trips from Whitehead to Addison,

could hardly believe it when we discovered we both had been born on Whitehead.

Not long after, I asked my mother if she remembered Wilbert Snow.

"Oh, yes," she said. "Young Wilbert. We never thought he would amount to much. Couldn't seem to do anything very well."

And in coastal Maine terms, Wilbert probably was not very good at lobster fishing and cutting granite—the only two occupations open to a young man in that area. All he ever amounted to was an outstanding professor of English, an acclaimed poet, author of several books, and lieutenant governor of Connecticut. One of his books was his autobiography, Codline's Child, which paints a colorful picture of his life in the Spruce Head area in the early 1900s.

because I was so young, but some of the events surrounding these jaunts were told so many times that they became a part of my life. The trips were always made during the summer months, when the weather on the Maine coast is relatively calm, but Mother related that on one trip before I was born, in the afternoon of their first day, they encountered heavy seas. There was no wind, just huge swells that seemed to appear out of nowhere. This was not an unusual occurrence. Sometimes storms far out at sea set waves in motion, and their energy is transferred over many miles. In spite of the unexpected rough seas, Father's new boat seemed to be handling them well until the peapod, being towed behind, rose on the crest of a swell and plunged directly at her transom. Just before striking, the pod veered away, but the painter was pulled directly under her stern, where it became entangled in the propeller and stalled the motor. She was dead in the water, creating a very dangerous situation. Not only were they adrift, probably near ledges, which are so prevalent, but they were in constant danger of being struck again by the pod. In those days there were no radios, but, fortunately, a nearby fisherman saw their predicament, took them in tow, and helped them tie up in a nearby harbor, where there was a boatyard with facilities for hauling a boat. Father's boat soon was out of the water, the painter was disentangled, and a thorough inspection revealed no further damage. With the boat back in the water, the motor fired immediately and they were ready to resume their trip. When Mother told me this story, I asked her if they stayed overnight to wait for the seas to go down. "Well," she said, "I don't remember, but, knowing your father, I doubt it."

After moving to Libby, Father used his boat a few more times to go to Addison, but then the trip was much shorter. Father loved to make these visits, and sometimes he wore his full lighthouse keeper's uniform. We have one picture of him in uniform and Mother dressed elegantly in a stylish suit and hat, standing in the doorway of a relative's house. On one of these trips from Libby, we acquired the first dog I remember—Sport, a mongrel cocker spaniel. We brought him home in a tiny wooden box.

For a number of years, Father stored his boat in the boathouse on Libby. There was no harbor where she could be moored. Later he sold her to a relative, but I don't think he ever received full payment.

We continued to take vacations to visit the relatives, but later, of course, we went by car. Father was a competitive person, and he enjoyed driving to Addison in a new car. Having been an orphan, raised in his sister's family, he seemed to gain a great deal of satisfaction from showing the relatives that he had done as well or better than most of the other young men from better homes with whom he had grown up.

But I was not wholly enthusiastic about these trips. Seldom were there other kids around with whom I could play. Besides, I was always all dressed up, so I spent most of my time sitting in a chair in some relative's stuffy parlor, listening to Father and the man of the house tell hunting stories. After a few of these trips, I had heard Father's tales over and over again. I did enjoy visiting my Grandmother Orrie and Grandfather Burlon (from whom I acquired my middle name), even though all Grandmother ever had for snacks were cold biscuits. One of my cousins lived with them, and he was about my age. The great attraction of "the Basin," the part of Addison where they lived, was tidal mudflats. Here, at high tide, the cold ocean water, having flowed in over the sun-baked flats, was warm enough for swimming. Except for the mud that squeezed between my toes, this was a real treat.

In retrospect, I realize that from these trips I gained a greater appreciation of my mother and father. On our isolated outpost, we did not see our parents as part of extended families. Seeing Mother with her own parents, and as the oldest girl in a family of twelve brothers and sisters—some of whom were still living at home—and noting that she was a loved and respected person, helped us regard her in a different light. She was doing a superb job raising her own brood of five, perhaps because she had had lots of practice helping to raise her brothers and sisters. It also brought home to us the fact that even though we seldom saw our many cousins, uncles, and aunts, we were, nevertheless, not just dwellers on a distant island, but also members of a large extended family. We never did get to feel really close to any of the Addison relatives, but we did get to visit our Aunt Meta and Uncle Charlie Cummings quite often. They owned a store in West Jonesport and had adopted one of our cousins whose mother had died young. Lloyd, who was about my age, made our visits fun, particularly because he seemed to have ready access to the store's candy supply. Another feature of their home that we all admired was a "tidal flush" toilet. Their store and home (they lived upstairs above the store) was built partially on posts extending over the tidal mudflats. Their toilet was in a small separate building that also extended out over the water. Each tide provided an automatic flushing system, eliminating all the flies and unpleasant odors. We thought it would be great to have a similar system on Libby, but we realized that moving our outhouse closer to the sea might jeopardize not only the building but also the occupant if a huge wave came in—as they so often did.

We never knew our paternal grandparents. Grandfather, who owned a small schooner, died on her deck in Boston, apparently the victim of a stroke. Grandmother died of cancer at almost the same time. At eight years of age, young Hervey had lost both of his parents. Although certainly not wealthy, Grandfather and Grandmother had had a comfortable home at the head of a small bay in Addison that Father always called Penelope Cove. His older siblings were old enough to be on their own, but he and his sister Nettie were not. So the ancestral home was turned over to an older sister and her husband. Hervey and Nettie then joined this poor family of thirteen children.

In a situation like that, children tend to bring up each other— or they fend for themselves. I think, in Father's case, that it must have been a combination of the two. However, he developed some skills and qualities that would serve him well in his career as a lighthouse keeper. One lesson he learned was to endure isolation. Each summer, while he was still very young, he was placed on an island in the bay at Addison as a shepherd for a large flock. This must have been intolerably lonely, but, in talking about the experience, he never expressed that. He also developed his hunting and fishing skills. His skill as a young hunter helped him not only to feed the large family of which he had become a member, but also to clothe himself. Apparently it was possible then to sell the fur of black cats (presumably feral ones). He told us that this was how he got enough money for shoes or a new pair of pants for school.

We also learned from his brothers and sisters that he was no paragon. One incident happened before his parents died. When they were away one day, young Hervey and one of his friends decided to do a little "fishing" from an upstairs window. However, they were fishing not for fish but for hens that roamed the yard. They collected some string—probably leftover lobster-net twine —fashioned some hooks out of bent pins, stuck pieces of corn on them, and proceeded to lure the hens under the window by sprinkling corn there. Eventually, a hen would pick up the wrong piece of corn and find itself being whisked through the air, cackling and flapping, to an upstairs chamber. When his parents arrived home, they found their flock of hens occupying the second story. I do not recall what punishment was meted out for this prank, but apparently Father never forgot the trick. He told of later catching seagulls in the same way, on board ship. Apparently one lesson he never learned was to be kind to dumb wild animals.

Seeing Father with his close relatives, we came to know that he, too, was loved and respected by his family. The head keeper of a large offshore light station held a position of importance, and it indicated high personal achievement.

Our best off-island vacations came after my sister Hazel married George Woodward and they moved to Franklin Island and then Wood Island. It might seem strange to say that we spent our most enjoyable vacations on other islands, but often farmers go to visit other farmers and city folks go to visit friends in other cities. We were island people and we loved visiting other islands—they were different and their differences made them exciting.

I remember little about our Franklin Island vacations except that our trip to and from the station was over a choppy sea in George's small Swampscott dory. This craft seemed so small compared to our big government boat that I was always very glad when we made a safe landing. The government did not supply a boat for this one-man station; the keeper had to provide his own.

The most memorable trips were to Wood Island. Our preparations for this trip began weeks ahead. I do not know why, but our house had to be cleaned from top to bottom before we could leave. I guess Father was afraid the inspector might come during his absence. Then Mother cooked huge quantities of food to eat on the way and to help my sister feed our big family. One delicacy that Mother made was date turnovers, a date mixture folded into small pieces of pastry. They alone were almost worth the trip.

The night before our departure, we always prayed for good weather. Even before then, we prayed that Father's leave-of-absence papers would arrive on time. Frequently they were delayed, and sometimes we got as far as Starboard still without the papers in hand.

By four-thirty in the morning, we were up doing last-minute packing. Carrying all our luggage to the boathouse was hard work, but our spirits were high, even if the bags were heavy. Sometimes we left in fog so thick that Father would say, "You can't see your hands before you." But on other mornings, the sky would be clear and slightly streaked in the east with color. Birds would already be singing, particularly my favorite Tom Peabody bird, which sang, "Toooooom, Peabody, Peabody, Peabody." Later, I learned that this was the song of the white-throated sparrow, and I never hear one now that I do not think of those dawn departures from Libby. Soon we would be making the crossing, the government boat carving her way through the crystal-clear water to Starboard. Before the sun was high, we would be on our way, suitcases strapped on the sides of our touring car.

For several years, I had detested riding in touring cars, because my mother had not been willing to cut my shoulder-length curls and my hair constantly blew in my face. Not until I was five did she yield. I clearly remember the day she set up my high chair in the sewing room, carefully wrapped each curl around her finger, tied it with a small piece of ribbon, and tearfully and tenderly cut it off. It had been a long, hard struggle to convince Mother that I was no longer a baby, but at last I was a real BOY!

One of the reasons we had an open car at first was Father's distrust of cars that surrounded their occupants with glass. He vowed he would not own one, but when Hazel and George arrived for a visit with a sporty new sedan, he began to soften his stand. Much to the relief of all of us, we soon were enjoying the comfort of "closed" cars.

It was more than two hundred miles from Starboard to Biddeford Pool, George's landing place. On the first part of our journey, the roads were unpaved, and passing cars enveloped us in clouds of dust. Even people in closed cars had to ride with the windows open to keep cool. Further slowing our progress were the ferries, which carried us across the rivers in Sullivan and Bucksport. It was a great advance for travelers on Route 1 when bridges were built at these sites.

Mother always packed well-planned meals for us to have along the way. And the forested areas, of which there were many on our route, provided "natural" toilet facilities. In the early part of the journey, Father knew where there were boiling springs near the road to supply us with fresh, cool water.

I am amazed now that we were able to make that trip in one day. On our first trips, we could hardly believe the sizes of the communities we went through, and we literally did go through them—right down their main streets. Ellsworth appeared to be enormous compared to Machias. But when we got to Portland, all the towns and cities we had seen were diminished to villages. To me, growing up on an island, and having visited only Machias, the three largest cities in the United States were Portland, Bangor, and Ellsworth, in that order. Later, at eighteen, on my first trip to New York, I could hardly believe the sizes of Boston, Providence, and the Connecticut coastal cities. But New York City was beyond the imagination of a simple island lad. On the way home, the giant metropolises I had seen before seemed to have shrunk.

When we reached Biddeford Pool, George would be waiting for us. I will always wonder how Father found his way, because I do not recall seeing any road maps or route numbers—just road signs pointing to the next town. It was always late when we arrived; the trip took at least fourteen hours. Then we still had a boat trip and a half-mile walk the length of Wood Island, which was about the size of Libby. Its boathouse was on the extreme eastern end. Landing on Wood was quite different, however, because the slip was almost flat. The bank where the boathouse was located was only a few feet above high water.

Although we would be exhausted by the time we reached the house, we always had sufficient energy to respond to our big sister's warm welcome. After scrubbing off the layers of road dust, we were soon sitting around the dining room table, enjoying a bounteous meal that Sis had prepared. That first night we always slept well, even though we kids bunked on the floor—it was not easy to make room for two extra adults and four children.

We were up early the next day, all fatigue of the journey magically gone, ready to begin exploring the island. And we had a good guide. George had two children from a first marriage, and his son Coleman was between Irwin and me in age. He knew all the secrets of Wood Island. It was quite different from Libby, although one similarity was that it had almost no trees. The island was low and had no cliffs or beaches, but it did have warm water for swimming. The best place to swim was at the boathouse, where we spent a lot of time. A short distance away was Negro Island, where hundreds of gulls nested. We swam over there, although I am sure that it was not safe, because no one was around to help us if we became fatigued or had a cramp. On Negro Island we faced the hazard of diving gulls protecting their nests. They never struck us, but their dive-bomb attacks were frightening.

Having no other place to climb—and we were inveterate climbers—we explored the upper reaches of the boathouse. Here I sustained an injury that taught me a lifelong lesson. I jumped from one of the top levels to the floor and landed with such force that my knee came up and hit my upper lip. I sustained a bad bruise that became a gigantic scab. When we went back to the mainland, I suddenly became aware that other kids were looking at me, then slyly calling their mothers' attention to the strange-looking boy they had just seen. It was embarrassing, but I learned what life was like for a person who has a handicap or visible disfigurement.

Another different opportunity on Wood was the chance to fish from the rocks. On Libby we always had to use a boat, but here we could throw in a line almost anywhere and haul in small fish called cunners. Apparently these fish did not wander into the cold waters off Libby. Pollock were the only fish of this type we were able to catch there.

A second exciting feature of Wood Island was a collection of houses presumed to be haunted. The light station had been established in 1808, making it one of the oldest on the Maine coast. At some time during this early period, the island had been farmed and the remains of several houses were still standing. Wood Island had an unsavory reputation among the local folk; it was a good thing we did not know much about the murders, the drowned sailors, and the misfortune that seemed to befall anyone who lived there. We just enjoyed exploring the ruins and imagining all sorts of mysterious happenings.

Father enjoyed these trips, and he and George spent a lot of time discussing lighthouse business. Being a keeper on a station like this was a far different assignment from Libby. Wood Island was a one-man station with a light and a fog bell. The bell was powered by a weight hoisted to the top of a conical tower. There were no watches to stand and little fog. The island is in a relatively protected area only a short row from the mainland. But it can become a treacherous place in storms, because the water is shallow, causing seas to break nearly everywhere around the

Keeper Wass with Tim. The object that looks like a pipe in his right hand is an oil can. (Father's solution to all mechanical problems was to "put some oil on it." This applied not only to heavy machinery but also to our toys.) He is wearing his lightkeeper's cap, which was unusual—perhaps he donned it for the picture—but he nearly always wore the white cotton gloves.

When the men finally refused to use the unsafe government boat any longer, it was replaced by this one. The occasion was one of the few times we had company on Libby. The man walking up the runway was Pastor Newman Wilson, from Jonesport. The ladies in the bow are his wife and daughter, and the other passengers were friends who accompanied them.

I took the upper photograph and developed it myself when I was about twelve. It was taken from the top of the tower and shows the layout of the dwellings. The house in the foreground was ours; by 1980, when the photo below was taken, it was the only house still standing. The white line extending out from the building was the sink drain, which emptied onto the ground. Just beyond that, the square object on the post was the mirror Father used to keep an eye on the light while he was on watch.

Mabel Wass, Philmore, and
Keeper Hervey H. Wass, 1921.

We children spent many hours at the saltwater pond. Our boats were quite exact replicas of the workboats of the time. Left to right: Irwin, Millie Foss, Arlona, and Philmore. Junie Foss is standing in front. In back are Leo Foss and my cousin, Orrie Crowley, who lived with us for a time.

The tower and whistlehouse. This photo was taken after the fog signal had been converted from coal to diesel; the tanks held the diesel oil.

This is how the slip and boathouse looked from an approaching boat. The white structure to the right was a bulkhead to protect the slip from cross seas.

Winona, Irwin, and Philmore astride Katie. George Woodward, the Second Assistant Keeper who married Hazel, stands at Katie's head.

Justin and Ada Foss.

A picnic at the black sand beach. Father, Philmore, Mother, Winona, Irwin, and George Woodward. (Hazel took the photograph.) Note the lobster tail protruding from the bucket.

Ada and Leo Foss, Mrs. Sargent, cousin Orrie, Irwin, Mrs. Sargent's daughter, Winona, and Arlona and Millie Foss. We were sitting on the bulkhead at the slip watching the *Hibiscus* unload. I believe it was on this same day that Arlona fell off the bulkhead.

Irwin at age thirteen.

Philmore, Mother, Winona, Irwin, and Father setting off with the picnic bucket.

Philmore at ages five (left) and eight (right).

Our boathouse and slip had little protection from wind and waves. Although the bulkheads usually prevented seas from breaking across the slip, especially severe storms could wipe out the timbers, making our landings and launchings even more precarious—and sometimes impossible.

The tower and whistlehouse as they now stand.

island. Many ships were wrecked here during the heyday of coastal trading.

Mother enjoyed visiting her older daughter, helping her with the meals and knitting and crocheting while talking about family matters.

The highlight of any trip to Wood Island was a visit to nearby Old Orchard Beach, where there was an amusement park. The family had talked about this magic place, but at first I could not quite understand what it was. My original image of it was of an actual orchard, with gray, gnarled trees. But when we looked across the bay at night and saw the brightly lighted area along the beach, it certainly did not look like an old orchard. What a wondrous experience it was to visit my first amusement park. I still remember Noah's Ark, electric bumper cars, and, most of all, the roller coaster. Washington County had no such exciting parks.

On our trips to see Hazel and George, we often stopped in South Portland on Day Street to visit Aunt Nettie and Uncle Will Merritt. Father and Aunt Nettie were very close, having shared the experience of losing their parents when they were very young and joining a large family of which they were not really members.

Aunt Nettie, through great good fortune and wise judgment, had married William Merritt, who was intelligent and ambitious. He went to sea as a young man, and it was not very long before he became captain of a ship. This created a turning point in Father's life around 1893. What a thrill it must have been for a twenty-year-old man with little work experience to be asked by a highly respected uncle, "Hervey, how would you like to go to sea with me next spring?"

I cannot even imagine Father's elation. Here was his chance to make something of himself. He had tried blacksmithing, but decided that that career was not for him—although he learned many skills that were useful later in lighthouse work.

Most of the coastal trading schooners were tied up during the winter months, so Father and Uncle Will set off for Boston in the spring. His experiences during the next ten years greatly expanded his horizons. Places like New York, Baltimore, Newport

News, Charleston, and Vera Cruz (Mexico) became very familiar to him. He was following a long tradition of young Maine men. During the previous century, there were countless small-town Maine men (and women who accompanied their husbands) who knew nearly every port in the world and many who had been around it several times. Father never had the opportunity to explore as far as that, but he traveled much farther than most of his contemporaries. A few decades later, not many young men knew more than their local waters—except for the few who might have "run" lobsters to Boston from Nova Scotia. Nor would these new generations have any of the skills that had enabled their ancestors to take five-masted schooners around Cape Horn. The coast of Maine, which once played such a vital role in world trade by building and manning ships, in the twentieth century became a very provincial place where most people's horizons were limited by the boundaries of their towns.

Father was soon appointed chief engineer on his ship, in charge of all the steam engines and hoisting apparatus used to raise sails and to load and unload cargo—a very responsible position for a young man. As I mentioned earlier, these skills also served him well in operating the boat-hoisting machinery and the steam boilers we uses to blow the fog signal on Libby.

During one year in Camden, Maine, Father helped to build a five-masted schooner, the *Jennie French Potter,* and then sailed on her as chief engineer. We always felt we knew this ship well, because Father kept a large picture of her in his office. It now hangs in my study. I never knew why Father left Uncle Will's employ—perhaps to better himself. Certainly there was never any rift between them.

Listening to Father talk with Uncle Will was quite different from hearing his conversations with other relatives. True, they sometimes told hunting stories, but they also talked about their experiences at sea. Observing them together, we became aware of the close relationship they shared. Later, we came to realize that Uncle Will became the father young Hervey never had, and from him he gained many of his skills and ideals. Perhaps we, too, were indebted to this man who exemplified honesty and clean living. He never smoked nor used alcohol, an example that Father followed and that has been passed down through our family. Although many ship's crewmen during those years were rough characters, Father followed his own set of ideals. He always told us, "When you find yourself in a new place, don't go to bars, go to church. That is where you will meet good people." Of course, we knew little about bars since this was during Prohibition, but we got the message. I can just imagine young Hervey, finding himself in a strange port, getting dressed up on a Sunday morning and heading for church. He did make good friends that way.

Some of the stories swapped by these two former sailors enthralled us. Uncle Will was a large man, with both the size and the determination to enforce his orders as captain. One day, as he came up out of his cabin, he looked down on both sides of the companionway. On one side he saw a sailor with a knife in his teeth and on the other side, an antagonist carrying a belaying pin, which was used to secure rigging. Without hesitating, he reached down on both sides and grabbed each of them by the collar with his huge hands. Then he brought their heads together in a mighty crash and dragged them off to the brig. This kind of story was far more exciting than hunting tales about the big buck that got away.

A story we loved to hear Uncle Will tell was the tale of his ship being sunk by a German submarine after World War I. All during the war, he had made regular runs up and down the coast and to ports in South America. German submarines were on the prowl, but he never encountered one until after the Armistice. He was sailing off Newport News, Virginia, when a submarine surfaced. The German U-boat captain apparently had not been notified that the war was over, for he ordered Captain Merritt to abandon ship. Uncle Will, having no other options, ordered his men into the lifeboats, and they all rowed clear. The German sailors then boarded his ship, wired her with explosives—

apparently they were out of torpedoes—and blew her up. Uncle Will was a gifted storyteller, and he told this tragic tale with such humor that we always thought of it as rather funny. The humor came when he described the sheer panic on the part of the sailors who went out in Coast Guard and naval vessels to hunt down the sub. He said they were dropping so many shells— which went rolling around their decks—that they were in more danger from each other than from the Germans.

But the tragedy was revealed starkly in two pictures taken by one of the navy men. The photographs hung on the walls of our home for many years. The first showed smoke pouring from several openings of the proud five-master and the bow settling slightly. The second showed more smoke and the ship tipped at a sharp angle just before she made her final plunge. I suspect that Uncle Will made a great deal of money during the war with this ship, which I believe he owned, so he probably could afford to lose her. After the war, sailing vessels were of little value. I believe that later he was recompensed for his loss through reparations from the German government.

Uncle Will also seemed to be sensitive to the needs of us kids. One afternoon, when he must have noted we were getting restless, he asked us if we would like to go to a movie and a show in Portland. We, of course, needed no urging. The Keith Theatre, which had both movies and a vaudeville act, was our destination. Uncle Will's daughter, Florence, with great skill, maneuvered Uncle Will's large touring car through the traffic to a parking space near the theatre. I can still remember the scent of the leather upholstery in that fine car. The movie, too, was unforgettable: *Lobo the Wolf*.

We always enjoyed visiting Uncle Will and Aunt Nettie in their large, comfortable home. It was sturdy, as any sea captain's home would be, and I presume it still stands. Knowing them gave us another window on the large world beyond our island's shores.

Although I later would have the opportunity to visit places of interest in many parts of the world, the thrills and excitement of these trips have never exceeded the joy of our early island-to-island vacations. Returning to Libby after one of our journeys, life always seemed a little dull, but it was always good to be home, and we soon settled back happily into our island routines.

9

ANIMALS SERVED AND ENTERTAINED US

OUR cow and our horse were so inseparable that as a child I always thought they were mates, and I concluded the same thing about cats and dogs, although they were not nearly as compatible. So when the cow showed up at the barn one day without Tim, our horse, and no one could remember having seen him for several hours, we became concerned and started a search. The search did not take long. Behind the barn was a steep gulch with two small promontories extending into it and a green grassy area created by the excess water drainage just above it. In the grass were deep grooves that made us suspicious. We carefully eased our way down this slope, looked over the edge, and saw Tim—on the beach where he had fallen. Although he appeared to be hurt, he was still alive, and the next problem was to get him out. Father, having done a lot of hoisting in his years at sea, devised a way to do it, but he knew he would need help.

The Coast Guard on Cross Island quickly responded to his emergency call, sending over a boat with a crew of men. Fortunately, it was a calm day, so they could make a landing on the beach where Tim had fallen. High above Tim, Father and one crewman were able to arrange a heavy timber to bridge the gap between the two cliffs. Then they fashioned a sling out of heavy canvas. The crew at the bottom got Tim to his feet and slid the sling under his belly. Father then lowered a hook with pulleys and heavy ropes, which they secured to the canvas. Now came the moment of truth. Could a horse weighing many hundreds of pounds be lifted to the top of the cliff and swung to where he could get a footing on the grass? The men below put a strain on the lines but stayed well clear so Tim would not come crashing down on them if something let go. It was a tense moment. Slowly but surely they raised him—his body swinging slowly back and forth, his head up, and his eyes all white with fear. When he was well on his way to the top of the cliff, Tim suddenly let out a great sigh and slumped. His whole body went limp and his head hung down to his hooves. The strain and the fall had been too much for his old heart. Tim had expired.

There was no need to hoist any longer, so the men lowered Tim's body slowly, and it fell in a heap on the sand. Since there was no place to inter him, burial at sea seemed the obvious way of disposing of his remains. Fastening a line securely around his body, the men carried the end of it out to their boat and turned on the engines full force. Tim began his slow "march to the sea," and soon he was afloat. They towed him well clear of the island, gave him an appropriate salute, and set him adrift. Fortunately, the tide was ebbing, and soon he was spinning slowly toward the horizon. I hope that, with the help of various sea creatures, his body disintegrated rapidly. Otherwise, the occupants of a ship striking it in the night would have had a real surprise.

I am told that I expressed my sympathy and concern for old Tim that night at the supper table. With tears in my eyes, I allegedly said, "Poor old Tim fell down in the gulch and hurt his tern [stern]." Tim was commemorated on Libby by having the gulch where he had fallen named "Tim's Gulch."

Father always needed to have a horse to haul coal, oil, and other supplies from the boathouse—where the lighthouse tender landed them—to the storage areas in each home and in the whistlehouse. Since the work was light and infrequent, Father looked on the mainland for horses that were close to "retirement." If they were basically sound, the easy life on Libby would extend their lives by several years.

Katie, our second horse, was a slow-moving chestnut, obviously on her last legs. Living the good life on Libby, she revived and served us for several years. But she also grazed too close to the edge of a cliff near the Tip-End, and one day she fell off. As with Tim, when we missed her, we organized a search party. Soon we found her on the sand at the bottom of a fifteen-foot embankment. She was standing, obviously not hurt. We all returned to the house to help Father carry down some block and tackle. As we drew close to the gulch again, we could not believe what we saw: Katie was grazing contentedly on the rich green grass, obviously unperturbed by her adventure. We never could figure out how she had managed to climb back up the embankment and greatly admired her courage in doing so. Perhaps she had more energy than she ever revealed to us. (The only time we ever saw Katie move fast was when our cousin Orrie took long-distance aim and fired a BB gun at her. Orrie was horrified when her shot actually hit the target, and so was Katie. She took off at a gallop for the other end of the island.) Even though Katie was not hurt from her fall, we commemorated her dramatic self-rescue by naming the area "Katie's Gulch." We never made a conscious decision to name these places for our two horses, but when we wanted to mention one of those areas, it was easy to refer to it as the gulch where Tim or Katie fell over the cliff. Eventually it became easier to apply their names directly.

Father's last horse was the one we remember most vividly. As usual, he let it be known on the mainland that he was looking for a horse in its declining years, and soon he had a call. On our next trip ashore, Father went to see Maude, and she looked ideal for Libby—rather docile, gaunt, but still looking basically sound. Arrangements were made for purchase and transportation. Soon Maude was roaming around at will on Libby, enjoying complete leisure and a diet of probably the richest grass she had ever grazed on.

We paid little attention to our horse and our cow—they were just there, part of the island scenery. Of course, the cow had to be brought to the barn morning and evening for milking, and, occasionally, when we had something to haul, I was given the job of going to get the horse.

One day, knowing Father intended to use Maude in a day or two to haul supplies, I decided to see where she was feeding. I found her standing high on a bluff behind the barn, looking shoreward into the wind. I could not believe my eyes. With her mane blowing, her neck arched, and her nostrils flaring, she was a magnificent horse. In her few months on Libby, she had filled out, her air of defeat had disappeared, and she looked like a wild mare in a western movie. I went and got Father so he could see her. He was as surprised as I, remembering the dispirited creature he had led from Bucks Harbor down to Starboard and brought by boat out to Libby. He decided that at last we had a good horse on Libby, but he was in for a real surprise!

A few days later, Father asked me to bring Maude to the barn. I followed my usual procedure, got a rope and a halter, and went looking for the horse. I had no difficulty finding her. When she saw me, she threw her head in the air and started moving away slowly. Every time I approached, she stepped away just out of reach. I decided that the only way I could catch her was to find a place near the fence where I could corner her. I was getting tired of this game, which she seemed to enjoy. Slowly I herded her toward a corner, and when she could go no further, she surrendered meekly and let me put on the halter. Feeling quite proud of myself and Maude, I led her to the barn, where Father was waiting for me. He had opened the barn doors where the wagon was kept so he could back Maude in between the shafts.

First Father put on her harness, well worn and patched from many years of use. Maude graciously accepted the bit in her mouth and Father then backed her up so he could fasten the pulling section of the harness to the wagon. I was rather relieved

to see that the horse appeared docile through all of this, showing none of the spirit that I had detected when she was cavorting
about the fields.

I noted that Father had been cautious as he had worked around
Maude, and he did not climb to the cart seat when all was in
readiness. He stood a little to one side, lightly flipped the reins
on her back, and quietly said, "Giddap!" Maude reared on her
hind legs, stood almost straight up, and then made a giant leap
forward. Expecting something like this, Father kept a firm grip
on the reins. With another leap, Maude fell to the ground, hopelessly entangled in the now-broken harness. Expecting to have to
deal with a wild, kicking horse, Father stood well away, but
Maude never moved. She did roll up her eyes as if to say, "Well,
you got me into this mess. Now get me out." I felt sorry for her,
lying there, her great chestnut sides heaving more from fear than
from exhaustion.

Cautiously, Father loosened the harness from the wagon. Then,
again standing clear, he pulled gently on the reins. Maude got to
her feet and stood quietly as if nothing had happened. Father,
seeing that she was not vicious, patted her nose and then carefully took off the harness and releasd her. She trotted away
quickly and joined the cow, as if nothing had happened. She
obviously was not hurt—except for her dignity. The same could
not be said for the harness, which needed major repairs.

Father knew he had a problem on his hands, and he determined, the next time he went ashore, to learn more about Maude's
history. What he learned explained her strange behavior. She
had been raised, along with another colt, as a pet, never having
been broken to a harness or wagon. Evidently the owner had died,
so the horses, fully grown, had been sold. The new owner apparently had starved them and worked them into submission. By
teaming up each of them with another horse, he had been able to
use them in the woods for hauling logs. This easily accounted for
Maude's strange actions. She was a pet until harnessed to a wagon. This was a frightening experience for her, so she bolted, but
never with any intention of inflicting harm.

A short time after this, Howard Colbeth, the government worker, was on the island doing repairs. When he heard about our problem horse, he said he had had lots of experience with horses. He agreed to tame Maude for us. For several weeks, Howard "courted" Maude— fed her many pounds of sugar lumps—and finally announced that he and Maude had come to an understanding. He was sure that, after all his kindness, she would cooperate and pull the wagon peaceably.

The next day, he brought Maude up to the barn, where Father had just the front wheels waiting. He did not want to risk his whole wagon. Again, with no evidence of alarm, Maude backed into the shafts and allowed herself to be fitted into Father's newly repaired harness. Howard talked to her soothingly all the while. The entire island population had gathered to see the "show," but we all kept well in the background.

Howard took a turn around his hands with the reins (a mistake), stepped to one side clear of the wheels, and, with a gentle, soothing, "Giddap," flicked the reins. With the memory of all the torment she must have suffered surging through her brain, Maude leaped forward, dragging the two cart wheels and Howard behind her. She headed straight for the nearby pasture fence and crashed through it, breaking free of both Howard and the cart. Howard was fortunate not to be hurt. After that episode, he said very little about his ability as a tamer of wayward horses.

Father decided to consult with horse experts on the mainland. They had many different suggestions, particularly about types of harness fittings and bits useful in controlling spirited horses. One that I recall was a martingale, designed to keep a horse from putting its head up to bolt. Another was a W bit, which, when pressure was exerted on the reins, opened up, spreading inside the mouth and inflicting great pain.

Being a kindhearted man, Father must have hated to use these devices, but he had to haul supplies. Using all his new controls, he was able to force Maude to work. Obviously, she was not happy about it, but her hurt overcame her fear. It saddened me to see this spirited creature subdued, sometimes with blood oozing from the corners of her mouth. We thought she had submitted, but we were wrong; she was just awaiting her chance to escape.

One of Father's major tasks was to haul barrels of oil for the fog signal from the boathouse to the whistlehouse. This required the help of a horse. Heavily loaded and held in place with a greatly strengthened harness, Maude was behaving quite well. I am sure Father thought he had won in this battle of wills—until the day that Maude seized another opportunity to gain her freedom. On a return trip to the boathouse, Father always loaded in a cartful of empty barrels, which were tied in place with cord. During a moment when Father's attention was distracted, Maude bolted. Why she did not go straight down the road where she always went, no one knows. Instead, she headed straight up a rather steep incline toward the tower. Rather than going to the inside of the tower, she swerved to the right—to the outside, where there was only a narrow strip of land between the tower and cliff. The lightly loaded wagon was swerving from side to side. When she reached the tower and saw the cliff's edge, she swung sharply to the left, but the centrifugal force sent the cart sailing out in the opposite direction. The harness held the cart, but Father's cord did not hold the empty barrels. They flew into the air and over the edge of the cliff, bounded off the rocks forty feet below, and either went rolling into the sea or were smashed. What a sight! Never had such a spectacle occurred on Libby, and I am glad I was there to see it. Fortunately, harness and cart held together, and after Maude had exhausted herself in her dash around the island, Father was able to lead her back to the barn, take off her harness, and set her free again. Maude had won another round.

But Father refused to give in. Besides, the oil had to be hauled. It was his responsibility. Up to this time little had been said about Maude's escapades being dangerous. Howard was the only person who had come close to getting hurt. But now there was talk about danger to the children, should Maude break loose near where they might be playing.

A few weeks later, Father was ready for the return trip with empty barrels when Maude again bolted. This time, having gone the tower route before, she again avoided the road, which she apparently had come to dislike, and headed down through a narrow passage between our house and a fenced gulch. No one knew how they happened to be there, but two small children were playing in this confined area.

When they saw Maude bearing down on them, the children ran toward the house. This might not have saved them, but since the cart was swerving from side to side, it moved away at just the right time. They were saved purely by chance. Everyone was horrified at what might have happened.

I do not think Father used Maude after that. I cannot recall her final end, but I suspect another island horse was given a burial at sea. Fortunately, most of the oil had been hauled by this time.

Maude was the last horse we had on Libby. Father decided it was time to modernize, so he bought an old Model T Ford truck. We could not believe it—an automobile on Libby Island. To transport it, we had to build a platform across the sides of a seine boat, and another to get the truck off and into the boathouse, but Father, being good at engineering such projects, managed to get the truck landed safely. Knowing nothing about cantankerous Model Ts, Father found his new truck almost as frustrating as Maude had been, but by consulting Model T "experts," he somehow got the truck to run long enough to haul the supplies. But "she" never was half as much fun as Maude.

As I mentioned in chapter 5, during most of the years we lived on Libby, we kept a cow, and sometimes one of the other keepers also kept one. Later, when we were on the mainland going to school, Father decided that the cow required too much work, so he resorted to what we considered a poor substitute: canned milk.

After several months of lactation, cows gradually dry up. We knew nothing about this process, but we did know that Father frequently would buy a young bull on the mainland and bring him to Libby to freshen our cow. The resulting calf gave us a "beef critter" to slaughter in the fall. Its carcass was kept frozen in the barn and used as needed. Bringing out the bull nearly always created some excitement, and I remember one incident particularly well. Father and Justin Foss went through their usual procedure of borrowing a seine boat to bring out the newest bull. They landed at the "cowhole," led him off the boat and up the beach, then let him go. He raced for the grassy top of the island and took a run around a high knoll. At that point, he turned and faced the mainland. Apparently deciding he did not like island life, he let out a loud bellow and headed for the water. Before Father could stop him, he jumped in and started swimming for Starboard. It took considerable time to launch a peapod and overtake him. As he swam in the waves, rolling from side to side, his feet would come out of water—like the propeller of a motorboat in high seas—and he would kick the air. When they reached him, he had swallowed a considerable amount of water. Putting a rope around his neck, they pulled him back to the island. When he got out of the water, he was no longer so lively, but they did not let him loose. Instead, one of the men led him to the barn and locked him in. To be sure that he would forget his longing for mainland life, they kept him incarcerated for three weeks. After that, he joined our island cows and seemed quite contented.

Some of the bulls that came to the island seemed to resent their loss of freedom—or perhaps they were just plain ornery. Anyway, they liked to chase us kids, so we had to keep our eyes on them if we were in the pasture, which of course covered much of the island. Once when Roland Cheney was walking up from the bar and went to step up on the grass, he found himself facing a snorting, pawing bull. Everywhere he went to try to get up on the island, the bull blocked his way. Finally, he found a fence that extended down almost to the water and was able to get around the end and out of the pasture.

Since we kids assumed that the horse and the cow were mates, we never made any connection between the cow and the bull. We knew that from time to time calves appeared, and we loved them, but when we asked where they came from, we were told that the cow or the bull dug them out of the earth-covered stumps that abounded on the island. Since they both did a lot of pawing at these old stumps, this explanation sounded reasonable.

We never had a cow fall off a cliff—perhaps they were more intelligent that the horses—but one cow gave birth to her calf on the edge of a bank, and it went rolling onto the rocks below. Fortunately, someone found it quickly and was able to bring it back to its mother. Even that did not alert us to the true purpose of the bull or to where the calves came from. We thought the cow had dug into a stump too close to the edge of the island.

These bulls also were a part of our winter food supply. When December came and it was cold enough to freeze meat, Father would butcher the animals and divide the meat among whichever families had contributed to their cost. By this process, our food supply was augmented considerably during the cold winter months when rough seas made it difficult to go ashore. Besides, it was comforting, and sometimes entertaining, to have cows in the pasture—even though the bulls sometimes resented our intrusions. They were company.

Dogs were very much a part of our island life, and we never were without one. The first was Sport, the mongrel cocker spaniel we got on one of our boat trips to Addison to visit Father's and Mother's relatives. Sport never grew to be very large. I do not remember that he was especially friendly, but I do have some clear memories of him.

One winter, Father spent many hours making Irwin a miniature set of sleds similar to those used to haul logs in the woods. There were two small sleds with a frame running across them to carry logs, ice, and other cargo. Irwin had wanted the sled so he could harness Sport to it and do some "freighting." Father and Mother had also made a dog harness, probably out of old rubber boot tops. Finally, all was ready for the first big freight run. Sport (not enthusiastically) allowed himself to be harnessed to the sled, and he and Irwin took off down to the beaches for a load of mussels to feed to the hens. The trip went without incident, and soon I saw them coming up through the snow-covered grass, Sport straining at his load but hauling it obediently. Irwin deposited his cargo and was just about to start off for another when someone let the cat out. Sport had never liked the cat—or perhaps he just liked to chase her. In one great leap, he wrested himself out of Irwin's grasp and took off after her. When the chase was finished, so were Irwin's sleds. As I recall, there was not even enough left to repair.

This was not the only unpleasant encounter Irwin had with Sport, who loved to follow him around. No matter where Irwin was, Sport could follow his trail and "smell him out." One day, Irwin was sitting in the outhouse, probably looking at the Sears, Roebuck catalog. Sport, having picked up Irwin's trail, was following it with great enthusiasm when he encountered the closed outhouse door. With one leap, Sport burst open the door, exposing Irwin, who was very embarrassed. In a burst of anger, he grabbed Sport by the scruff of the neck and stuffed him down the hole next to him, which was "papa size." The minute he did this, Irwin regretted his rash action, because there was no way to get Sport out except by the same way he went in. So Irwin had to reach down, grab him by the scruff of the neck once again, and haul him up through the toilet hole. Sport emerged, kicking and whining, totally decorated with excrement and Sears pages.

To add to Irwin's embarrassment, just as he opened the door to the outhouse, Father appeared. After Irwin told him what he had done and why, Father was very amused. He did not scold Irwin but told him to give Sport a bath, because he was going hunting and would need a clean dog. So Irwin had to get a bucket of water and soap and give his hunting dog a bath. Then all three of them went off on the hunt.

I had heard that story all my life, but I never knew, until I began writing this book, why Irwin had played this "dirty" trick on his dog.

Sport had one very strange trait—he loved to dive under water and retrieve rocks. Whenever we took him near the Salt Water Pond, he would dive and retrieve one rock after another. It was a compulsion, and as he grew older, his teeth were all worn down, which made him a very poor bird dog. He could not hold a bird if he caught one.

Sport was replaced by a springer spaniel that we named, appropriately, Springer, but he would never spring after anything—especially the birds we had shot. Although these spaniels usually are excellent retrievers, our dog could not be trained, so Father took him back to the farmer where he got him. He then bought another dog, an Irish rattailed water spaniel. When we got the puppy, she was a tiny ball of curly, chocolate-brown fur. It was love at first sight. We soon knew that we would cherish this dog—and we did, through most of our childhood on Libby. Arnie named the dog Peter Pan, but of course the Pan was quickly dropped. (And since Peter was a boy's name, most of the time we thought of Peter as a "he.")

When we had to leave the island to go to school, we missed Father, but we missed Peter just as much. When we returned, they were both equally glad to see us—and we, them. Peter and Father became so close, sharing the same domicile over so many years, that we were always sure they could communicate.

They communicated especially well when hunting. Peter was an excellent hunting dog and she enjoyed the hunt as much as Father did. At the slightest indication that Father was going to the bar to hunt for ducks, Peter would start cavorting around the kitchen. All Father had to do was to walk to the corner where the guns were stored and Peter would be on her feet. Then, if he went to the cupboard and took out shotgun shells, she would run for the door, ready to go. It was very humiliating to me, as a beginning hunter, to realize that I could make exactly the same moves and Peter would open her eyes, look at me, and then go back to sleep.

Hunting ducks required great skill on the part of both the hunter and his dog. To approach tidal pools where ducks might be feeding, Father had to crawl several hundred yards over slippery rockweed on his hands and knees and—for his final approach—on his stomach. Peter seemed to know instinctively that she too had to keep low and to stay behind him. When the ducks took flight, with a great "whoosh" of wings, Father would pick the lead duck and work his way back in the flock. The gun would spout fire, smoke, and lead shot. With each blast, a duck would fall and a bright red shotgun-shell casing would fly out of the magazine.

With the first shot, Peter would spring into action. Some of the birds might land in the water and she would retrieve those first. By this time, it would often be near dark, which was dangerous for Peter, especially when she tried to pursue a crippled bird into heavy surf. A bird with only slight wing damage would wait until it was almost within Peter's grasp, then flap away, each time going farther offshore.

One cold winter night, Father was sure that he had lost Peter when she pursued a bird out of sight. He called repeatedly, but his voice was drowned out by the crashing waves. Heartbroken, he returned home, convinced that he would never see Peter again. There was no joy when he entered the kitchen with the ducks but without Peter. Supper that night was a sad affair. As we all sat in subdued silence, we heard a light scratching at the door. It was Peter, ice still clinging to her curly brown coat. She was exhausted but unhurt. Had she been lost, our lives on Libby would have been far less satisfying.

Peter was a rare breed, and I have no idea how the man who sold her to Father happened to be breeding them. I never saw one anywhere else until about 1968, when I walked into a sailboat showroom and one came bounding over to greet me. I could hardly believe my eyes. The owner of the shop said he had two, and that there were only about two hundred of them in the United States.

Capturing baby crows and ravens and raising them as pets was common among country boys in Maine when we were growing up. One day, when we were returning to Libby from Starboard, we heard two ravens calling loudly and flying around the western head of Stone Island. Going in close to investigate, we saw the problem. Their nest, built on a shelf high on the cliff, had been dislodged and had fallen into the water. One baby raven was dead, apparently drowned, but the other was flapping around in the water, very much alive. After several unsuccessful attempts, Father managed to catch it. Having had a pet crow himself as a child, he wanted us to have a similar experience, so he decided to take the raven home to try to raise it. Our new pet gave some trouble on the way, trying to escape, so Father finally tied it to one of the seats.

Not knowing what to feed Billy, as Irwin had named him, Father suggested bread and milk. Apparently Billy thrived on this, because he soon matured and took to his wings. A raven is nearly twice the size of a crow, it croaks rather than caws, and in flight it maneuvers its wings like a hawk, alternating between flapping and soaring. Crows flap their wings steadily.

Billy was free on the island, but he showed no desire to leave and seemed to enjoy joining in our activities. When we were picking cranberries, we would hear a whir of wings and he would land near us and come waddling over to see what we were doing. When he discovered we were picking the bright red berries, he would watch our fingers and try to grab a berry before we did. He did not swallow these berries—he stored them in his crop. When no more would fit, he would fly away a few feet and disgorge them deep in the vines—undoubtedly for later enjoyment. A favorite game we played with him was "catch," using cranberries. He would almost never miss one, even when he was ten or fifteen feet away and we threw them over his head. He merely flew up and caught them on the wing.

Billy was not all fun. Sometimes he was a nuisance, especially when he followed us on our hunting trips. On one occasion, Irwin and Peter had been successful in killing a duck. Rather than carry it, Irwin hid it behind a rock, because he knew that ravens are scavengers and will pick clean anything that they find. Spotting a flock of oldsquaws swimming close to the shore, he left and started stalking them, but apparently they smelled or saw him and swam away. It was very cold and the wind was blowing hard, so Irwin and Peter huddled together in the shelter of a rock before starting the long walk home. Suddenly, they looked up and were surprised to see feathers floating in the air. They ran as fast as they could over the slippery rocks and found Billy astride their duck, ripping out the feathers with his beak. Having picked off all the breast feathers, he was just about to begin feasting. Croaking loudly in protest, he took to the air. The duck was saved.

On another hunting trip, knowing Billy's tricks, Irwin hid the duck much more carefully and then took Peter for a long walk over to Big Libby. On the way home, they crossed on the other side of the bar, so Irwin sent Peter after the duck. She always remembered where birds were hidden, or could smell them, and would bring them back without a toothmark, but this time she did not return. After waiting a long time, Irwin decided to go see what had happened to Peter. Just before he got to the hiding place, he saw Peter coming toward him, acting very ashamed because she was bringing a skeleton, not the plump duck they had left. Only the head and feet remained—the bones had been picked clean. Peter must have been reluctant to bring in the "remains" for fear that she would be blamed for the sorry state of her master's duck.

Except for his relationship with our family, particularly Irwin, Billy lived the life of a wild bird. He had selected a shelf of rock near one of the beaches as his lair, thus giving him some protection from the cold and snow. One day he alighted on the railing outside the kitchen door and began to croak, begging for food. Irwin went out with five soda crackers, which he put down on the snow, wondering how Billy would handle them. Much to his surprise, Billy kept picking them up and putting them down, until finally he put one on top of another. Apparently this was what he had been trying to accomplish. After that, he quickly placed the others on the pile. Then, using his underbill like a forklift, he scooped up all five and flew off home to enjoy them in comfort.

Billy entertained us for many hours with his antics, but he had one very bad habit: lighting on our rainshed roof and depositing his droppings on the shingles. This could not be tolerated, since some of the rain from this roof went directly into gutters to fill cisterns from which we got our drinking water. Irwin had the unpleasant task of taking a broom and a bucket of water and climbing up on the roof to clean up the mess. I do not quite see how this prevented the residue from reaching our water supply, and perhaps Father did not either, so a decision had to be made. We heard that a family on a nearby island was interested in having a raven for a pet. Fortunately, the island was some distance away. So we had to say a sorrowful goodbye to Billy, who had added an element of unique interest to our island life. Father had been right—keeping a raven was a wonderful experience.

Another unforgettable experience with animals did not occur on our island but on Big Libby. The sheep that were left there all winter had no caretaker. But the feed was good because the snow cover was light, and a simple building had been provided for their shelter.

After a storm, Father and Irwin were on one of their frequent gunning trips and crossed the bar over onto Big Libby. The snowstorm the night before had been severe, with high winds, and the blowing snow had created huge drifts off the edge of the island. As they were walking along Big Libby's shoreline, awed by the enormous wall of snow that had formed, they noticed something even more strange: motion in the snowdrift. They quickly went to investigate and found twenty-six sheep huddling together, almost invisible in the deep snow. Retreating from the biting winds, they had somehow gone over the island's edge and stayed there, partially protected from the cold but not from the snow. Moving about continually, trying to keep warm, they had trodden the snow into a solid ice-covered pack, four or five feet deep. Two of the sheep apparently had laid down, while the others continued to pack snow around them. Only their heads were sticking out. Father and Irwin knew that they had to free these two sheep to save them from suffocation. The only object they could find for chopping ice was a long bolt left from the wreck of the *John C.*

Myers. They cut around the sheep until they were free, but the animals could not stand up, because their wool was weighted down with ice and their legs apparently were paralyzed.

The next problem was getting all the sheep up through the drift, which had a sheer face and extended about ten feet beyond the island's edge. Father and Irwin knew that they first had to make a near-vertical path through this snowbank. After a lot of tromping with their feet—since they had no shovels—they finally broke through. Father, from his boyhood experience as an island shepherd, knew that a flock of sheep almost automatically would follow a leader. But apparently he had forgotten that if, for some reason, they did not follow, the leader would quickly become lonely and rejoin its friends. Father decided that if they could get one sheep through the snow to firm ground, the others would follow its lead. They selected a sturdy-looking potential leader and pushed him with enormous effort through the drift, until he finally was on solid ground. Separated from his mates, who showed no inclination to follow him, this "leader" ran around frantically for a few minutes. Then, looking down and seeing all his friends below, he gave a mighty leap and disappeared completely into the giant snowbank. It took Irwin and Father a half hour of frantic digging to extricate this "fallen leader"; otherwise, he would have suffocated.

In their next attempt to save the flock, Father and Irwin got three of them in a line on their "road" and pushed them up onto the bank. With company, these sheep stayed there, and, with a little encouragement, the others (except for the two that had been frozen down) quickly climbed up what now was a well-defined path. The only way to get the last two up was to carry them. That was a real struggle, but finally they also were up on the island. These two were still quite incapacitated, so Father put them close together behind a large rock, hoping their strength would return. Nothing more could be done for them, and already the flooding tide had almost closed the gut. Even though thoroughly chilled and exhausted from their exertion, they knew they had saved twenty-six sheep from almost certain death.

This gave them a warm feeling to counteract the cold and an exciting story to tell when they reached home.

The next day, they went back in the peapod with a load of hay and found the sheep in about the same location. To their amazement, the only way they could tell the "frozen" ones was by the extra ice on their coats. In the spring, the owner of the flock, having heard about the rescue, presented Father with a lamb. This was the only sheep we ever had on Libby. Its wool supplied us with several pairs of warm mittens. Also, it was fun to have another animal to observe and care for. And even though Peter had chased the sheep on big Libby, she never tried to harm our new pet. A solitary sheep—or even two, when Junie was later given one—apparently did not trigger her hunting instincts.

This was not our only sheep rescue. Several times when we were looking up and down Big Libby with our spyglass, as we always did, we would see some white puffs looking like snowcaps on a tidal ledge. We always knew instantly what had happened. The sheep often wandered along the shore—perhaps liking the taste of salt or eating the seaweed. Not being knowledgeable about tides, they would find themselves marooned and finally would climb to the highest rock they could find. It was a major job to row the peapod around to where they were, but the real challenge was how to get the frightened sheep into a small boat without dumping both sheep and rescuers into the water. Seldom was the sea completely calm, which increased the difficulty. Sometimes, even after they were aboard, the sheep would panic and jump out into the water. The water in their wool multiplied their weight quickly, but fortunately their hides made good handholds, so we could pull them back over the side and then subdue them until we could get them back to land. Many precious "woolies" were saved by the lightkeepers of Libby.

Libby was almost devoid of wild animals. It is surprising that we did not even have rats and mice inadvertently brought out on boats with boxes of food and other freight. The only wild animals we had were mink, which had to swim nearly three miles to

Libby, with only one island stopover on the way. Once there, they found an ample supply of prey: birds, fish, and crustaceans.

We had never seen any mink until one winter when they began to appear. Peter occasionally would flush one out, and we found a dead one that apparently had climbed into a lobster-bait barrel and had been unable to get out.

On a hunting trip down to the bar, Irwin finally had an opportunity to shoot a mink. He came home quite proudly, bringing it instead of his usual game birds. Having trapped fur-bearing animals as a boy, Father knew just how to skin it out and make a stretcher for the hide. Soon Irwin had a precious mink pelt, for which I believe he got about ten dollars. I thought that was fantastic and I wished that I, too, could kill a mink, because I certainly could use ten dollars, a small fortune. Irwin's pelt would have brought even more except that it had been damaged severely by shotgun pellets.

A few months later, I was near Katie's Gulch on an "explore" around the island when I had to go down onto the rocks to relieve myself. While resting on my haunches, I caught a glimpse of movement in the side of a small cliff. I looked closely and could see a black nose and two shiny black eyes peering out at me. Here was the mink I had been wishing for, but how could I capture it, since I had no gun? I dressed myself as soon as possible, without taking my eyes off the hole, and glanced about for a weapon. I found a short, stubby pole. First I tried jabbing at the mink as it looked out of its hole, but it was too quick for me. Every time I jabbed, it stuck its nose out of a second hole. We went back and forth this way several times. Then I devised a new strategy. I feinted at one hole and, without even looking, drove my weapon into the other. I knew I had struck something. I pulled my pole back cautiously and a beautiful mink fell out on the sand. I stood over it, with my pole ready, but there was no sign of life. Apparently it had been killed instantly. I picked it up and started for home, so proud of my prowess as a hunter that I even forgot to feel sorry for my prey. Its fur was a rich, shiny brown and felt soft over my arm.

Irwin and Father could hardly believe my story, but I had the mink to prove it. Father skinned it and stretched the hide for me. It was not as big as Irwin's, and the fur was not as heavy since it was springtime, but the pelt was perfect—no bullet holes. I think I got about eight dollars—the easiest money I ever earned.

Libby would have been a much more lonely place, indeed, had it not been for the animals. They added a rich variety to our island experience and a warm sense of companionship. When there are few people with whom one can associate, friendship with animals becomes much deeper and more significant.

10

A

LIGHTKEEPER'S
CHRISTMAS

THE dark days of December were brightened by the Christmas spirit, which came early on our lighthouse island and lingered in our hearts a long time after the day itself had passed. Perhaps the first sign of the approaching holiday was the increasing amount of time each member of the family spent studying the mail-order catalogs from Sears, Roebuck and Montgomery Ward. Most of the shopping would be done by mail. We did not get to Machias often because of the severity of the winter weather, and, at any rate, stores there were few and the choices limited. For us children, the real excitement began when Mother began to spend some of her evening hours thumbing through the catalogs. We knew better than to try to sneak a look over her shoulder, but we still knew when she had finished the letter containing her order. The order included not only presents for each of us but also other items like special candies, and new Christmas tree ornaments to replace old ones that had lost their glitter from years of use.

The next pre-Christmas excitement began when we planned our buying trip ashore. This would be our chance to peruse the wares in the mainland stores, to shop for holiday (and everyday) food, and, most important, to get our Christmas tree. But any activity that involved leaving the island depended upon the vagaries of the weather, so the Christmas shopping trip often came unexpectedly.

The general plan was that one of the keepers would go ashore once a week, but these trips often were postponed during the winter because of high winds and seas, or because unfavorable tides prevented launching or landing at our slip. With only eight hours of daylight in December, choosing a day to go ashore was difficult.

Father had one absolute rule: no launching or returning to Libby Island after dark. (This rule was violated only twice that I can remember: once when Father and Mother were attending a funeral, and much later when Irwin and I, enamored of two young ladies in Starboard, lost track of the setting sun and returned by rowboat in fog and darkness. It was a calm summer evening, but we were given a stern lecture and never did it again.)

We would always look forward with anticipation to the day when Father would make a weather survey (he was an excellent weather prophet), check the tide tables, and make an announcement: "Maybelle, it looks like a good day to go ashore."

Going ashore was always exciting, but the Christmas trip was the most thrilling one of all. First, the house had to be put in order. Then one of us would be sent to tell the other keepers and their families that we were going ashore so they could prepare their grocery lists and let us know what other errands we could do for them, such as mailing letters.

Not only did the house need to be put in order, but each of us had to scrub and get into "going ashore" clothes, the warmest we had. The tide, the wind, and the waves might keep us on the island, but seldom the temperature. Father always had to do a number of chores relating to the light or the whistlehouse, and invariably we would all be ready and waiting when he would come in and announce that he had to shave. Although we were impatient, at least we were certain there would be no further delay, since shaving always came last.

The only sad family member would be Peter. But at least she

would not be as sad as when she knew we were leaving for more than a day. Somehow, she could sense the difference.

The walk from the house to the boathouse was about a third of a mile, with no protection from the wind. For the first hundred feet after leaving the warm kitchen, we were protected by the rainshed, but at its far end, we faced the full, punishing cold. On our seemingly endless walk, the cow often distracted us from our stinging faces. As we went through the pasture gate into her domain, she would kick up her heels, curl her tail, and generally cavort as she followed us, breathing "smoke" like a fire-eating monster. Such antics made us all laugh and forget our discomfort until we reached the shelter of the boathouse.

During the winter, the government boat was hauled directly from the top of the slip into the boathouse on loose iron rollers, so the first step in launching was to open the huge, rolling doors. Sometimes the doors opened to reveal a frightening scene, with waves crashing against the shore and throwing spray high in the air. We often returned to the house at this point, Father having decided it would be too dangerous to try to launch the boat.

The twenty-four-foot hull looked enormous, held upright by triangular wooden braces. With one man slowly releasing the winch, the boat would begin to ease backward down the slightly inclined floor to the top of the slip. All of us who were old enough to have any lifting power helped hold her upright. The crucial part came when, with the edge of the building acting as a fulcrum, the gigantic hull seemed to point nearly straight up before leveling off on the slip timbers.

Before letting her down, Father usually tried the engine to be sure it would start. (Often he would have brought a teakettle of boiling-hot water to pour over crucial engine parts.) After repeated crankings of the huge flywheel, the engine finally would catch, creating clouds of acrid smoke and a deafening staccato from the exhaust.

Once Father was sure the motor would restart after the boat was in the water, we were all loaded in. Then the boat would slide down the greased slip, our progress controlled by one of the other keepers holding a four-by-four timber under one of the cog-wheels on the winch—creating an effective, if not very scientific, brake. By the time the boat hit the bottom, the timber would be smoking furiously.

The slip leveled off a little near the bottom, so it was easy to stop the boat at that point. With the stern just barely in the water, Father would again test the engine. This would result in much splashing as the propeller turned with the blades hitting the water. Father next signaled the man holding us on the slip to cast off the hook. He would then give us a push with all his strength to propel us beyond the rocks. One of us children would be assigned to hold the wheel straight to keep the boat heading clear. If there were any seas running, another kid would have a huge oar ready to paddle if the engine failed to restart. Father would rock the flywheel back and forth until, with a mighty lift, the motor started again. Then he would dash back to the steering wheel to direct our course into open water.

Once the motor was started for the final time, we could set our course for Starboard. In the winter, we usually had to use our compass when it was very cold because of the foglike sea smoke that obscured our vision. After we were underway, Father would raise the spray hood, which was made of canvas stretched over steel hoops. Mother and anyone else feeling the need for protection would sit under the hood on a low box in front of the engine, which gave out a little heat.

During the forty-five-minute run to Starboard, we suffered great discomfort from the cold and the flying spray, which even seemed to find its way through the hood. By the time we had tied up to the mooring, gotten into our peapod, rowed ashore, and pulled the pod up beyond the high-water mark, we were thoroughly chilled. But, as usual, a warm welcome always awaited us at the home of "Aunt" Alice and "Uncle" Jim Sprague.

Father would have to hike a quarter of a mile to where our car was garaged. If it started promptly, as it usually did, and he did not have to shovel too much snow, we soon would be on our way to Machias.

Sometimes it was not possible to go to Machias after all. This was before isolated country roads were plowed regularly. Instead, they were broken out by use. When the road was not passable, we would do limited shopping in a small local store. Our mail came to Starboard, so we did not have to be concerned about our mail orders. Hazel also mailed Christmas presents. A third source of gifts was the Maine Seacoast Missionary Society, which distributed presents to the families of all lighthouse keepers, as well as to children up to the age of sixteen, to low-income families, and to the elderly on Maine islands. (My mother received a gift from the organization on her ninety-ninth Christmas, long after she had left the island.)

Fortunately, the trip to Machias was reasonably comfortable. During the time we had touring (open) cars, Father never used them in the winter. But for many years our closed cars had no heaters, so they were only a slight improvement over the open vehicles.

When we did reach Machias, we dashed about gaily, buying groceries, last-minute gifts, shotgun shells, Christmas candies, and popcorn—all from a long list. Since we were bound by the government's six-hour-off-island regulations, we could never relax for a minute. There was no time for visiting friends.

Finally, car seats piled high with packages and grocery bags, we returned to Starboard. At the top of a long hill, just as we started the descent to the harbor, we would stop on Uncle Jim's land so Father could cut our Christmas tree. Father would go quickly from tree to tree, looking for the "right" size and contour. Since these were natural trees, it was difficult to find one that was well filled out and had no bare spots. After looking at several, he would make his selection, fell the tree with a few quick chops of his hatchet, drag it to the car, and lash it on the top.

Mother and the youngest children would wait at the Spragues' while the rest helped unload the car and carry the packages, bags, and boxes to the peapod. Sometimes we had a long way to haul the pod over sand, rocks, and seaweed. This was hard work with a loaded boat, but with all hands pushing, we soon would have her at the water's edge. The job was easier when there was ice on the sand.

Sometimes it took three trips to ferry passengers and purchases out to the boat. Mother would go out on the first trip, with most of the packages. While Father got the engine ready to start on the government boat, one of us would go back for the rest, including the Christmas tree, which would stay in the pod during the trip to Libby. We would fasten the painter of the pod at a proper length for towing, then head for home.

Even if it had been calm in the morning, a strong breeze would likely have sprung up by afternoon. A breeze running in the opposite direction from the tidal current would create a sharp chop. More of us would seek the shelter of the spray hood with Mother, but Father had no choice. He had to stay exposed and face it. I have a clear picture of him, face red with cold, water streaming down his cheeks, but wearing a happy expression. And why not? We had our presents, our tree, and lots of good food, and we were headed home for Christmas.

Back on the islands, with the boats secured and the heavy doors back in place, we would collect our precious bundles and head for the house. We usually left the tree at the boathouse until later. It was a long, cold walk, but our hearts were warm even if our faces, hands, and feet were not.

It was a great relief to all of us to know that our Christmas shopping was completed and we had our Christmas tree. Now, certainly, Santa Claus would come. We had escaped the wind and the cold when we entered the rainshed, but it was even more wonderful to enter our large, comfortable kitchen, warm from the glowing coal fire in the stove, which would have lasted all day. Peter would be so overjoyed to see us that she would try to jump up and lick our faces, while her long, whiplike tail lashed our legs until they stung. She was also ready for Christmas.

A few days before Christmas, Father and Mother would decide that it was time to bring up the tree from the boathouse. Once we kids got it as far as the rainshed, Father would begin the intricate task of building a base out of scrap lumber. These never came out quite the same from one year to the next, but building them was very much a part of the Christmas ritual—so much so that for years afterward, I refused to buy a stand and always built one for my family's Christmas tree.

Measurements also had to be taken so that the tree would fit into the "Christmas room." Father had a tendency to overestimate the height of the ceiling and underestimate the size of the tree he had selected, but he seldom cut anything off the bottom of the tree. Rather, he would cut the extra height off the top, so what we ended up with often resembled just the middle of a tree.

After the tree was installed, the trimming began. We had no electricity, so there were, of course, no electric lights. We did have beautiful, delicate ornaments, however: balls of many colors and flowers made of a thin tinlike material that Mother ordered one year from Sears. In place of tinsel icicles, we draped tinsel rope over the tree and also from corner to corner in the room. In the center of the room was a beautiful red paper bell. We also strung yards of popcorn on the tree to represent snow. Father would step back and say, "That is the most beautiful tree we've ever had." And certainly it was, as each Christmas seemed to grow more precious to all of us.

Over the years, we actually used two different rooms for the Christmas tree: the sewing room (which served mostly as an office for Father's bookkeeping) and the dining room, right off the kitchen. The sewing room was one of my favorite places. It had exposure on the south and east and was sunny and warm. It also faced the light in the tower, so it was well illuminated even at night. Our steam heating system also seemed to favor this room. Perhaps most of all, I remember the room's aroma. We stored apples in its large closet, and for several months each year, the sewing room was filled with the sweet aroma of apples. I do not know why we later used the dining room for our Christmas room. Perhaps it was to cut down on our use of coal during the Depression.

For Christmas dinner, we never had chicken, turkey, goose, pork, or beef. There was only one main dish acceptable to us: wild black duck. This was so much a tradition in our family that whenever we had duck at other times of the year, we always referred to that meal as "a Christmas dinner."

The task of securing the wild ducks, of course, fell to Father and Peter, who often were accompanied by Irwin. They hunted on a casual schedule at first, but as Christmas drew closer, Father would begin to hunt on every low tide when there was light. If he came home empty-handed time after time, all of us would begin to worry.

Sometimes, knowing how anxious we were that Christmas dinner be secured, Father would play a joke on us. He would come home empty-handed, talking about his bad luck and the ducks that flew away before he could get within range. After he had taken off his clothes, which would be wet from his crawling over the rocks, he would saunter out to the storage room outside our kitchen and bring in his game, throwing the ducks on the floor in front of the kitchen stove. He always did this (even without the subterfuge), indicating a successful hunt and hunter.

With our tree trimmed and the Christmas ducks ready for the oven, our excitement and wonder increased and a sense of peace entered our home and our hearts. We were together as a family, secure on our lighthouse island. There would be no mail, no newspapers, no radio to bring bad news. No one would come and no one would leave for perhaps two weeks. In fact, we probably could have lived for several months without any contact with the outside world.

One special treat we always had for Christmas was ice cream, made the day before. Our ice-cream freezer could make a gallon and required a considerable amount of ice, which we cut from shallow ponds. With an old ax, a crocus sack, and a sled, we would strike out for a pond. As we chopped away, ice dust would fly into our faces, but if we kept cutting along a line, soon a piece would break away. Since the pond water was shallow, the ice would be thin, and grass would cling to the underside of it. When we thought we had enough, we would haul it to the rainshed. The next step was to break the ice into small pieces, which we did by striking the crocus sack repeatedly with the flat top of the ax. This required considerable time and energy, but in the cold rainshed where we made the ice cream, anything that increased body heat was welcome.

While we were gathering and breaking up the ice, Mother would prepare the ice cream mix. She was severely allergic to eggs, so she used junket instead. When the mix was ready, she poured it into the metal ice cream container. This we placed inside the larger wooden outside container and then packed ice around it, adding layers of rock salt as we did so. I still do not understand why brine is colder than mere ice, but it is. The last step was to install the turning gears with the handle attached and begin the long, arduous task of grinding until the mix froze.

Mother would tell us to call her when the crank became hard to turn. This is when we would find out whether the ice cream would be strawberry, raspberry, maple walnut, or some other flavor. After we called Mother, we would carefully brush away the chipped ice, take off the cover, and peer inside. Already the ice cream would be beginning to form in swirls that looked like miniature snowdrifts. I liked it best when she dumped in a generous quantity of walnuts with maple flavoring. It was important to add the goodies after the ice cream had begun to freeze so they would not all settle to the bottom. After that, we again settled into the cranking routine. Occasionally, we would take a stick, poke down the ice around the metal container, and add more ice and salt. We took turns cranking, and as the handle became harder and harder to turn, someone would have to hold the freezer to keep it from spinning away.

Since we often began this process late in the afternoon, we did not finish until after dark. In late December, darkness came early. We would bring the family lantern out to the rainshed and light it. The flame gave off a warm glow around our work area and illuminated an even larger area of darkness. The dark, tunnellike atmosphere of the rainshed was eerie, so we were easily startled by unexpected noises from ice falling on the roof.

Mother or Father always came out and tested the handle to see if the ice cream was hard enough. Usually they would say it was not, much to our disappointment, and we would buckle down to more cranking. Eventually, it became impossible to turn the handle. Now came the packing process. We would drain off the brine through a hole in the wooden container and then punch down all the ice and pack in as much new ice and salt as possible, mounding the ice completely over the cranking mechanism. It would now keep this way for a long time.

Christmas Eve was a time of great excitement, because Santa Claus never failed to come to our island, regardless of weather. It could be snowing and blowing, with rough seas, but we firmly believed that Santa would come, airborne, with his eight reindeer and his sleigh full of toys for "good girls and boys." (And we were all sure that we qualified as long as Santa did not check the records too far back before Christmas.) After supper, we would bring in the ice-cream freezer and put it in the kitchen sink. Father would dig out the ice and take off the cranking mechanism, while we crowded around to peer in. How wondrous it looked and smelled. Mother would use a big spoon to scoop out large cereal bowls full of ice cream and we would return to the table for our first Christmas treat. Sometimes I would eat too fast and get a rather severe headache, which Mother would ease by placing her warm hands on my forehead.

By now, we knew, Santa could come at any time. The first sign of his arrival was the sound of the huge door being opened in the far end of the rainshed. This door had a weight on it for automatic closing, and we could always hear the weight moving up and down in its slide. Santa invariably greeted each of us with a "Ho! Ho! Ho!"—always, of course, asking if we had been good girls and boys. If we were brave enough, we said yes, but often we said nothing, only snuggling more tightly into Mother's or Father's lap.

No one today would have recognized our Santa. He was unique —no red suit or white beard. On his head he wore a white stocking-leg cap. His face was not bearded but instead was totally covered with what looked like the fine yellow wool of a sheepskin. Rather angular in appearance, Santa was clothed from head to ankles in a long, black coat, as if he had climbed down many chimneys before reaching Libby.

Santa never stayed long, but he always left us with the assurance that we would find presents around the tree in the morning. No one moved until the rainshed door slammed shut and we heard the sleigh bells recede in the distance. These were magical moments. It never occurred to us to question how Santa's reindeer got to our island over miles of stormy seas. In all the pictures we had seen, his reindeer and sleigh were soaring across the face of the moon, suggesting that they would not be stopped by a mere three miles of ocean.

We knew they landed because, when there was snow on the ground, we would find their tracks the next day. Of course, we did not know that Father had made the footprints with feet saved from a deer he had shot in November. A stick dragged through the snow made tracks for the sleigh. Father would even make long, straight "skid marks" to show where the reindeer had landed after their flight across the bay.

During the rest of Christmas Eve, we talked and played games. No family could have been happier than we were in our cozy kitchen, but one thing we never forgot: if it was Father's watch, every few minutes he or one of us would check the light to be sure it was burning steadily. Often he would sit in his large wooden rocking chair so he could see the light reflected in the mirror attached to a post erected outside the window. When it was foggy, he would have to remain most of the time in the whistlehouse, coming home to be with us only during short breaks. No matter what we were doing, the maintenance of the light and the fog signal came first. Just because it was Christmas did not mean that a ship might not be depending upon these guides to stay on her course and away from the rocks and reefs.

Breaking away from the warmth and love that surrounded us always was difficult, but we knew that the sooner we went to sleep, the sooner Christmas morning would arrive. After we were snug in bed, Mother's final preparation for Christmas would begin. First, she would get out the presents, which had been carefully hidden away in boxes in some closet that we were forbidden to go near. She never wrapped them but left them open in their containers with our names attached on tiny cards. (In those early years, I do not remember that we children gave gifts to each other. Perhaps it was too complicated with our limited shopping time.)

Next, Mother would stuff our candy bags, which she made out of old lace curtains. They held about two quarts of goodies and were pulled together at the top with red ribbon. The main ingredient of these bags was popcorn, but they also contained a variety of nuts, hard candies, ribbon candy, and chocolates. The bags were hung on stout limbs of the tree with our names attached. We children cherished these bags and carefully rationed the treats they contained. Even as late as Easter, we might have a few kernels of popcorn left. I never knew what time Mother went to bed on Christmas Eve, but it must have been very late.

I do know that as early as four o'clock, we started calling to see whether it was time for us to get up. By five, we usually received permission. Grabbing our clothes to put on by the stove, where it was warmer, we headed down the stairs, sometimes even sliding on the off-limits banister to get to the bottom faster.

When we opened the kitchen door, the room's warmth flooded over us. Father would have left the Aladdin lamp turned low and the covers ajar on the stove. This allowed the light of the glowing coal to spread a rosy color over the whole room, flickering on the walls and ceiling. Peter would greet us with enthusiasm, whacking our bare legs with her tail.

Our hearts beat with excitement as we entered the Christmas room, where a lamp would have been left for us to turn up. When it illuminated the room, an unbelievable array greeted us. The Christmas tree would be shining with its own beauty in a corner, with gifts and candy bags resting on its branches, and gifts would be everywhere—on tables, on stands, and sometimes even on the floor.

No joy in life has ever surpassed these marvelous moments, and I especially remember one Christmas when I received a toy train. Father had assembled the track and laid it around the trunk of the tree. When I looked, there was a glistening black locomotive, with freight and passenger cars attached, just waiting for the engineer to wind up the spring and, in his imagination, climb aboard, blow the whistle, and head off down the track. Another year, I found a steam engine complete with steam boiler, kerosene wick "fire" to heat the water, water valve, whistle, safety gauge, and many power tools that it could turn with small pulleys made of cords. I played with that engine for years and can still smell the burning oil and hear the steam releasing from the tank. It worked just like the steam engine in the boathouse. I spent hours polishing the gleaming bright brass tank.

Father and Mother were generous, and no one lacked for presents—toys, games, new clothes, sleds. Sometimes Father would have made something special for us. He made my sisters elaborate dollhouses and doll toys, such as swings. He also made bow guns, wheelbarrows, buck saws, and other toys, all of which were functional. Mother knew I loved to read, and she always bought books for me. I loved the Tom Swift series and the series about Bomba the Jungle Boy. Hazel almost always sent me books.

Mother usually would be the first adult to appear downstairs (especially if Father had been on watch during the night). She would be greeted with a chorus of thank yous and hugs and kisses. The night before, she would also have put out dishes filled with generous supplies of ribbon candy, hard candy, and other sweets, and we consumed quantities of these. But we were always ready for a hearty breakfast of oatmeal with milk, cream-of-tartar biscuits, jam, and fruit (usually an apple, sometimes an orange).

After breakfast, we would return to our toys and games, examining each other's gifts, but after lunch we would feel the need to go outdoors. If it was a sunny day and the wind was not blowing, we would be quite comfortable, but more often, the temperature was in the twenties, with a strong breeze. Then we had to bundle up. Our basic jackets were sheepskins, which had inner linings of wool, outer covers of green melton cloth, and high-standing collars also lined with wool. We would wear heavy trousers, several pairs of woolen socks that Mother knit, and "lumbermen's rubbers" (the kind with rubber bottoms and leather tops made fashionable by L.L. Bean). We also wore woolen mittens, perhaps even two pair, made by Mother. She always was busy knitting mittens and socks to keep us supplied.

As we went out the door, Mother would admonish us to be careful not to get hurt. In reviewing our lighthouse life with her in later years, I learned that she had an ever-present fear that one of us might sustain a serious injury. On a day when the sea was rough, it might have been impossible, or at least time-consuming, to get medical help. We had a well-stocked medicine chest, but to my knowledge no one was trained in first aid.

Nothing could be more beautiful than a bright winter day on our island, and nothing was more fun than trying out new skates on deeply frozen Big Pond, our only place for skating. Whether or not we had new skates for Christmas, we would spend Christmas afternoon (until we became too cold) skating. Our skates were the old-fashioned kind—runners attached with clamps and straps— and we spent much of our time putting them back on after they came off. Also, we wore them with leather-soled shoes, which were cold! The clamps would not hold on our rubber-soled boots. One of the greatest inventions for winter recreation was shoe skates, but for us children they came a bit too late.

As we played at our ice-cold games, always in the back of our minds were the warming thoughts of our comfortable home filled with newly acquired treasures. Early in the afternoon, the sun began to lose what little warmth it offered. No matter how warmly we were dressed, fingers and toes began to get numb, faces began to burn, and finally the chill would creep inside our thick sheepskin-lined jackets. It was time to go home. Mother would welcome us and help the younger ones to wriggle out of their snow-encrusted jackets, trousers, and boots. The first few moments could be painful as the blood began to return to toes, fingers, and cheeks already in the early stages of frostbite. Chilled to the bone, we would stand near the stove, or perhaps lie on the floor with our legs under it, to get thawed out. Peter, who usually was lying near the warmth, made a fine pillow. It did not take long for us to warm up because we were anxious to reclaim our gifts. By this time darkness would have settled and Mother would have put a light in the Christmas room so we could again enjoy our treasures.

Supper was served early, by 5 p.m., so that it did not interfere with the watch change. This meal usually was topped off with ice cream left from Christmas Eve. After supper, we played games, often with Mother and Father joining in. Again that wonderful feeling of peace and love would encompass us. No matter how hard the wind blew, whining and whistling about the house and rattling the windows, or how loudly the waves roared, beating against the cliffs only a few feet away, we felt perfectly secure.

Later, living on the mainland, we found Christmas quite different. There would be lots of activities: church Christmas pageants, concerts, carol singing, visits from friends and relatives —a round of happy times. Yet no one could have been happier than we were on Libby Island, in spite of our almost total isolation. As children, of course, we knew no other way of life. If Mother and Father missed the experience of joining friends and relatives in the Christmas celebration, we never were aware of it. In any case, they certainly succeeded in making our Christmases full of joy, wonder, love, and peace.

11

ISLAND
LEARNING

I CREPT along the upstairs hallway to the door of the "school-room" occupying the fourth bedroom in our house. Standing just outside the door, I could hear Mrs. Vera Sargent's voice as she asked questions and the lighter mumbled answers coming from the children who were lucky enough to be five or older. I was only four, but I desperately wanted to be in there with the rest of the kids. It was lonely when they were all in the schoolroom most of the day, and I figured I was as smart as most of them. I was ready for school. Ever since I could remember, I had been lugging around books, trying to get someone to read to me. I could "almost" read; all I needed was a little help.

I begged Mother to let me go to school but kept getting no for an answer, so every day I spent part of my time outside the school-room door, listening. Finally, they could stand my persistent pleading no longer. Mother and Mrs. Sargent decided that it probably would not do any harm for me to sit with the other children—if I promised to behave. And of course I did. The fact that I was below the magical age of five did not seem to matter. I had no difficulty keeping up with my friend Loni, who was about a year my senior. I loved school. (This love continued until I received a Ph.D. from Columbia University in 1951, and I have spent most of my adult life as a college professor.)

Mrs. Sargent was an itinerant teacher who came to Libby for short periods of time and then went on to other stations. She laid out the work, and the parents were supposed to make sure we did our assignments before she returned. It was a hit-or-miss kind of schooling that depended greatly on the seriousness of the parents in wanting their children to have a good education.

I do not know when this system was instituted, but in 1908, Alexander P. McDonald, a missionary for the Maine Sea Coast Missionary Society, had become very concerned about the education of lighthouse children in Maine. He indicated that in one area alone, he knew of a hundred children growing up without school opportunities. He lamented this because he felt that lightkeepers and their families were above average and were anxious for all their children to be educated. The state contended that it was the federal government's responsibility. The "guvment" said it was not its concern because the keepers knew what the conditions were, and they would have to provide educational opportunities the best way they could.

Perhaps McDonald's inquiry and the pressure from others had some impact. I believe our itinerant teacher was paid by the Maine Sea Coast Missionary Society. When we had a full-time teacher for a year in 1925-26, her salary was paid by the Lighthouse Service. Records also show that from time to time the town of Machiasport paid for teachers on Libby. When Father and Mother began renting places on the mainland in 1922, to ensure good schooling for us, the Lighthouse Service paid a small stipend per child to help defray the expenses.

The fourth bedroom in our house seemed to have been set aside for use as a schoolroom when the house was constructed, or perhaps it was adapted later. A stairway led from the room down into our end of the rainshed so that the children of the other keepers did not have to come through our house. There was only one window in the room, so a skylight had been installed in the roof. A large, potbellied coal stove gave off ample heat. We had no traditional seats and desks but sat at various-sized tables probably built by earlier keepers. The blackboards were just that—boards painted with black paint —and quite inadequate for writing. For individual assignments, we had slates, which worked well.

We had reading and math books and a few others on geography and history, but nothing for enrichment. Loni and I mastered our reading book so well that we could recite most of the stories. We particularly liked the one about the Little Red Hen, who planted wheat, made flour, and baked bread while all her barnyard friends stubbornly refused to help. When the bread came from the oven, she, of course, just as stubbornly refused to share it. And then there was Chicken Little, who was convinced that the sky was falling. Loni and I frequently recited these stories to each other when we were outside playing, and we thought it was funny that we could "read" without looking at the pages.

It was not easy for Mother to spend time each day teaching her children, in addition to doing her regular chores. Mondays were for washing, Tuesdays and Wednesdays for ironing, Thursdays for mending, Fridays for housecleaning, and Saturdays for baking. Although this was the typical New England housewife's schedule, Mother must have varied it some, because I have a clear remembrance of her "tutoring" while baking, and I am sure we did not do any lessons on Saturday. One minute Mother would be tending to her weekly batches of cookies. The next minute she would turn to Nonie, at one end of the table struggling with math problems, then to Orrie on the other to help her out of her difficulties. After this, she would return to the pantry to prepare her next lot of cookies. This was not always a happy scene. The kitchen would be steaming hot from the baking, and Mother's face would be very red and covered with flour and perspiration. Frequently, the girls would be in tears. I imagine this scene was duplicated in other families over the many years that children were taught at home on lighthouse stations.

As I mentioned in chapter 1, this was the type of education

Winona and Irwin had through most of their elementary grades. Fortunately, Hazel was already of high school age when we arrived at Libby, so she immediately boarded with a family in Machias to attend high school. On Whitehead, all three of them had been able to attend school with a full-time teacher. In fact, Whitehead was the only Maine lighthouse station with a separate school building.

I do not know what happened to the itinerant teacher program, but it ended for us in 1922, when I was five and ready for "real" first grade. Mother and Father rented a small summer cottage belonging to Alice and Jim Sprague so that we could attend school in Starboard.

On a recent visit to that school building, Irwin and I found it hard to believe how tiny it was. It had been an "all-grade" rural school.

I do not remember much about that early educational experience, but I do remember the cottage we rented. It had no foundation, and the walls were only the thickness of one-inch boards. At night, after the fire went out, the temperatures on the inside and the outside were exactly the same, and that was cold! In the morning, Mother would build a fire, break the ice in the bucket to get water for cooking, and prepare breakfast. We would all get as close as possible to the stove to eat—our faces burning from the heat and our backs shivering from the cold. I do not know how she kept warm during the day.

Every weekend when the weather was good, we went back to Libby. There was no way we could endure the cold after Christmas vacation, so we stayed on Libby and did not return until the spring term, which began in April. We missed the whole winter term, but Mother tried to help us with our lessons each day. How happy we were to be back together again on Libby, living in our "luxurious" home. I do not think any of us were very enthusiastic about leaving Libby in April, but we returned to our cold cottage to finish the year.

Starboard, in the spring, was pleasant after the cold began to subside. Our walk to school led us along the upper levels of a shingle beach, which in late spring was decorated with morning glories trailing everywhere. And we all enjoyed being able to play with other kids our own ages.

Three of us—Roland Sprague, Keith Sprague, and I—got into trouble one day. On the inside of the beach where we walked there was a freshwater pond, and someone had hauled an old skiff into it. We decided to take a row, only to find that the bottom had rotted away. As we felt the boat sinking from under us, we climbed out quickly and scrambled back to the shore, but not without getting soaked. There was no way we could conceal what we had done, to the great alarm of our parents. For this reckless deed, I was sentenced to stay inside, after school, for several days.

Another memory I have of that first experience of mainland living was a party for Jamie Sprague. (Jamie was Alice and Jim's son.) It was the first party I had ever attended, and it impressed me so much that I can still remember some of the games we played. There were no such activities to enjoy on Libby.

But, come June, except for Nonie, we could hardly wait to get back home to Libby with Father. Nonie, in spite of the cold, greatly enjoyed that year in Starboard, where she was in eighth grade. After Whitehead, she spent her fifth, sixth, and seventh grades totally cut off from young people her own age. This was a lonely existence for her, and she always resented being deprived of the friendships that both girls and boys need during these formative years.

One old Maine lightkeeper felt that the isolation of an off-shore light station was hard on the men but doubly hard on the women. He might have gone on to say that it was even more severe on girls and young women. They had no school activities, no Girl Scouts, no 4-H Club or other social and church activities.

The situation was quite different for Irwin and me. I had known no other kind of life, and Irwin, arriving on Libby at the age of seven, made an easy adjustment. It was a boys' world. Although Nonie helped Mother with cooking, sewing, and housecleaning, few of these activities offered her much satisfaction. When I first asked her, years later, to talk to me or to make a tape describing her life on Libby, her answer was curt: "I don't want to talk about Libby Island. I hated the place." I do not think she ever quite forgave "life" for imposing this limiting experience upon her.

Mother and Father placed a high priority on education, and by 1922 had become concerned that we were receiving inadequate schooling, even in Starboard. I am sure they spent many hours discussing what they should do, but finally they decided that Mother would live ashore during the school year so that their children could attend "regular" school in Machias. This meant a great sacrifice. We were a close-knit family, and this would separate us. Father loved his children and we loved him. Living apart would be a sad experience for all of us. Mother and Father were still very much in love—this was evident in the great regard they had for each other. Father helped Mother with nearly every phase of the housework, even cooking. And Mother did nearly all of Father's lighthouse reports, or helped him with them. They would surely miss each other.

They could have decided to rent a house or apartment in Bucks Harbor, Larrabee, or Machiasport—nearer to Starboard—but I'm sure they felt that the schools would be better in Machias. So they decided on Machias, on the west side of the river. I am not sure whether this was a conscious decision or merely where they could find a rental, but it was a life-shaping decision for me. The river marked the dividing line between those who attended the elementary school connected with Washington State Normal School and those who attended the town schools. The "Model School," as it was called, was used as a training center for student teachers, and the regular teachers there were the best that could be obtained.

During my years as a student in this school, I developed a great admiration for the student teachers, particularly the young men. Later, I came to know several of them as outstanding superintendents of schools in Connecticut. In these early years, I made up my mind that I, too, wanted to become a teacher, and I never had any doubts about my decision. Having set this clear direction early helped me later to make good progress in my chosen profession.

After I attended grades two and three in Machias, we all hailed with great joy the news that we were going back to Libby Island. Because of a change of keepers, there were nine children living on the island, enough to justify hiring a full-time teacher. Father and Mother were overjoyed at the thought of being reunited, and Irwin and I could not wait to return.

Early in September 1925, we gathered once again in the schoolroom in our house, ready for more island learning. Our teacher was Miss Carro Richardson, from Machias, who recently had completed one year at Washington State Normal School. She was an attractive redhead and this was her first assignment. It must have been a difficult decision for her to make, knowing she would be isolated on an island all through the long winter months. But we will always be grateful that she decided to do it, because it gave us all a wonderful year. Being on the island meant that Irwin and I had plenty of time to carry out our "salvage operations" on the *John C. Myers,* which was wrecked that year on Big Libby. Most of my vivid memories of Libby came from that year, when I was eight and in fourth grade.

Our schooling was quite different from what we had had for two years in Machias. There we had music and art and lots of individual attention from the student teachers. By comparison, our island curriculum was quite barren. For art, we mostly used stencil cards to make pictures of flowers and animals. Apparently the government was not very generous with enrichment materials.

Irwin was thirteen and in the crucial eighth grade, preparing for high-school entrance exams. Miss Richardson found that one essential text had not been provided, so she sent for it and they studied together. Although I'm sure it was illegal, she helped Irwin with that part of the test. In spite of his intermittent schooling, Irwin passed the whole examination and was admitted to high school the next year.

Miss Richardson liked Irwin because she loved to eat seabirds, and he often was her means of ensuring that they were served at our table when she was boarding with us. (She rotated among the three families.) In the schoolroom, he had a special seat near the window so he could look out on a section of the shoreline. I can almost see him now, raising his hand and pointing out the window—apparently a prearranged signal. The teacher would nod her head and he would quietly slip out the door. In about twenty minutes, I would hear gunshots. A short time later, Irwin would return and slide into his seat. Miss Richardson would look at him inquiringly and he would nod, confirming that wild seabirds would be served for dinner the next day.

There was not much for our teacher to do on weekends, so when the weather was fair, her uncle, Roy Sprague would take her ashore after he finished hauling his lobster traps. Then someone in her family would pick her up and drive her home to Machias. We liked this arrangement, because often the tide and weather were such that she needed to leave early and we got some unexpected time off from school. When this was a substantial amount of time, we sometimes had to make it up by going to school a little longer each day—which, of course, we did not like. She would return early Monday morning when Roy came around the island to haul his traps.

After a bit of detective work while writing this book, I was able to make contact with our island teacher, who now lives in Bar Harbor. She was quite surprised to hear from one of her island pupils. I asked her what she remembered most about her year on Libby Island. Her answer was, "The tremendous waves we sometimes had to go through to land on the slip. I wasn't scared then, but I would be now."

Our family greatly enjoyed being together again in our own home. With school just upstairs, there were no long hikes in the cold and we seldom went ashore during the winter months. It was truly an island year. We were living much the same as families had lived on Libby for the hundred years before we came—except that they usually had no school. Hazel, already married, was living on Franklin Island. Nonie was boarding in Machias so she could attend high school. But Irwin, Arnie (age two), and I were there with Mother and Father, making a cohesive family. Nonie would return home for occasional weekends and for all the school vacations. We looked forward to her visits. Sometimes she brought girl friends with her, and often I fell madly in love with them—depending, of course, upon how much attention they paid to me.

After the fourth grade, my schooling was in Machias, but we all joyfuly headed back home to our island on weekends in the fall and spring, during school vacation, and for three months in the summer. Most of the other keepers established their families on the mainland and they did not return to Libby as frequently as we did. We considered Libby our home, and we wanted to be there with Father at every opportunity.

It was on these weekend and holiday trips that we made our most hazardous crossings to and from Libby. When we lived on the island all the time, we could choose our days for going ashore. There was seldom any compelling reason to go, since we had plenty of food, and mail and other errands could always wait. But school was different. We desperately wanted to get to Libby when we were not in school, and Father was just as determined to get us back to Machias so we would not miss any school.

With the greatest joy, we kids greeted an oncoming storm, hoping it might prevent us from returning to the mainland. A huge snowstorm came one year after Christmas. It kept us from leaving the island for several days and piled up high drifts on the mainland, blocking the roads. Although Father hated to have us leave, he hired a Bucks Harbor farmer who had a horse and sleigh to take us to Machias. The crossing was one of the coldest trips I remember. Mother heated soapstones and wrapped them well so they would retain the heat. We put our feet on these, but there was nothing to keep our hands warm and to protect our faces from the biting wind and salt spray. As I remember, the temperature was about ten degrees. After landing, we hauled up the peapod and immediately hiked up the beach to the Spragues' house, where we were welcomed into their warm kitchen. "Aunt" Alice put the soapstones into the oven to reheat them and soon our driver arrived. We were delighted to see a sprightly horse—unlike the slow-moving nags we usually had on Libby—and a well-kept sleigh and harness adorned with bells, which were ringing merrily in the brisk winter air. We wrapped scarves around our faces, crawled into blankets, and covered ourselves with a huge bearskin rug. The trip was thirteen miles, but the horse, running most of the time, kept up a good pace. Fortunately, much of the road was through deep woods and valleys protected from the wind. We reached Machias without frozen hands or feet, although the cold gradually had penetrated our covers. I believe our driver's name was Irving Johnson, but I do not remember what he looked like, because he, too, was wrapped in his own personal cocoon.

I well remember a pre-Christmas trip when I was marooned in Starboard. Father, having heard predictions of bad weather, came early to the mainland to take Mother back to the station. They left me in the care of a neighbor in Machias so I could finish school. I think Irwin's school already had closed for the holidays. The only means of public transportation to Starboard was with the mail—a slow ride for a small fee. Having to stay in school the extra days was bad enough, but when Saturday came and I got to Starboard, I found a telephone message from Father, telling me that Libby was being bombarded by heavy seas and it was impossible to launch the boat. I was to stay with the Spragues. Every morning I would get up, full of hope, and call Libby, only to find that the weather was still bad and I would have to wait another day. At this news, I would sink into deep despair. Not that "Uncle" Jim and "Aunt" Alice were not kind to me, but I wanted desperately to be home. Finally, there was a calm day, and nothing ever looked better to me than the gray-hulled government boat coming around Ingalls (Starboard) Island toward the town of Starboard.

We had another dangerous episode on one of these December trips. Heading out from Starboard in bitter-cold winds, we encountered heavy seas between Ingalls and Stone islands. One of the dangers of a winter crossing, if seas were breaking over the boat, was ice. And with the water flying, it was not very long before ice began to form on the peapod. Soon a particularly vicious wave capsized her. Pulling in under the lee of Stone, Father and Justin were able to right her and bail out much of the water. By this time the seas were running so high that Father turned and headed back to Starboard. The waves continued to threaten us, and the situation grew increasingly dangerous, because the ice was now forming on the government boat. We finally reached our mooring and safety, but we could not get back to Libby for several days. Again the Spragues had not wholly unexpected guests, and the keeper on the station had to run the light and fog signal by himself until we returned. That was about as close as we ever came to having a serious accident.

Another hazardous Christmas trip occurred when we were much older. (I was a sophomore in high school and Irwin was taking a postgraduate course.) A bad storm had come up unexpectedly. As we drove over the top of the last hill on our way to the landing in Starboard, we could see the whitecaps in the bay. By the time the car was stored in the garage, tiny needles of snow were stinging our cheeks. The weather reports forecast a heavy snowfall, with high winds and drifting.

When we had all the supplies ready to load into the pod, we expressed concern to Father that the car might be snowed in for the rest of the winter—there were no powerful plows to clear roads in those days. Lack of a car would have been a great inconvenience. Father would have no way to get to town, and (of more immediate concern to us) we would have no transportation to basketball games and dances. Father thought a minute, looked out over the harbor to where our boat was swinging slowly in the wind, and said, "I'm going to need both of you to help land on the slip and get the boat into the boathouse. If the weather isn't too bad after that, you can row back and take the car to Machias before the storm blocks the road." The thought of rowing back in the storm did not worry us. If Father said it was safe, we would do it.

Soon we were headed out of the harbor—Mother huddled under the spray hood with Arnie, Father at the wheel, and Irwin and I watching the peapod to see that she was not taking on water.

As we hit the open ocean, the signs of the impending storm were evident everywhere. The northeast wind was increasing steadily and the seas were starting to build. We could see them beginning to crash on the outside shores of Ingalls. The sky had become ominously gray, lightened only by the falling snow. We made the crossing without incident and soon were at the winch, hauling the boat into the boathouse. Once she was secure, we had to make our decision.

After talking with Father, we decided to attempt rowing back. Mother was quiet, but we could tell that she was concerned. The sky was getting darker, and night was coming on fast, so we would have to hurry. Checking our oars to make sure we had two sturdy pairs with snug-fitting oarlocks, we eased the pod into the waves breaking on the slip. As Father shoved us off, he said, "You'd better follow along the shore until you get to Big Libby—then it won't be far across to Stone. Once by Stone, you should be all right."

Fitting our oars into their locks, we soon were rhythmically stroking our way along Libby's northeastern shore. The tide was low enough that the bar offered us some shelter. Father stood and watched us, but we must have disappeared quickly as our gray boat merged into the slate-colored ocean and sky.

We were in good spirits. Rowing together, we ordinarily could make the three-mile crossing in a little over an hour, and there was no doubt in our minds that we could make the trip safely. By this time, both snow and wind were more intense. The fog signal had begun its somber booming, muffled by the storm. Soon we could no longer see the boathouse.

The full fury of the wind did not strike us until we pushed the boat beyond the shelter of Big Libby's bluff head. When it hit, both of us turned and looked across the channel. Already the dark, forested shape of Stone Island was merging into the gray-whiteness of the snow-filled horizon. The whitecaps were streaking the water's surface and larger waves were beginning to strike the boat. There was no need for discussion. We might make it across in a storm like this, but it would be dark in less than an hour. If we lost our oars or became disoriented, no one would ever find us. It was a gray world, and it would be impossible to distinguish our boat from its surroundings. Either we would be swept into the surf, which we could hear surging over the bar, or we would be blown out to sea, where we would surely be lost. No one could survive long in an open boat in weather like this.

With a few swift strokes of our oars, we headed for our boat-house. It was already a relief when we were back under the lee of Big Libby and out of the wind. In another fifteen minutes, we touched out on the slip, hauled up the pod, and, thoroughly chilled, headed for the house. As we topped the hill, the light from the tower was barely visible through the snow, which already amounted to several inches.

When we entered the kitchen, we must have looked like walking snowmen. Mother took one look and ran to us, giving us each a hug and a kiss. We could tell she had been crying, and we guessed that she also had been praying that we would turn back.

As always, we had a happy Christmas, but the news from the mainland was not good. The storm had brought several feet of drifting snow, making it impossible to open the road to Starboard. The road was closed for the winter, much to our disappointment.

But our adventure with this storm was not over. A few days after Christmas, Irwin and I decided again to attempt rowing ashore. We wanted to get back to Machias and open the house so that it would be warm when Mother and Arnie arrived. School was due to open in a few days. This time, we knew that the hardest part of our trip would be hiking through the snow from Starboard to Bucks Harbor, the first village on the way, and then walking in the cold to Machias.

Our peapod crossing was swift. We secured the boat on the beach at Starboard above the high-water mark and started the slow, four-mile walk to Bucks Harbor. The road had been trodden by horses and sleighs, but the snow was light and continued to drift. Sometimes it was ankle deep, sometimes knee deep, and sometimes up to our thighs. I do not remember ever having been so tired, but we kept going. The worst part was getting over Howard's Mountain, fighting gravity and the snow. Finally we made it to the top, and on into Bucks Harbor. From there, the road was more open, but the walking was still tiring. I do not remember how many hours it took us to reach our destination, but what kept our spirits high was the dream of building a fire in the kitchen stove, thawing out, and getting a hot meal. It was dark before we climbed the steep driveway to our house. We collected kindling from the barn and soon had a fire going.

Just as we were beginning to congratulate ourselves, however, a cloud of steam rose from the stove. We could not imagine what it was—our wood was bone dry. Opening the stove covers, we saw the source of the steam. The firebox had pipes running around it to heat hot water, and these apparently had frozen and burst while we were gone. This was our first year in the new house Father and Mother had purchased, and it was also our first experience with indoor plumbing.

Now our only source of heat was the fireplace in the living room, where we soon built a fire to thaw us out. I do not remember what we had for supper, but whatever it was, we had to eat it cold. It was not until midnight that we finally crawled into our cold beds. Fortunately, the next day we were able to get the pipes repaired. Mother arrived with Arnie a few days later. Father had hired a horse and sleigh to take them the first four miles and someone to drive them the rest of the way.

Our automobile was securely barricaded that winter behind many snowdrifts. We spent hours developing schemes for rescuing it. I even envisioned construction of a plank road that we could rebuild continuously in front of the car. All of our ideas were futile. We had to wait until the sunny days of spring melted away the snow and dried up the mud before we would have "wheels" again. In the meantime, we walked, but it made us appreciate Father's usual generosity in letting us use the car. Most young men our ages always walked.

With all of our comings and goings, the thirteen miles of road between Machias and Starboard became thoroughly familiar. During the summer months, it was a very passable road, but most of our traveling on it was during the school year. We traveled by every possible means. We often walked; we went by bicycle or skis; and sometimes in winter we would go by sled so we could slide down all the hills. We traveled through the snows of winter and the ice and sleet of spring and late fall. Every hill, curve, mudhole, and jutting rock was etched sharply on a memory map in our minds, because we had experienced difficulties with all of them. Hills were always a hazard except in summer, and curves hid approaching traffic—both cars and horse-drawn wagons. We had to blast away with our car horn several times before turning each corner. The road between Bucks Harbor and Starboard, for most of its distance, was one lane. One car usually had to move into the ditch to let another pass. Sometimes getting out again was not easy.

Going to Libby and back during spring vacation, we usually encountered *mud*. All of the roads were unpaved, and in the spring huge mudholes developed, especially between Starboard and Buck Harbor. Father knew where the holes were, and, as we approached one, he would shift the car into second or low gear, floor the accelerator, and try to charge through it. Sometimes we were successful but sometimes we got stuck up to the hubs—not an uncommon occurrence on country roads in those days. One useful skill we learned as boys was "mud engineering"—how to get a car out of a mire. Sometimes a horse and wagon would come by and the driver would hook on and pull us out, but more often we had to depend on our own ingenuity. We would cut brush and line the road with a heavy layer. If we could find flat rocks, we used them to stiffen the mud soup. Since other cars usually would have been stuck in the same hole, we could just rearrange their escape materials. The final step was somehow to get a firm foundation under the car for a jack. Then we could raise the rear wheels and place rocks, limbs, logs—anything substantial we could find—underneath them. When we thought we were ready, Father would start the car and take off in low gear under full power. We would push with all our strength and often become spattered with mud from head to foot in the process. If we were lucky, the car would go flying out, swerving from side to side but landing on dry ground.

Father's time restrictions always made this situation much worse, and the possibility that the tide would be off the end of the slip was another worry. Because of being delayed by mud on the mainland, we frequently had to leave the government boat at the mooring and land on the slippery rocks at Libby with the peapod. This was a dangerous feat, especially for Mother.

Another hazard was ice, which was much more dangerous than either mud or snow. We usually encountered it in the early spring and late fall as we returned from Libby, trying to avoid missing any school. When rain fell at temperatures below freezing, it instantly froze on the roads, which were usually hard-packed snow, making them into elongated ice ponds. There were no road crews spreading salt and sand—the remedy was chains stretched over the tires. Chains were fragile equipment and often broke, so every driver had to carry tools and extra links for making repairs on the road. In these conditions, too, Father charged up the steep hills, hoping to go fast enough down one slope (without landing in the ditch) to reach the top of the next. I think we dreaded ice more than either snow or mud. It was a great relief to all of us when the winds of March and the sun of April melted the ice and snow and dried up the mudholes.

There were some major educational and social disadvantages in being lighthouse children. All five of us had grade school educations that might well be classified as fragmented. All of Nonie's education, until she reached high school, was either on White-head or Libby. Irwin spent part of one year in the tiny rural school in Starboard, two at the Model School in Machias, and the rest on Whitehead and on Libby with the itinerant teacher and Miss Richardson. I was more fortunate to have had six of my first eight grades at the Model School. Hazel received all her schooling on Whitehead and in Rockland before we came to Libby. Only Arnie received all his schooling on the mainland.

All of us, except Hazel, seemed to have suffered some negative influences from this fractured island educational experience. I always felt somewhat apart from the other kids in my school—largely, I think, because my life experiences had been so different. Most of their fathers were employed in the lumber industry—cutting trees in the forest, driving logs downriver in the spring, and working in the sawmill in the summer. My whole background was oriented to the sea, theirs to the land. But then I also had adjustment problems in the other direction. I can remember returning to the island for vacations and feeling awkward around boats. Boating skills are peculiar—there seems to be a rhythm or balance of movement about them that can be lost rather quickly. Then, after being on the island for several weeks at a time, particularly in summer, I can remember feeling uncomfortable and strange when I returned to the "busy" streets of Machias. I sometimes was not sure whether I was an island boy or a city lad.

My frequent departures from town also ruptured friendships constantly. All the summer swimming activities in the Machias River were lost to me, as were the almost continuous games of baseball. I never acquired the degree of skill in swimming, diving, and baseball that the other kids had—and of course they knew nothing about my skills in handling a boat in rough water, building lobster traps, or rock climbing. No matter how hard I tried, I never was able to catch up in the "accepted" games. Irwin had many of the same feelings and experiences, because he also found it difficult to join in.

Another negative factor of our island experience was that we never really had a family or a comfortable place to live in Machias until my last two years in high school. We were there on a kind of tentative basis, knowing that our real home was on the island. Since we had a fine house on Libby, Father rented tiny, very inadequate mainland places. After living in two, we moved to the other side of the river to live on the second floor of a house with another family. Later, we moved downstairs to a larger apartment.

When we made the move to the other side of the river, I decided, on my own, to continue attending the Model School so I could finish seventh and eighth grades there. Since I was a "lighthouse child," not limited by town boundaries, I could go to any school. But this further kept me feeling somewhat separate from other kids my age, now on both sides of the river.

Father, in particular, never encouraged us to participate in town activities. A musician started a band—the Machias Boys Band—and I was anxious to join, but Father said there was no point in it because I was on Libby in the summer. When I became interested in the Boy Scouts, he voiced the same opinion, but this time I stood firm, telling him I might miss some activities but much of the program took place during the school year. I was right, and I learned a great deal from my scouting experience.

Although Mother lived ashore during the school year from the time that I entered fifth grade, in a way she still lived on a self-imposed island. She did not feel that she quite "belonged" in Machias, since her husband was on Libby. She never joined any clubs, had no close friends, and just lived to care for us kids. Had she lived in Jonesport, where she had relatives and could have participated in church activities, I think her life might have been quite different. With Father absent and Mother choosing isolation, we children were very much on our own in Machias.

Shyness was a characteristic that we Wass kids shared. Hazel escaped quite well, but I think it affected the rest of us in varying degrees. Irwin, in particular, had a difficult time with any kind of "performance" in school. One time, he was assigned a poem to recite at a school program, and he defied Mother, his teacher, and even the redoubtable principal, by failing to show up. He knew the poem perfectly. In fact, he practiced it so much that I learned most of it by listening to him. (He still remembers the poem and recited it to me recently without error.) But he would *not* stand before a group of people and recite it. He still tries to avoid speaking before groups.

Shyness was one of my problems then, too. One of our high school principals decreed that every student should participate in the annual speaking contest, usually reserved for juniors. We all had to learn a piece and "try out." On the day that a friend of mine and I were scheduled to recite, we watched for a chance, and when the teacher left the room, we jumped out the window.

But Irwin was influenced more deeply by our island years that I was. I made an important discovery in high school: I could perform in plays. As long as I was acting and not being myself, I had little difficulty, so I participated in dramatics all through high school and college. Later, having chosen a career in teaching, I found that "acting" before students was not as difficult as standing before my peers. But there were always times when it was an onerous burden to have to appear, "prepared," in front of college and graduate-level classes. Fortunately, I was able to overcome this fear enough to enjoy my career as a teacher.

In spite of these negative social and educational experiences, Libby Island provided us with some learning opportunities that would enrich all of our lives. Our island environment was a rich learning laboratory, a source of knowledge in such fields as animal husbandry, carpentry, boathandling, weather forecasting—not to mention lighthouse keeping, hunting, and fishing. In addition, we gained a set of values that, with few exceptions, has served us well.

We learned a great deal by observing our fathers at work every day and often lending a hand when needed. With a little added instruction, by the time we were ten, we could have operated the light in the tower and the diesel engines in the whistlehouse to blow the fog signal. We knew the "marks": when certain islands were no longer visible, the fog signal had to be started. In fact, we often reported this information to Father when he was working inside. And we knew about standing watches, because we often relieved Father when he had other duties to perform.

We were also familiar with every phase of maintenance work, because we helped with most of it. We polished brass, scraped and painted woodwork, and learned the skills of simple carpentry through building lobster traps and our camp.

We learned to be skilled hunters and fishermen, as I have already described, and we learned to use guns safely. We could identify songbirds and shore birds. Every phase of lobstering was a part of our island learning, and in the process, we also became familiar with many varieties of fish, crabs, periwinkles, and seaweeds and learned to distinguish which were edible. Fishing also was an acquired skill, and we learned not only how to catch fish, but also how to preserve them by salting and drying.

As weather prophets, we were not as skilled as Father, but we could recognize most signs of approaching bad weather and predict when it might clear. We came to know and respect the power of the sea by observing its destructive force in wrecking great ships. And we knew something about the construction of ships from crawling through every nook and cranny of wrecks.

By the age of ten, we could handle a sixteen-foot peapod, frequently in choppy seas. We also learned to steer the government boat and could hold a course to Starboard and return, knowing the rudiments of navigating by compass. Also, we understood the power of the tidal current and how to correct for the distance it would set our boat off course. We knew about handling ropes, could tie a bowline with our eyes shut, and could cleat a line in seconds. We did not become expert sailors, but we learned the principles from sailing our own fully rigged toy sloops and the peapod, which had a portable sail.

Farming was an essential part of our island experience, and we learned every phase of it except handling the plow. We could plant, cultivate, weed, and harvest. Caring for a cow and a horse, milking, making butter, and butchering—all were things we did or observed many times. With a little extra effort, I could have learned even more about some of these activities, but I was never interested in farming.

There is no doubt that we could have learned even more had we urged Father and Mother to teach us. Both of them had many skills that we did not learn. But there were also rich learning opportunities that we missed in this island environment because Father and Mother and our teachers were not entirely knowledgeable about their surroundings. There could have been excellent lessons in biology, ornithology, ichthyology, oceanography, geology, and botany—but, of course, lessons in these fields were far beyond them. What they knew was largely the folk-learning of Maine farmer-fishermen that had been passed on from one generation to another.

As I have already mentioned, another great source of learning for me on Libby was reading. I early became an inveterate reader—so much so that Father often would say, "Philmore, if you don't get your nose out of that book and get outdoors and do something, you'll never amount to anything." This also was folk-wisdom, shared, I'm sure, by many Maine coast parents. But not by my mother. Reading material was scarce, although we did have a government-sponsored circulating library. These books came in a big wooden box that, set up on its end, became bookshelves. When the keepers had exhausted one box, they could exchange it for another. Most of the books were a bit too adult for me, but through these libraries I did become acquainted with Edgar Rice Burroughs and his mythical apeman, Tarzan.

One summer, Mother knew that I had just about run out of things to read, so she wrote a letter to the Maine Sea Coast Missionary Society, telling them that her son was a great reader and had exhausted the book supply on the island. She asked them if they had any books and magazines that might be appropriate for a boy my age. I have no idea why she thought they might be able to help.

We had completely forgotten about her letter when one day a large, black boat appeared off the island. She was larger than any lobsterboat I had ever seen and did not look like a lobster smack or sardine boat. The captain blew her whistle, signaling that he wanted to land, so our whole family, plus the other keepers, their wives, and kids, gathered quickly at the boathouse. Father soon recognized the boat as the *Sunbeam* from the white cross on her bow. Her tender was lowered into the water and the captain came ashore. I could not believe my eyes when I discovered that he was carrying a number of boxes marked BOOKS. His cargo was an answer to Mother's letter. It was a personal supply of reading material for Philmore Burlon Wass. During the following weeks, I was quite willing to share all of this—but there were not many other young readers on Libby.

The thrill of that experience has never left me. If I had ever had doubts about being a person of worth, that one event certainly dissolved them. I still have some of the books and am thrilled when I occasionally open one and see the MSCMS stamp. In recent years, I spoke to the Reverend Stanley Haskell, former head of the society, and personally thanked him for the organization's long-ago generosity to an island boy. He told me that, over the years, they had frequently taken books to children living on isolated Maine outposts.

Another part of our schooling on Libby was religious education. Mother's grandparents had been converted to the Reorganized Church of Jesus Christ of Latter Day Saints (RLDS) when missionaries traveled by boat along the coast of Maine, holding meetings in all the coastal towns and villages. Father had joined later, after he and Mother were married. The Maine interpretation of this faith was quite puritanical, so we were brought up by a strict code regarding language and respect for the Sabbath.

Each Sunday, during all the years we spent on Libby, Mother set aside time to instruct us in matters concerning God and the church. She wrote to church headquarters in Independence, Missouri, for special pamphlets called "quarterlies," which provided the materials for our lessons. Even though Irwin and I are five years apart in age, we were taught with the same book.

Our activities were strictly limited on Sundays, making it a long, tedious day for us kids, who were "all dressed up" and just sitting around. In the afternoon, when anyone was there who could play the piano, the "old folks" had a hymn sing in the parlor. I can remember feeling very lonely during these times, because there was no one around with whom to talk.

Some Sundays, to break the monotony, Father (who probably was bored too) would lead the whole family on a walk around the shore. We loved these treks. Father would point out birds and identify them. On warm Sundays we would sit on the sand at the beach and sometimes have a picnic, but we were not allowed to go swimming, no matter how hot it was. It was permissible to make candy. Nonie and our cousin Orrie usually would make fudge, and occasionally divinity—a creamy white fudge with walnuts. One batch, I remember, absolutely refused to harden. Finally, they put it in a big baking tin in the center of the kitchen table, and all of us gathered around with spoons and ate from the common dish. I loved this, because no one could keep track of how much I ate.

We greeted Monday with great joy—having regained our freedom, at least until the next Sunday. It took me a long time to outgrow this type of Sabbath observance, but eventually I recognized the absurdity of the practice. With some difficulty, I abandoned the restrictions, although it was a long time before I felt comfortable going skiing on the Sabbath. In analyzing our Sundays on Libby, I now realize that making Sunday a different day, painful as it was, probably added zest to each week and variety to our lives.

Another aspect of our religious training was concern for "the end of the world." I cannot imagine putting such matters in a child's religious curriculum, but I got the notion from somewhere that the world would end in one giant fire. One night, after I had gone to bed, I was awakened by a violent thunderstorm. The flashes of lightning were so bright they illuminated my whole room. After one brilliant flash, I got up and looked out the window. Whether or not the lightning had struck a tree in Starboard, I do not know, but I thought I could see fire. And then the thought struck me like the thunderbolts I had just seen: *The end of the world has come and the big fire has started.* I cringed in my bed, digging as deeply as possible under the covers. About that time, I heard a scratching sound on the stairs, and it kept getting louder. I was sure the end had come now and that "Old Scratcha" was coming after me. I felt paralyzed with fear. A few seconds later, I felt something pushing at my arm, which was under the covers, and then I heard familiar sounds. Cautiously taking the covers off my head, I saw Peter (to my great relief and delight). The scratching sound had been her toenails on the stairs. No dog ever was given a warmer welcome. All my fears vanished. Together we would face whatever was coming. Peter had been scared, too—so frightened that she had disobeyed the strict rule that she was never to leave the kitchen. I was glad that she had.

Had we lived in an environment that included other people, other ideas, and perhaps respected relatives following different sets of values, I might have questioned our beliefs earlier. But since they were the only beliefs I was exposed to, they were etched deeply in my mind.

There were, however, many positive benefits from this early religious education. We learned love, compassion, and forgiveness —as taught by Christ and modeled by our parents.

After attending a business college in Bangor for two winter terms, Irwin decided, in 1934, to join the Coast Guard. Shortly after he was assigned to Cross Island Coast Guard Station, he decided that he wanted to become a member of our family faith. I do not know what impelled him to make this decision, since we seldom had an opportunity to attend our own church, but somehow a seed had been planted. He asked me if I would like to join at the same time, and I readily agreed. He was twenty-one and I was sixteen. Few young men of our ages were at all interested in church-related activities. After World War II, it was said that there are no atheists in foxholes. I suspect that a similar saying might be attributed to many of those who lived on island lighthouse stations. We were confronted, almost daily, by forces over which we had no control.

So in June 1934, Irwin and I were baptized in the icy-cold waters of Moosabec Reach, between Beals Island and Jonesport. Our witnesses were many church members whom we had come to know and love on our infrequent visits.

All five children in our family became members of the RLDS church, and three of us have continued to be active in its work.

As young children, and then young men and women, we always were given a great deal of freedom. I do not remember Mother or Father ever haranguing us about our behavior or laying down any strict rules, except about the Sabbath. We seemed to follow almost instinctively the pattern they had set. One aspect of our freedom was in the use of the family car. In our teenage years, Irwin and I often stayed on the mainland while Mother joined Father on Libby. Or in the summer we stayed on the island to work during the week and then went ashore on the weekends. Of course, our major interest was girls, and we pursued them throughout Washington County—always, of course, believing that the most attractive ones lived in the next town. Perhaps we were not quite as circumspect as we might have been in that pursuit, but as far as Father's car was concerned, we took the very best care of it, never exceeding safe speed limits or driving recklessly. Father had taught us to drive carefully, and we followed his example.

Perhaps another reason our parents' values affected us so deeply was that we were influenced little by peer pressure. In our early years on the island we *had* no peers. Family values were the only values we knew, and by the time we went to the mainland, these values had been thoroughly instilled in us.

Looking back on my island learning, I always have felt that I had a richer and more varied educational experience than most of my contemporaries. As a student at the Model School, I found that I always possessed more general information than most of the other kids. Often, when a teacher asked a question, I could come up with an answer not from the textbook, but from some other book I had read or from an island experience. Years later, when I was on the faculty of the University of Connecticut, I participated in the doctoral exam of one of my former student teachers in the Model School. We were joking about the reversal of roles. He remembered me as a student and asked if I knew that the student teachers were warned to watch out for "that Wass kid," because he could ask some very embarrassing questions. When we studied anything about the ocean, I was often the authority in the class, not the teacher. When I took Graduate Record Exams at the University of Iowa, I received my highest scores in biological science, despite having been a social science major. I had never had a college-level course in biology. What I knew came from "island learning."

Concluding my book with this chapter seemed appropriate because often it was the requirements of formal schooling that ended family life on Maine islands. But I shall be forever grateful that we lived as long as we did on Libby, because I think it gave all of us a unique outlook on life that no other experience could have provided.

A·F·T·E·R·W·O·R·D

THE era of manned lighthouse stations in Maine, which began in 1791, will soon end. The first lighthouse station was established in that year at Portland Head. In the next hundred years, sixty more were added, and by 1907, when the last station was built, the total was eighty-five.

Why so many lighthouses in a state with few large seaports? One answer lies in the lumber being shipped from the port of Bangor. In 1860, more than three thousand ships arrived there to load lumber. Ellsworth was another major lumber-shipping port. Often fifteen or twenty schooners would be waiting off the mouth of the Union River for a tow to the loading docks. In addition to lumber, granite was being shipped from mid-Maine islands and lime from the Rockland/Thomaston area. Lighthouses were built not only to protect the lives of seamen but also to save ships and their cargoes. Even with all the light stations, the average life of a sailing ship was less than fifteen years.

When these industries waned and land transportation improved, the number of ships diminished, and so did the number of lighthouses. By the 1930s, fewer than seventy Maine stations remained in operation. In *Lighthouses of Maine*, published in

1986, author Bill Caldwell lists sixty-two lights still in operation.

Correspondence with the commander of the First Coast Guard District reveals that in 1987 nine light stations remain manned. All of these stations have either mainland or coastal island locations, and all of them are to be automated by 1990.

A story that began in 1791 with the construction of Portland Head light will end 199 years later. There will no longer be lightkeepers (and their wives and children) dedicating their lives to the safety of those who travel on the sea. I am proud to have been a member of one of those families, and I hope that this book will engender an increased appreciation for the services all light-keeping families rendered over two centuries, not only in maintaining Maine's light and fog signals but also in directly saving hundreds of lives.

There is no question about the increased efficiency of the new automated lights and fog signals, but one lighthouse buff raises these questions:

> The light I've tended for forty years,
> Is now to be run by a set of gears . . .
> And I wonder now, will the grass stay green?
> Will the brass stay bright and the windows clean?
> And will that automatic thing
> Plant marigolds in early spring?
> —Edgar Guest, *Detroit Free Press*, 9/12/85

And one further question might be added: Will any strong hands be there to rescue any person unfortunate enough to be wrecked on one of these island outposts?